Library of
Davidson College

GAME PLAYING
WITH BASIC

GAME PLAYING WITH BASIC

DONALD D. SPENCER

President
Abacus Computer Corporation

HAYDEN BOOK COMPANY, INC
Rochelle Park, New Jersey

*To my wife RAE
and our six game players*
SANDRA, SUSAN, SHERRIE, STEVEN,
LAURA, and MICHAEL

510.76
S745ga

Library of Congress Cataloging in Publication Data

Spencer, Donald D
  Game playing with BASIC.

  Bibliography: p.
  Includes index.
  1. Basic (Computer program language). 2. Electronic digital computers--Programming. 3. Mathematical recreations--Data processing. 4. Games--Data processing I. Title.
QA76.73.B3S669   793.7'4   77-24610
ISBN 0-8104-5109-3

Copyright © 1977 by HAYDEN BOOK COMPANY, INC. All rights reserved. No part of this book may be reprinted, or reproduced, or utilized in any form or by any electronic, mechanical, or other means, now known or hereafter invented, including photocopying and recording, or in any information storage and retrieval system, without permission in writing from the Publisher.

Printed in the United States of America

79-552

4 5 6 7 8 9   PRINTING

78 79 80 81 82 83 84 85   YEAR

PREFACE

Games have been with us almost since the dawn of man. The ancient Chinese and Egyptians devised many mathematical and logical games such as Nim, Awari, Tower of Hanoi, Fan Tan, Go, etc. Medieval Europe was responsible for many games played for recreation in nobles' courts. Gambling games have been popular in casinos throughout the world for years on end. Who in the United States does not know how to play Tic-Tac-Toe, Checkers, or Monopoly? Who does not, now and then, indulge in playing with solvable puzzles of one kind or another?

Games and mathematical recreations share three characteristics: First, they are logical or mathematical; second, they are fun; third, they all appear to be quite useless. The first two characteristics require no reasons for being, but some might ask why anyone should indulge in anything that is of no practical value. An indirect defense may be built up from the fact that the most staid mathematics, educational, and computer science publications publish material that is strictly recreational in nature, giving such amusements a kind of endorsement. Moreover, a very cursory examination will disclose a few interesting facts about games and recreational mathematics. Prime numbers, for example, have no practical value. It may be decades, if ever, before they can be put to use for anything. However, the study of prime numbers and their properties has filled many a gap in the field of *number theory,* that mathematical discipline which studies the basic properties of all numbers.

Magic Squares have been involved with superstitious beliefs and proven an interesting source of amusement for centuries. They even offer practical rewards for agricultural and nuclear scientists. The study of the patterns of certain types of Magic Squares has shown how to reduce the number of experiments required to obtain plant growth and radiation data. Many games and mathematical recreations still seem to be useless, but who can say what next year or the next decade will bring?

Up until the invention of the digital computer, game playing was limited to human beings. Today, students, teachers, programmers, analysts, and game playing novices are spending a considerable amount of time programming computers to play games. The educational value of both playing

PREFACE

and writing computer games is substantial. They make ideal supplemental learning experiences when learning about problem solving, probability, computer programming, statistics, logic, and decision making.

The reader of this book will be introduced to computerized game playing and the BASIC programming language. The easy-to-learn and easy-to-use BASIC language is ideal for use as a game playing language. The reader will see how this language is used to direct a computer to play such games and puzzles as Tic-Tac-Toe, Battle of Numbers (Nim), Craps, Roulette, Blackjack, slot machines, Magic Squares, the 15 Puzzle, Tower of Hanoi, Knight's Magic Tour, and many others.

Regardless of whether the reader is a secondary school student, college student, teacher, analyst, programmer, layman, or businessman, he should find games of particular interest to him. Chapter 8 of the book contains 26 games for reader solution, including 3-D Tic-Tac-Toe, Nim, Morra, Hexapawn, King's Tour of the chessboard, Poker Dice, Nine Men's Morris, the 50 Puzzle, Poker, Palindromic Numbers, Boule, and Craps.

I am indebted to many readers of my earlier game playing book, *Game Playing with Computers,* Hayden Book Company, who have taken the time to correspond with me on different solutions to many of the games. Many of their ideas were incorporated in this book.

I would like to thank my wife, Rae, for typing the manuscript and Ken Herrin for keying and executing the BASIC programs on the computer. I also wish to thank Ed Johnson, Embry-Riddle Aeronautical University, and Jack McCabe, Mainland High School, for providing terminal and computer time for running the BASIC programs.

One word of advice for those readers who will use the games described in this book: Be sure you fully understand a game before attempting to write a game playing computer program. Always draw a flowchart of the game logic *prior* to the coding of the solution in the BASIC programming language. These simple steps will allow you to more fully enjoy playing games with a computer.

Happy game playing!

DONALD D. SPENCER

CONTENTS

1 MEETING THE COMPUTER   1
    1.1   The Digital Villain   *1*
    1.2   Game Playing with Computers   *1*
    1.3   Minicomputers and Time-Sharing Systems   *3*
    1.4   Writing the Game Program   *4*
    1.5   Game Playing Programs   *6*
    1.6   Using the Computer   *10*
    1.7   Game Programs for You to Try   *11*

2 TALKING IN BASIC   12
    2.1   The BASIC Language   *12*
    2.2   The GO TO Statment   *15*
    2.3   The IF-THEN Statement   *17*
    2.4   READ and DATA Statements   *18*
    2.5   The INPUT Statement   *20*
    2.6   Using Library Functions   *22*
    2.7   Arrays   *24*
    2.8   The RESTORE Statement   *26*
    2.9   Subroutines   *29*
    2.10 Summary   *30*

3 IT'S GAME PLAYING TIME   31
    3.1   Tossing a Coin   *31*
    3.2   Rolling Dice   *33*
    3.3   Mouse in a Maze   *35*
    3.4   Sam the Drunk   *39*
    3.5   Battle of Numbers   *40*
    3.6   Dealing a Poker Hand   *46*
    3.7   Fox and Geese   *49*
    3.8   Tac Tix   *50*
    3.9   Tic-Tac-Toe   *52*
    3.10 Go-Moko   *56*
    3.11 Knight's Tour   *56*
    3.12 Sharky, the Card Player   *60*

4 NUMBER RECREATIONS   61
    Introduction   *61*
    4.1 Guess the Number   *62*
    4.2 Prime Numbers   *64*
    4.3 Chinese Remainder Theorem   *68*
    4.4 Perfect Numbers   *69*
    4.5 Fibonacci Numbers   *70*
    4.6 Amicable Numbers   *72*
    4.7 Mind-Reading Tricks   *74*
    4.8 Square Numbers   *76*
    4.9 Armstrong Numbers   *77*

5 GAMBLING GAMES   78
    Introduction   *78*
    5.1 Slot Machines   *78*
    5.2 Blackjack   *82*
    5.3 Roulette   *89*
    5.4 Craps   *92*
    5.5 Keno   *98*
    5.6 Baccarat   *99*
    5.7 Wheel of Fortune   *101*

6 PUZZLES   102
    Introduction   *102*
    6.1 Tower of Hanoi   *102*
    6.2 The Colored Cubes Puzzle   *105*
    6.3 The 15 Puzzle   *106*
    6.4 Pentominoes   *113*
    6.5 Buried Treasure   *113*

7 MAGIC SQUARES   119
    Introduction   *119*
    7.1 How to Make Magic Squares   *120*
    7.2 Odd-Cell Magic Squares   *120*
    7.3 Even-Cell Magic Squares   *125*
    7.4 What Numbers Will Magic Squares Add Up To?   *129*
    7.5 Magic Squares Starting with Numbers Other Than One   *129*
    7.6 Multiplication Magic Square   *133*
    7.7 Geometric Magic Square   *136*
    7.8 Other Interesting Magic Squares   *139*

8 GAMES FOR READER SOLUTION — 142

    8.1   Magic Square   *142*
    8.2   Buzz   *142*
    8.3   Typing Monkey   *142*
    8.4   Prime Number Polynomial   *143*
    8.5   Poker Dice   *143*
    8.6   Guessing Game   *144*
    8.7   Morra   *144*
    8.8   Twin Primes   *145*
    8.9   Mersenne Prime Numbers   *145*
    8.10   Milkman's Crate   *145*
    8.11   The 50 Puzzle   *145*
    8.12   Lucky Prisoners   *145*
    8.13   The Four Checkers   *146*
    8.14   Poker   *147*
    8.15   Palindromic Numbers   *147*
    8.16   Magic Square Checker   *148*
    8.17   Boule   *149*
    8.18   Craps   *150*
    8.19   Five Field Kono   *150*
    8.20   Knight Interchange   *151*
    8.21   Symmetry Game   *151*
    8.22   Nine Men's Morris   *153*
    8.23   King's Tour of the Chessboard   *153*
    8.24   Hexapawn   *153*
    8.25   Nim   *154*
    8.26   3-D Tic-Tac-Toe   *157*

Bibliography   **159**

Index   **161**

chapter 1
MEETING THE COMPUTER

1.1 The Digital Villain

A computer is a device that can perform a wide variety of jobs, ranging from mathematical calculations as simple as addition to complex problems in the sciences, engineering, the humanities, and the social sciences.

Although computers come in many shapes and sizes, they are all similar in many ways. Each computer must be able to *read in* instructions and data, *remember* the problem being solved and the data to use, *perform calculations* (and other manipulations) on the data, *print out* the results, then *control* the entire operation. Thus, for a machine to process data it must contain five logical elements: (1) a means of input, (2) a means of output, (3) an arithmetic unit, (4) a means of storing data, and (5) a control unit. These elements must all work together in solving a problem since numerical data and instructions are constantly being sent back and forth between them. The whole process is under the control of instructions that are specified in a *computer program*.

Since natural languages (for example, English, German, Japanese) contain idioms that permit more than one interpretation, special languages with no ambiguities have been developed for writing computer programs. The BASIC language (an acronym for *B*eginner's *A*ll-purpose *S*ymbolic *I*nstruction *C*ode) is chosen for use in this book because, of all the widely available computer languages, it is the one most easily understood. The BASIC language is described in Chap. 2.

1.2 Game Playing with Computers

Today, people all over the world are spending a considerable amount of time programming computers to play games. Why? One reason is that game programs provide excellent problems for learning how to solve problems with computers. Beginning computer users can grasp such problems in a minimum amount of time and can therefore devote more time to learning about the computer, algorithm development, programming languages, and techniques of problem solving.

Another reason why we use computers to play games is that games often provide good analogies to actual situations involving human beings and their environment. Gaming can be applied to business management, scientific experiments, and military war games. Business executives play games with digital computers to simulate the operation of their business. Games of this type allow executives to keep abreast of their employees and to learn more about their companies. Consider the problem of developing a plan for planting several crops and distributing the produce after it has been harvested. Without the use of a computer, the problem would have to be solved by a trial and error method, and it might take as long as a year before it was known if the plan chosen was successful. With a relatively short space of time, however, a game situation simulating the actual situation on a small scale can be programmed for a computer and many different plans checked to decide upon the proper one.

Information learned from programs such as Chess, Checkers, Go, and Go-Moko may very well apply to other problems. Consider the problem of the maintenance and repair of electronic equipment. Assuming that all parts of a chassis could be checked or monitored by automatic means, a computer could be programmed to do the automatic checking function. Using a learning program similar to a Chess, Go, or Go-Moko program, the computer could indicate which parts are likely to go bad first for a specific chassis, and also which sections appear to be weakest. For example, in a certain run of radios, a lot of weak transistors may have been used. The computer can be programmed, after a few of these are found to be bad, to look at this part first each time one of these radios comes up. After the run is over, the computer will return to its normal pattern. The computer might reveal that in audio amplifiers it is the power supply units that go first and hence immediately check all such units in all audio amplifiers of any design. These frequency-of-occurrence techniques along with standard techniques such as signal tracing and analysis of symptoms of malfunctionings could make a computer acting as a technician more efficient than a human technician.

War games have been used by military organizations for many years for training personnel and testing military plans. War gaming was used by the Germans and Japanese prior to World War II. However, it was in America (about 1950) that computers were first used to develop simulations of military operations.

It is difficult to determine exactly how techniques of game playing programs can be applied to actual problems. Perhaps these programs will solve many problems that human beings have thus far been unable to solve. Such was the case when a computer was directed to execute a geometry theorem-proving program. This program found proofs for theorems in plane geometry. When the program was used to prove that the two base angles of an isosceles triangle are equal, it produced a proof which was very surprising to the programmer who developed the program. The proof it produced was shorter than the proof that is usually given in basic geometry textbooks. Of course, the programmer could have studied the program and determined exactly what proof would have been generated by the program. This may have taken years to do, however, as the program was designed to solve many different problems.

The programming of digital computers to play games has led to many important insights and to a number of new programming techniques. It has also led more or less directly to today's work on *artificial intelligence,* which is right to the forefront of computer technique.

Games and recreations may be classified in a variety of ways. In this book the following terms are used to identify the types of games and recreations one may come across.

MEETING THE COMPUTER

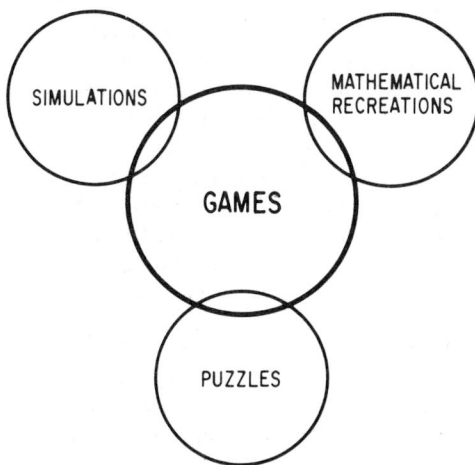

Fig. 1-1 Relationship of puzzles, mathematical recreations, simulations, and games

1. A *puzzle* is a problem that has a baffling quality that one must exercise substantial mental ingenuity and thought to solve. The Tower of Hanoi and 15 Puzzle are two examples.
2. A *game* is an amusement involving competition under a specific set of rules. The competition may be against another person or machine (such as in Chess or Tic-Tac-Toe), against oneself (such as Solitaire), or against laws of chance (such as Blackjack or Craps).
3. A *mathematical recreation* is a logical problem that is fun and often appears to be quite useless. Prime Numbers, Magic Squares, and Perfect Numbers are examples of mathematical recreations.
4. A *simulation* is a model or representation of a real-life situation, event, or process that is performed by a computer. For example, one may use the computer to simulate the operation of a slot machine or the roll of two dice.

One might think of puzzles, games, mathematical recreations, and simulations as having a certain overlap, as shown in Fig. 1.1.

1.3 Minicomputers and Time-Sharing Systems

Computers come in a variety of sizes and shapes, but there are two general types the game playing user is likely to encounter: the minicomputer/microcomputer system and the time-sharing system.

A *minicomputer* is a low cost digital computer that is about the size of a television set. A minicomputer system often consists of just a minicomputer and one or more *terminals*. The terminal is usually a typewriter-like device; however, it could be a keyboard display unit or some other input-output device. The terminal is the means by which one communicates (or plays a game) with the computer. Although there is some limit to the size of problems that a minicomputer can handle, it is able to solve many complex problems including games and recreations such as Tic-Tac-Toe, Blackjack, Go-Moko, Magic Squares, and others.

The *microcomputer* is similar to the minicomputer. It is a low-cost machine that consists of one or more microprocessors (a central processing unit on a chip) and a memory device (such as a ROM or RAM). Microcomputers are rapidly becoming more popular with personal and home computer users. Many of them can be purchased for only a few hundred dollars a unit. They are also available in kit form.

A second type of computer system you are likely to encounter is the *time-sharing system*. Time-sharing is based on the principle that there is enough capacity in a computer system for multiple users, providing that each user terminal is active only a small fraction of the time. Each user of a time-sharing system has the illusion that he is the only person using the system. Each user can run his program on line as he would with a minicomputer. How does a time-sharing computer system take care of several users simultaneously? Each one has control over the computer for a specified quantum of time. The computer picks up orders from one user, works on his problem, say for 1/200 of a second, and stores the partial answer. It then moves to the next user, receives his orders, works on the second problem for 1/200 of a second, and moves to the third user, etc. When a problem is completed, the answer is printed on the user's terminal. The computer system accomplishes this work so fast that the user feels the system is working for him full-time.

In a typical time-sharing system, the users communicate with a central computing facility by means of remote terminals. The computer may be a short distance from a terminal, or it may be several thousand miles away. Communication between remote terminals and the central computer is via common telephone lines.

1.4 Writing the Game Program

The computer is a piece of machinery to be used as a tool. However, most other tools are easier to use; it is usually possible to install them, read the instructions, start them, and get promptly to work. It is not possible simply to push a computer's "start" switch, however, and have it perform useful work. A newly installed computer might be compared at best to a five-year-old child, for a child is at first capable of doing very little, but he can in degrees be taught to do a variety of useful things. The more a child is taught, the more complex the work he can do. The computer can also be taught to do many things, but only by a process involving considerable planning, effort, and time. The "teaching" of a computer must be done through the form of programs. Because it can respond only to a basic set of simple instructions, problems for the computer must be broken down into a great number of detailed steps.

The following analogy will help the reader understand the extent to which problems for computer solution must be broken down. Suppose that you wanted to add two numbers, say, 36 and 41. This operation certainly sounds simple enough. However, let us examine the thought process required to perform it. First you must determine that you are going to add two numbers. Do you know how to add? If not, you must learn before proceeding. Next you must obtain the numbers to be added. If they are unavailable, then you cannot add. Write down the first number. Write down the second number. Are the numbers aligned correctly? If not, then erase the second number and rewrite it. Repeat this process until the numbers are aligned properly. Then draw a line below the numbers. You are now ready to add the numbers to compute the sum.

This set of instructions for a simple written addition is roughly analogous to the program of instructions that must be provided for a computer. Every process, no matter how elementary, must be broken down into simple steps that the computer understands.

A game program presented to a computer is a complete set of instructions that solves a particular game. The set of instructions is not always unique, for there may be more than one way to solve a given game. A computer does not do any thinking and cannot make unplanned decisions. Every step of each game it handles has to be accounted for by a program.

A game need not be described by an exact mathematical equation in order to be solvable by a computer, but it does need a definite set of rules that the computer can follow. If a game requires intuition or guessing or is so hard to define that it cannot be put into precise words, the computer cannot solve it. A great deal of thought must be put into defining the game exactly and setting it up for the computer in such a way that every possible alternative is taken care of within the program.

When you begin to develop a game playing program, you must be familiar with several aspects of the situation:

1. You must thoroughly understand the rules of the game and be able to determine if it is possible to solve it on a computer.
2. You must know what operations can be performed by the computer available.
3. You must understand what the output of the game is to be.

Before we begin the discussion of how to write game playing programs, let us enumerate the steps that are involved:

1. Understanding the game
2. Developing an algorithm to play the game
3. Drawing a flowchart
4. Coding the program
5. Executing the game program on the computer

Each of these steps will now be briefly discussed.

Step 1: Game definition Before a game can be solved on a computer, the following questions must be answered:

1. Can the game be solved with a computer?
2. How can the game be solved on a computer?
3. Can the computer in question solve the game?
4. What are the inputs and outputs?
5. What programming language will be used?

Step 2: Develop an algorithm Once the game has been defined, it is necessary to design a systematic problem-solving procedure. Such a procedure is called an *algorithm,* which is a sequence of operations that, when applied to given information, will produce a desired result.

Step 3: Flowcharting Once the game has been defined and an algorithm developed, a *flowchart* should be drawn to illustrate in symbolic figures the logic of the solution to the game. Flowcharts are perhaps the best method available for expressing what computers can do, or what you want them to do. Simple and easy to prepare and use, they eliminate any ambiguities. Several flowcharts are shown in Chapters 3, 4, and 5.

Step 4: Coding the program The flowchart is used as a guideline to the actual coding of the game in a *programming language* (BASIC is used in this book). The program, which is a list of computer instructions, will cause the computer to play the game.

Step 5: Communication with the computer After the program has been written, the operator must input the program and the known data into the computer and instruct the machine to execute (perform, run) the program. If the program contains no mistakes, the computer will execute the program and output the desired result. If the program contains mistakes, the program writer must find out why the program failed, make necessary corrections, and try again. This process is called *debugging* the program.

1.5 Game Playing Programs

A computer may be programmed to play or simulate games in many different ways. It may be pitted against a human player as in a game of Tic-Tac-Toe or Chess. It may be asked to generate the solution to a mathematical recreation such as a Magic Square. It may be used to simulate the operation of a roulette wheel or slot machine. It may also be used as a bookkeeper between two players or teams as in war and business games. The most popular form of play with a computer is for it to participate in the game as an active player. In this type of play the human player indicates each of his moves to the computer on an input unit. The computer then computes its move and outputs the move to the human player. The output units usually used are a typewriter or display device although other output units can be employed. The computer keeps score by recording both its own moves and those of its opponent.

In games where no known algorithm exists, such as Chess or Checkers, the computer looks several moves ahead, examining all possible combinations of its own moves and those of its opponent, and selecting that move which is most advantageous according to some computable criterion of selecting a position. This method simulates the action of a human player, who, like the computer, is confronted with millions of possible situations resulting from just a few moves. Each contestant starts with 16 different pieces, any one of which may be moved after the game has opened up. Each one of these moves affects the moves open to the opponent. In an average game of Chess, each player makes about 40 moves, each of which is governed by about 30 possibilities, resulting in about 10^{120} possible variations per game. The size of this number staggers the imagination, and few computers are large enough to analyze all possible sequences of moves.

The difficulty in programming a computer to play a game depends largely upon the complexity of the game. Games with simple, known algorithms, such as Tic-Tac-Toe or Nim, can be programmed without much trouble. However, programs for playing games like Checkers, Chess, and Go are extremely complex because the strategies for such games are extremely complex. Since not even a Chess master can outline a precise algorithm for evaluating the desirability of certain moves, it is easy to imagine the complexity of a Chess-playing program.

A few games and recreations that have been programmed for play on computers are discussed in the following paragraphs. The rules for playing many of them are covered elsewhere in this book.

Tic-Tac-Toe The idea of playing Tic-Tac-Toe on a machine was conceived as far back as the nineteenth century. Charles Babbage, an English mathematician, wanted to build a machine to play Chess and Tic-Tac-Toe to help finance his efforts to build a true computer. Today, Tic-Tac-Toe and three-dimensional Tic-Tac-Toe have been programmed for play on hundreds of general purpose computers. An algorithm exists that prevents a human player from winning the game. At best he can only tie the computer.

Pentominoes A polyomino is a figure formed by joining equal squares along their edges. Pentominoes consist of five contiguous squares, and it is possible to construct 12 different pentominoes. A Pentomino game is played by arranging the 12 pentominoes into various size rectangular boxes: 3 by 20, 4 by 15, 5 by 12, or 6 by 10. Computers have been used to generate many solutions to the Pentomino game. In fact, a computer program has found that there are two solutions for the 3 by 20 configuration, 1010 for the 5 by 12 configuration, and 2339 for the most popular size, the 6 by 10 rectangular configuration.

Knight's Tour The strange moves of the Chess knight make his operations fascinating. He is permitted to move one or two rows up or down and, depending on this first part of the move, two or one columns left or right. In other words, if the first part of the moves involves one space, the second involves two, and vice versa. An interesting game is to move the knight to every square on the chessboard without landing in any square twice. This game is called a "Knight's Tour." There are many different tours and computers have been used to determine many of them.

Prime numbers An integer greater than one is called a prime number if and only if the only positive integers that exactly divide it are itself and the number one. The prime numbers less than 25 are 2, 3, 5, 7, 11, 13, 17, 19 and 23. How does one determine if a number is prime? One way is to write down a large number of integers and simply cross off the composite numbers (numbers that are divisible by numbers other than themselves and the number 1). This simple procedure was devised by Eratosthenes 2000 years ago. This procedure is relatively easy to use when one wants to determine only a few prime numbers; however, it would be rather a lengthy operation to determine all the primes less than 200,000 or to determine if 209267 is a prime number. A computer can easily determine if a number is prime by using a method similar to that of Eratosthenes. A computer was used to determine a 961-digit prime number ($2^{3217}-1$), that 1,000,000,009,649 and 1,000,000,009,651 are twin primes (prime numbers with a difference of 2), and that $2^{11213}-1$ is a 3376-digit prime number.

Go The Japanese game of Go is a popular game among computer users. It is played with black and white stones on a board containing 361 intersection points (19 by 19 squares). The object of the game is to surround vacant intersection points.

The rules of Go are simple and no mathematical theory of the game is known. It is estimated that there are around 10^{172} different board positions possible during the course of a game. It is easily seen that it would be impractical to calculate all these configurations. This is one of the reasons that Go is such an interesting game to play with a computer.

Go is probably the most difficult of the board games, and no really successful Go-playing program has yet appeared. However, Thorp and Walden (1970) investigated some of the logical aspects of the game; Zobrist (1969) described a program that plays a legal game and has "reached the bottom rung of the ladder of human Go players"; and Ryder (1971) described a program that uses heuristic search techniques to play a "fair beginner's" game. It may be several years before a program can be written that will be "skillful" at playing the game.

15 Puzzle The 15 Puzzle consists of a square box containing 16 squares, 15 of which are occupied with tokens bearing the numbers 1 to 15 and one of which is blank. Any one of the numbers to the immediate right, left, top, or bottom of the blank square can be moved into the blank space. The object of the puzzle is to start with a specific number arrangement and finish with a different arrangement. There is one slight catch to the puzzle: there are 10,461,394,944,000 number arrangements that are impossible to obtain. There are also the same number of possible arrangements. A computer can be programmed to determine if a specific number arrangement of the 15 Puzzle is possible or impossible.

Go-Moko Go-Moko is a two-player game played on a Go board. Each player places stones, on alternate moves, on an intersection of the board. The object is to obtain five adjacent stones in a row either vertically, horizontally, or diagonally. The player doing this wins the game. Several computer programs have been written to play this game. Some programs have been written using a smaller board, for example, a 9 by 9 board.

War games   War games have been used by military organizations for many years. Computers have been used in gaming theory since about 1950. Computers are used in War games to evaluate military strategies, weapon systems, tactics, and organizational concepts. They are used to simulate activity ranging from the tactical moves of a small military unit to a large full-scale war using many armies. As an example of a recent computer war game, consider *Grand Strategy*, a game of international conflict developed for the U. S. Department of Defense. The global cold war conflict incorporates three power alliances of 39 nations with conflicting interests. The action takes place over a simulated 10-year period, divided into weekly events. In this game, all nations can win peace and prosperity. The roles of the players are as political, military, and economic leaders of the nations.

Nim   The ancient mathematical game of Nim has always been a favorite of computer users. Prior to 1945, several machines were built especially to play Nim. Since the invention of the digital computer, many computer programs have been written to play it. Nim is played by two people or one person and a computer playing alternately. Before the play starts, an arbitrary number of objects are put in an arbitrary number of piles, in no specific order. Then each player in his turn removes as many objects as he wishes from any pile (but from only one pile) with a minimum of at least one object. The player who takes the *last* object is the winner of the game.

Chess   Nearly twenty-five years have passed since Claude Shannon described how a computer might be programmed to play Chess. Shannon and others thought that if a computer could be taught to play Chess, it could be taught to perform other intellectual tasks. Researchers excitedly began preparing their programs, but they underestimated the depth and difficulty of the Chess problem and overestimated the power of their machines.

These early frustrations have to some extent been eased. And what was mere theory in the early fifties is an annual tournament now. The first nationally organized ACM* computer chess tournament took place in New York City in August 1970. Three years and three tourneys later, the electronic chess masters met in Sweden for the first international face-off.

In 1974, computer chess had a new world champion. After four years of domination of computer chess in the ACM sponsored U.S. Computer Chess Championships, CHESS 4.0 of Northwestern University was defeated by the computer controlled teletypewriter of CHAOS from Univac.

It was the program KAISSA from the Soviet Union which swept the tournament with a perfect score of four points in the four-round tournament.

The tournament site was in central Stockholm. The games were analyzed for the audience by David Levy, the tournament director, on special display boards supplied by the Swedish Chess Federation. At each teletypewriter, display terminal, or telephone was a flag showing the competing country. Thirteen programs were entered in the tournament and were run on computers located all over Europe.

Checkers   Checkers can be played between a human player and a computer. The checkerboard is divided into 64 squares, colored alternately light and dark, and each side is provided with a set of twelve counters, one set red and the other black. At the beginning of the game the board is so placed that each player shall have two of his

---

*Association for Computing Machinery, a professional computer organization.

counters on squares at the edge of the board on his left, the counters being placed only on the dark squares of the first three rows on opposite sides of the board. The counters are moved alternately on the dark squares only, in a diagonal forward direction, one square at a time. The object of the game is to capture all the opponent's counters and remove them from the board or else pen them up in such a manner that they cannot move.

The game of Checkers is less complex than Chess since it involves simpler moves, with only about eight possible moves for the average position instead of the more than 30 possible moves for an average chess position. Still, it has been estimated that there are around 10 *duodecillion,* that is,

$$10,000,000,000,000,000,000,000,000,000,000,000,000,000$$

possible moves in an average game. Several checker playing programs have been written for computer play.

Blackjack   Blackjack (Twenty-One) is the most popular card game played in casinos throughout the world. Contributing to its popularity is the fact that it is played at a rapid rate, and money can be exchanged quickly. It is a simple game to play once all the basic rules are known. For a specific combination of the player's two up cards and the dealer's one up card, there is only one course of action for the players. In principle, it is easy for a computer program to use the same logic.

Until 1961, it was not generally known how to overcome the house odds at Blackjack. Then Dr. Edward O. Thorp wrote the book, *Beat The Dealer*. This book, which at one time was on the best seller list of *Time* magazine, included a basic strategy for playing Blackjack properly. Thorp's system was based on the fact that the odds change after certain cards have been played. Playing his system in a Las Vegas casino, Thorp won $2000 in about four hours. He was soon barred from various Blackjack games because his winnings were too consistent. Thorp had used a computer to work out all the odds changes as certain cards were removed from the deck and to produce the percentages for or against the player in each situation.

In the mid-1960's, Dr. Allen Wilson, a research scientist in San Diego, California used a computer to compute Blackjack statistics. He also wrote a book on this and other casino games entitled *The Casino Gambler's Guide*. In 1973, Lawrence Revere, a Blackjack expert, wrote a book entitled *Playing Blackjack as a Business*. The strategies in this book were devised with computers by Julian H. Braun, who also wrote the original strategy detecting program for Dr. Thorp. It required more than 9,000,000,000 computer dealt hands to devise the strategies in Revere's book.

Magic Squares   A magic square is an array of integers arranged in a square such that the sums of the integers in each row, each column, and each main diagonal are all equal. Magic squares were known to the ancients and were thought to possess mystic and magical powers because of their unusual nature. Producing these magic squares by a computer is an interesting and challenging problem.

Russian Roulette   In a game program called RUSROU, the computer simulates a revolver loaded with one bullet and five empty chambers. You spin the chamber and pull the trigger by inputting "1" or, if you want to quit, input a "2". You win if you play ten times and are still alive. Let's play this game:

THIS IS A GAME OF RUSSIAN ROULETTE

HERE IS A REVOLVER
PRESS "1" TO SPIN CHAMBER AND PULL TRIGGER. PRESS "2" TO GIVE UP.

GO? 1
—CLICK—
? 1
—CLICK—
? 1
—CLICK—
? 1
—CLICK—
? 1
—CLICK—
? 1
—CLICK—
? 1
—BANG—YOU'RE DEAD!

Other games There are literally hundreds of games that have been programmed for computer play. Many are covered in this book. Others may be found in this author's *Game Playing with Computers, Second Edition* (Hayden Book Co.) as well as in other books listed in the Bibliography.

1.6 Using the Computer

Let us now see how a computer is used to play with a mathematical recreation.

Step 1: Get the computer ready to execute programs typed in the BASIC language. The exact steps will depend upon which computer you are using.

Step 2: Type in the following BASIC program:

```
10   FØR N=100 TØ 999
20   LET A=INT(N/100)
30   LET B=INT(N/10)-10*A
40   LET C=N-100*A-10*B
50   IF N <> A↑3+B↑3+C↑3 THEN 70
60   PRINT N;"=";A↑3;"+";B↑3;"+";C↑3
70   NEXT N
80   END
```

If you made a mistake typing the program, press the RETURN key (assuming you are using a teletype terminal) and retype the entire line over again. Ignore any error messages that are printed.

Step 3: To obtain a listing of the program, just type LIST. The computer will type back all the BASIC statements in the program. If you see something you don't like in one of the statements, just type it over. The *last* version you type of a statement is what will be stored in the computer's memory. All other versions are erased.

Step 4: You are now ready to observe the computer *execute* your program. Simply type RUN, and away we go! In this example, the computer finds all three-digit numbers that have the properties of the following number:

$$153 = 1^3 + 5^3 + 3^3$$

The computer printout is as follows:

```
153 = 1  + 125 + 27
370 = 27 + 343 + 0
371 = 27 + 343 + 1
407 = 64 + 0   + 343
```

Step 5: After you are finished using the computer, turn it off. The exact steps needed to do this will depend upon the computer you are using.

1.7 Game Programs for You to Try

Even though you may not have yet learned to write your own programs for a computer, you should become familiar with using the teletype terminal or CRT display terminal.

Just for the fun of it, key in and execute one or two of the following BASIC programs. This will give you practice in using the terminal and seeing how a computer executes a program. I won't explain what the program will do. You will find out after you type RUN. Remember that you are not expected to understand how these programs work. (We will start writing BASIC programs in Chap. 2.)

PROGRAM 1

```
10  LET S=0
20  FOR N=112 TO 1000 STEP 14
30  LET S=S+N
40  NEXT N
50  PRINT "THE SUM OF ALL NUMBERS BETWEEN"
60  PRINT "100 AND 1000 THAT ARE DIVISIBLE BY 14"
70  PRINT "IS";S
80  END
```

PROGRAM 2

```
20   FOR N=0 TO 7
30   FOR R=0 TO N
40   LET C=1
50   FOR X=N TO N-R+1 STEP -1
60   LET C=C*X/(N-X+1)
70   NEXT X
80   PRINT C;
90   NEXT R
100  PRINT
110  NEXT N
120  END
```

PROGRAM 3

```
10  LET S=0
20  FOR N=112 TO 1000 STEP 14
30  S=S+N
40  NEXT N
50  PRINT "THE SUM OF ALL NUMBERS BETWEEN 100"
60  PRINT "AND 1000 THAT ARE DIVISIBLE BY 14"
70  PRINT "IS";S
80  END
```

chapter 2

TALKING IN BASIC

2.1 The BASIC Language

BASIC is a widely used programming language that is ideally suited for programming game programs. It has been implemented on all time-sharing computer systems, most minicomputers, and several medium and large scale machines.

Consider the following problem. A sheet of paper is 0.5 millimeters thick. A stack of this paper is to be started by laying down two sheets. The next addition to the stack is to be double the first, or four sheets. The third addition is to be double the second, or eight sheets. If this progression is continued until 32 additions have been made, how high would the stack be? The following program computes the answer to this question and illustrates some of the more commonly used BASIC statements in the process. The program was typed on a teletypewriter terminal, similar to the one shown in Fig. 2-1.

```
10   REM MOUNTAIN OF PAPER
15   PRINT "NUMBER","HEIGHT"
20   PRINT "OF SHEETS","IN MILLIMETERS"
25   PRINT
30   LET S=2
35   LET A=2
40   FOR D=1 TO 32
45   PRINT S,S*.5
50   LET A=2*A
55   LET S=S+A
60   NEXT D
65   END

RUN

NUMBER          HEIGHT
OF SHEETS       IN MILLIMETERS

2               1
6               3
14              7
```

TALKING IN BASIC

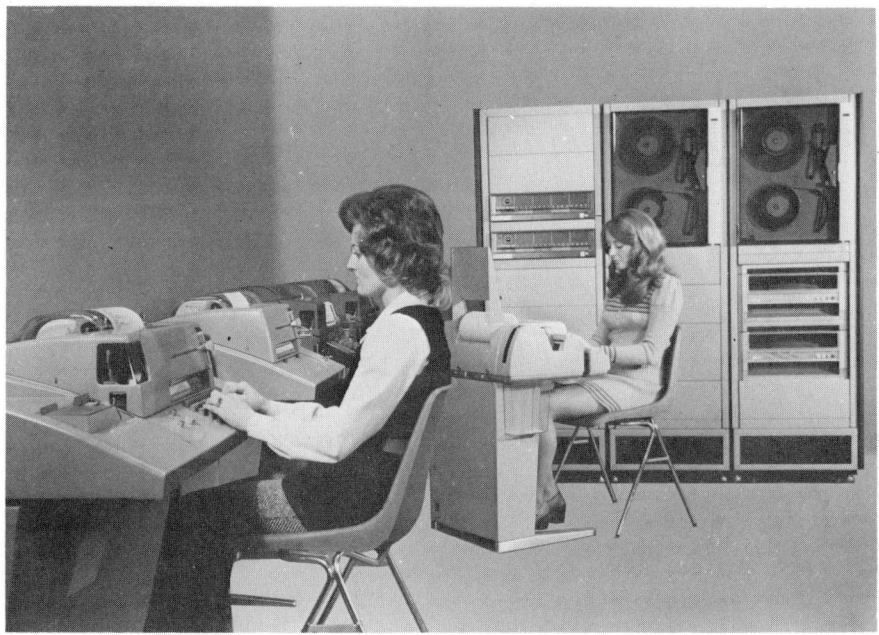

Fig. 2-1 Minicomputer time-sharing system

```
30                  15
62                  31
126                 63
254                 127
510                 255
1022                511
2046                1023
4094                2047
8190                4095
16382               8191
32766               16383
65534.              32767
131070.             65535.
262142.             131071.
524286.             262143.
1.04857E+06         524287.
2.09715E+06         1.04857E+06
4.19430E+06         2.09715E+06
8.38861E+06         4.19430E+06
1.67772E+07         8.38861E+06
3.35544E+07         1.67772E+07
6.71089E+07         3.35544E+07
1.34218E+08         6.71089E+07
2.68435E+08         1.34218E+08
5.36871E+08         2.68435E+08
1.07374E+09         5.36871E+08
2.14748E+09         1.07374E+09
4.29497E+09         2.14748E+09
8.58993E+09         4.29497E+09
```

Although all BASIC program statements must have *line numbers* assigned by the program writer, *sysiem commands* enable the user to communicate with the operating system of the computer. Thus, the command RUN at the bottom of a program is a system command that instructs the computer to process the program. The printed answer following RUN is the computer's response to this command.

The program determines that the stack of paper is 4.29497E09 or 4,294,970,000 millimeters high. This converts to 4,294,970 meters, or about 4,295 kilometers high. In other words, this stack of paper will be 1,451 times as high as the Sears Tower in Chicago, the tallest building in the world.

The first statement in the program is a REM statement, which enables us to insert a program. The REM statement is not executed by the computer; it merely provides information to anyone reading a program. The general form of the REM statement is

line number   REM   *comment*

where *line number* is an integer between 1 and 99999 and *comment* can be any arrangement of numbers, alphabetic characters, or special symbols such as $+, >, *, ?, /, \uparrow, =$, etc. Every statement in a BASIC program must have a line number. The computer will process the program in line number order, for example, line number 10 first, line number 15 second, line number 20 next, and so on.

After three PRINT statements (lines 15, 20, and 25), which will be discussed later, we find BASIC *arithmetic assignment* statements (lines 30, 35, 50, and 55). The word LET is used to introduce this type of statement. On line 30, the variable S is assigned a value of 2; on line 35, the variable A is assigned a value of 2; on line 50, the product of 2 times A is assigned to A; and on line 55, the value of A is added to the variable S.

In BASIC, a variable name consists of either a single letter, such as A, B, C, ..., Z, or a letter followed by a single digit, such as A0, A1, A2, ..., B0, B1, B2, ..., etc.*

Lines 40, 45, 50, 55, and 60 put the program into a looping or iterative process. The FOR–NEXT statements in BASIC are always used together and have the general form

line number   FOR v = n_1 TO n_2 STEP n_3
            BASIC statement
            BASIC statement
            BASIC statement
            BASIC statement
            BASIC statement
line number   NEXT v

where v is a variable name acting as an index, n_1 is the initial value given to the index, n_2 is the value of the index when the looping is completed, and n_3 is the amount by which the index should be increased after each iteration through the loop (if the step is 1, this portion of the statement may be omitted as it is on line 40). In our example, the index (D) is initially set at 1 (n_1) and the program steps called for in lines 45, 50, and 55 are executed. The end of the loop is reached in line 60. If a test shows that D (in this case 32) has not been reached, the index is increased by 1, and the next pass through the loop occurs. When the looping has been completed and the height of 32 additions of paper has been computed and totalled, program control moves to line 65.

The word PRINT is used in output operations to display program results. A statement that reads

            100   PRINT X, Y, Z

---

*Later on in this chapter you will be introduced to another kind of variable name, the subscripted variable.

TALKING IN BASIC

would cause the values of the three variable names to be printed across the page, with X beginning at the left margin, Y beginning 15 spaces to the right, and Z beginning 30 spaces to the right. The width of many terminal printers (such as the teletypewriter) is 75 characters, and the use of commas in the PRINT statement automatically establishes a format of five columns of 15 characters each. This implicit format specification feature of BASIC is especially appreciated by problem solvers who are not professional programmers. The statement in the program

        45   PRINT S,S*.5

would cause the value of S to be printed at the left margin and the value .5 times S to be printed 15 spaces to the right.

If you wish to have the output data printed in a more compact form, a semicolon can be used instead of a comma. In other words, the semicolon serves a function similar to that of the comma, but it specifies that a different spacing be used between printed values.

So far we have discussed the printing of values only, that is, data represented in the program by variables. It is also possible to print *messages* exactly as they are written in the program. Quotation marks serve a special purpose in statements used to print messages.

A PRINT statement containing quotation marks is the only one in the BASIC language in which blanks are counted, and the computer will print the message enclosed in quotation marks exactly. For example, the statement

       100   PRINT "COMPUTERIZED GAME PLAYING IS FUN"

will cause the message,

       COMPUTERIZED GAME PLAYING IS FUN

to be printed. Statements 15 and 20 in the Mountain of Paper program will cause the headings,

       NUMBER   HEIGHT
       OF SHEETS   IN MILLIMETERS

Messages and variables can also be mixed in the same PRINT statement. For example, when the statement,

       200   PRINT "ROULETTE NUMBER NUMBER=", N

is processed by the computer, the *message* "ROULETTE NUMBER =" will be printed at the left margin of the paper, and the *value* of N will be printed at the right. Commas (or semicolons) must be inserted between the items to be printed. If N represents a value of 22, then the printed message would appear as

       ROULETTE NUMBER = 22

On line number 65 we find an END statement. Every BASIC program must be terminated with this statement, to which the highest numbered line number in the program is assigned. This statement identifies the end of the program and consequently terminates computer processing. Figure 2–2 gives the flowchart for this BASIC program.

2.2 The GO TO Statement

The simplest BASIC statement for altering the sequence of execution is the GO TO statement. This statement has the general form,

       line number   GO TO *line number*

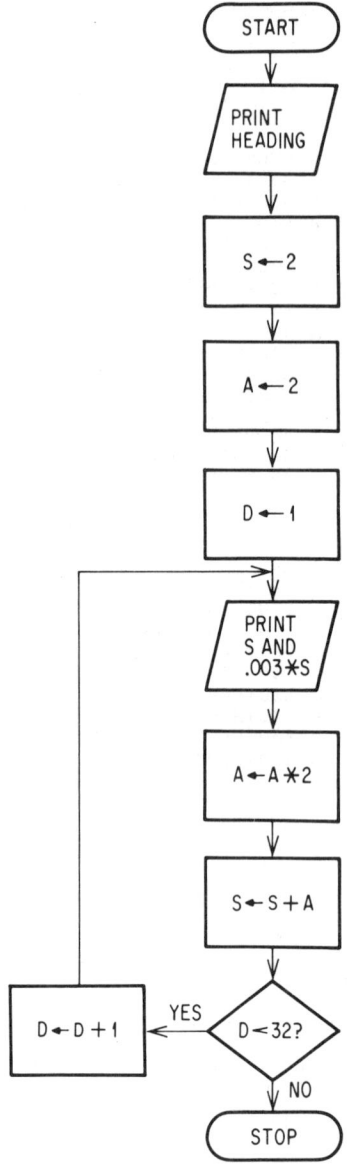

Fig. 2-2 Flowchart for the tall stack of paper problem

Suppose, for example, that we want to print the message,

GEORGIA IS A SOUTHERN STATE

many times. The following program will print this message and keep returning control to statement 10 where the message is printed again. When will this program stop printing the message? Well, let's run the program and see.

TALKING IN BASIC 17

```
10 PRINT "GEØRGIA IS A SØUTHERN STATE"
20 GØTØ 10
30 END

RUN


GEØRGIA IS A SØUTHERN STATE
GEØRGIA IS A SØUTHERN STATE
GEØRGIA IS A SØUTHERN STATE
GEØRGIA IS A SØUTHERN STATE
GEØRGIA IS A SØUTHERN STATE
GEØRGIA IS A SØUTHERN STATE
GEØRGIA IS A SØUTHERN STATE
GEØRGIA IS A SØUTHERN STATE
GEØRGIA IS A SØUTHERN STATE
GEØRGIA IS A SØUTHERN STATE
GEØRGIA IS A SØUTHERN STATE
GEØRGIA IS A SØUTHERN STATE
GEØRGIA IS A SØUTHERN STATE
GEØRGIA IS A SØUTHERN STATE
GEØRGIA IS A SØUTHERN STATE
GEØRGIA IS A SØUTHERN STATE
GEØRGIA IS A SØUTHERN STATE
GEØRGIA IS A SØUTHERN STATE
GEØRGIA IS A SØUTHERN STATE
GEØRGIA IS A SØUTHERN STATE
GEØRGIA IS A SØUTHERN STATE
GEØRGIA IS A SØUTHERN STATE
GEØRGIA IS A SØUTHERN STATE
GEØRGIA IS A SØUTHERN STATE
GEØRGIA IS A SØUTHERN STATE
GEØRGIA IS A SØUTHERN STATE
GEØRGIA IS A SØUTHERN STATE
```

As you might guess, the program will continue printing the message until the teletypewriter is worn out. In the next section, you will find a statement which will allow us to repeat a previous statement but stop the process at some predetermined point.

2.3 The IF–THEN Statement

The general form of the IF–THEN statement is

    line number   IF   *expression relation expression* THEN *line number*

Both *expressions* are evaluated and compared by the *relation* in the statement. If the condition is *true*, program control is transferred to the line number given after THEN. If the condition is *false*, program control continues to the next statement following the IF-THEN statement.

In the IF–THEN statement, the following six relations symbols are used to compare values:

Symbol	Relation
<	less than
<=	less than or equal to
>	greater than
>=	qreater than or equal to
=	equal to
< >	not equal to

The line number following the word THEN may be the line number of any executable statement (not DATA or REM) in the program.*

Consider the following BASIC program. This program illustrates program control using the IF–THEN and GO TO statements and three FOR–NEXT loops.

```
10 REM SUM OF TWO SQUARES
20 FOR N=1 TO 50
30 FOR A=1 TO 7
40 FOR B=1 TO 7
50 IF A*A+B*B<>N THEN 80
60 PRINT N;"=";A*A;"+";B*B
70 GOTO 95
80 NEXT B
90 NEXT A
95 NEXT N
99 END

RUN
```

```
 2 = 1 +  1
 5 = 1 +  4
 8 = 4 +  4
10 = 1 +  9
13 = 4 +  9
17 = 1 + 16
18 = 9 +  9
20 = 4 + 16
25 = 9 + 16
26 = 1 + 25
29 = 4 + 25
32 = 16 + 16
34 = 9 + 25
37 = 1 + 36
40 = 4 + 36
41 = 16 + 25
45 = 9 + 36
50 = 1 + 49
```

This program finds all the numbers less than 50 which can be written as the sum of two squares. For example,

$$20 = 2^2 + 4^2$$

In the fifth statement in the program, the relation of "not equal to" is used in the IF–THEN statement to determine whether $A^2 + B^2$ is not equal to N. If the conditional part of this statement is satisfied ($A^2 + B^2$ not equal to N), then program control will be transferred to the statement at line number 80. If the condition is not satisfied (that is, $A^2 + B^2$ equal to N), program control will commence with the next in-line statement (line number 60). The GO TO statement at line number 70 transfers program control to the statement at line number 95, thus bypassing the statements at line numbers 80 and 90. A flowchart of this problem is shown in Fig. 2–3.

2.4 READ and DATA Statements

Look at the following program:

---

*This is not true in all BASIC systems.

TALKING IN BASIC

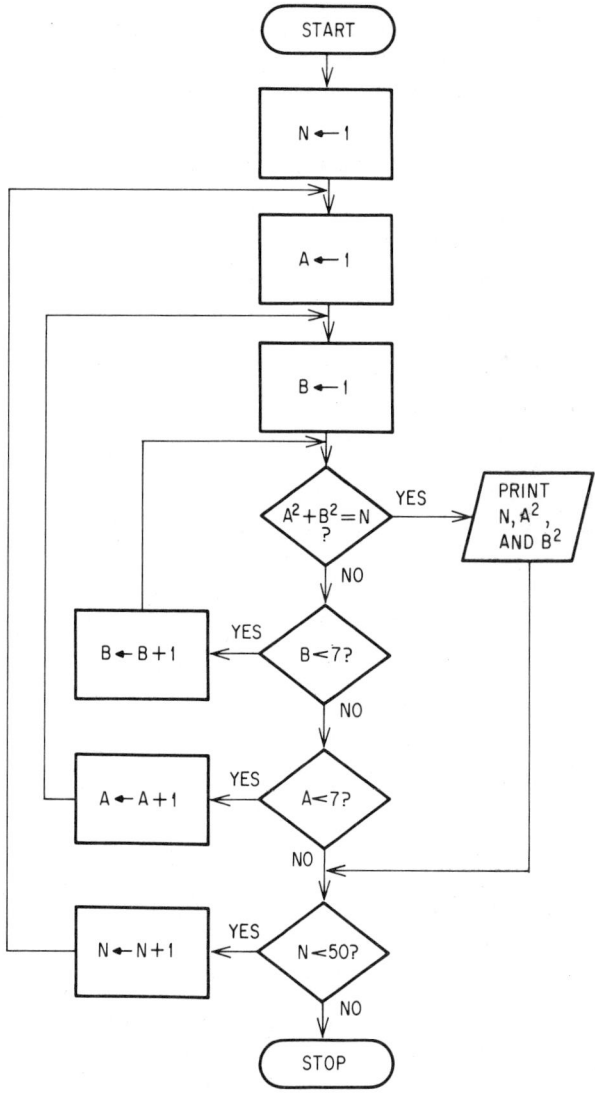

Fig. 2-3 Flowchart for program control example

```
10   READ A,B,C
20   LET Y=A*B*C
30   PRINT "Y =";Y
40   DATA 27,94,66
50   END
```

How does it work? The READ statement tells the computer that some variables follow which haven't been assigned any values as yet. To find their values, the computer searches for a DATA statement where the values are listed. In this particular program, at line number 10, the computer "sees" the READ instruction and then the A; it searches for a DATA statement, finds it, and then stores the first value in the DATA statement in the storage location for variable A:

```
10 READ A
20
30
40 DATA (27)
50
```

Values for B and C are found in the same way:

```
10 READ A , B , C
20
30
40 DATA (27) , (94) , (66)
50
```

When finished with the statement at line number 10, the computer has given A the value 27, B the value 94, and C the value 66. At line number 20, using A, B, and C, the value of Y is calculated and in the following statement, the value of Y is printed.

The general form of READ and DATA statements is

> line number   READ   *list of variable names*
> line number   DATA   *list of data values*

where the values to be assigned to the variable names identified in a READ statement are found in a DATA statement.

2.5 The INPUT Statement

In the last section we saw how data were assigned to variables using the READ and DATA statements. A more flexible way of assigning data values to variables is found by using the INPUT statement. This statement allows data values to be entered while the program is being executed by the computer. Here is another version of the program shown in Sect. 2.4:

```
10    INPUT A
20    INPUT B
30    INPUT C
40    LET Y=A*B*C
50    PRINT "Y =";Y
60    END

RUN

?27
?94
?66
Y = 167508.
```

The INPUT statement causes the computer to print a question mark and than to *wait* for you to type a number. In the preceding program, 27 was typed after the first question mark, and the computer assigned this number to A because the corresponding INPUT statement was

              10   INPUT   A

Similarly, 94 was assigned to B, and 66 assigned to C.

The three INPUT statements in the previous program could have been represented by only one INPUT statement, as shown below:

```
10   INPUT A,B,C
20   LET Y=A*B*C
30   PRINT "Y =";Y
40   END

RUN

?27,94,66
Y = 167508.
```

In this example the INPUT statement causes the computer to print a question mark and then to wait for you to type three numbers, separated by commas. A 27 was typed after the question mark, followed by a comma, the number 94, a comma, and the number 66.

It is often desirable to print a message identifying what variables are to be typed, as shown below:

```
10   PRINT "TYPE VALUES FOR A,B AND C"
20   INPUT A,B,C
30   LET Y=A*B*C
40   PRINT "Y =";Y
50   END

RUN

TYPE VALUES FOR A,B AND C
?27,94,66
Y = 167508.
```

If you use a semicolon at the end of the PRINT statement preceding the INPUT statement, it will cause the question mark to appear on the same line. Here is an example illustrating this point:

```
10   PRINT "I AM THINKING OF A NUMBER."
20   PRINT "WHAT IS THE NUMBER";
30   INPUT N
40   IF N <> 6 THEN 70
50   PRINT "HURRAY - YOU GUESSED THE NUMBER"
60   GOTO 80
70   PRINT "WRONG NUMBER"
80   END

RUN

I AM THINKING OF A NUMBER.
WHAT IS THE NUMBER?14
WRONG NUMBER
```

2.6 Using Library Functions

Functions are computer programs that are stored inside the computer. There are several of these available in BASIC, and the collection of functions is often called a *library of functions*. In this section we will discuss only three of the library functions found in BASIC. Other library functions include programs to compute square roots, trigonometric values (sine, cosine, arctangent, and tangent), logarithm, sign, and e^x. A description of these functions may be found in any BASIC text.

The *integer part* function INT associates to its argument (whatever number lies within the parentheses) the greatest integer* that is less than or equal to that argument. For example,

$$INT(7.3) = 7$$
$$INT(13.68) = 13$$
$$INT(48) = 48$$
$$INT(-6.9) = -7$$
$$INT(.004) = 0$$

The general form of the INT function is INT(X), where INT is the *name* of the function and X is the *argument* of the function.

The *random number* function RND causes the computer to select a *surprise* number between 0 and 1; in other words a number like .843214, .061237, or .551366 (see Fig. 2–4).

Fig. 2-4 Random numbers between 0 and 1

It's as though the computer spun a number wheel, like the one shown in Fig. 2–5, to get the value for the RND function. We're never quite sure what number will be selected.

The general form of the function is RND(X), where RND is the *name* of the function and X is the *argument* of the function. On some computers, the value of the argument is not important; on other computers, it makes a difference. A negative number, such as -1 or -43, will produce random numbers on most computers. The following program produces 30 random numbers between 0 and 1:

```
10    FOR N=1 TO 30
20    LET R=RND(1)
30    PRINT R,
40    NEXT N
50    END
```

RUN

5.95831E-02	.305312	9.21001E-02	.224408	.946787
.792589	.60074	.758426	.922355	.951629
.446311	.605791	.923159	2.33573E-02	3.16814E-02

*A whole number without a fractional part, for example, 267 is an integer while 58.3 is not.

Fig. 2-5 Wheel of Fortune

.6214	2.89415E-02	.861596	.843385	1.44611E-03
.940583	.756067	.959186	.581024	.376345
.126482	6.73708E-02	.221578	.323577	.275226

Many game programs require the use of random numbers in ranges other than from 0 to 1. For example, assume that you want to simulate the numbers in the game of Keno, which range from 1 to 80. This can be accomplished in BASIC very easily by writing the statement,

```
10    LET   K = INT(1 + (80 * RND (-1)))
```

If you want to simulate the numbers of a roulette wheel,* you could write the following program:

```
10  FOR R=1 TO 115
20  PRINT INT(37*RND(1))+1;
30  NEXT R
40  END

RUN
```

17	37	4	15	10	27	2	36	33	35	5	32
5	11	32	7	22	34	32	4	30	21	4	34
5	3	8	19	23	6	17	9	12	16	27	26
17	26	4	13	37	20	8	14	35	19	2	22
28	7	16	8	18	2	32	36	37	26	3	13
27	7	14	25	7	2	36	25	8	2	34	7
22	25	28	29	16	32	24	3	29	1	11	33
28	13	6	31	37	37	3	6	8	34	13	6
9	33	2	8	30	23	22	2	34	14	17	33
27	37	37	33	24	36	11					

*The number sequence of an American roulette wheel is 1, 2, 3, ..., 36, zero (0), and double zero (00).

In this case the number 37 is used to simulate the zero (0) on the roulette wheel.

The statement,

$$10 \quad \text{LET} \quad D = \text{INT}((6 * \text{RND}(-1)) + 1$$

will produce numbers in the range from 1 through 6 or, in other words, a simulation of the roll of a die. The statement

$$10 \quad \text{LET} \quad D = \text{INT}((6 * \text{RND}(-1)) + 1 + \text{INT}((6 * \text{RND}(-1)) + 1$$

will produce numbers in the range from 2 through 12, thus simulating the roll of two dice.

The *absolute value* function ABS gives the "absolute value" of the argument. The function is written ABS(X), as follows:

$$\text{ABS}(3) = 3$$
$$\text{ABS}(-3) = 3$$
$$\text{ABS}(0) = 0$$
$$\text{ABS}(-623) = 623$$

The following program asks two players to guess which number between 1 and 50 the computer has randomly picked:

```
10  REM A NUMBER GUESSING GAME
15  PRINT "PLAYER 1 - GUESS IS";
20  INPUT P1
25  PRINT "PLAYER 2 - GUESS IS";
30  INPUT P2
35  LET C=INT(50*RND(1))+1
40  PRINT "COMPUTER SELECTED"; C
45  IF ABS(C-P1) <> ABS(C-P2) THEN 60
50  PRINT "BOTH PLAYERS WERE EQUAL"
55  GOTO 80
60  IF ABS(C-P1)<ABS(C-P2) THEN 75
65  PRINT "PLAYER 2 WAS CLOSEST"
70  GOTO 80
75  PRINT "PLAYER 1 WAS CLOSEST"
80  END

RUN

PLAYER 1 - GUESS IS?6
PLAYER 2 - GUESS IS?36
COMPUTER SELECTED 9
PLAYER 1 WAS CLOSEST
```

This program used the functions INT, RND, and ABS. The INT and RND functions were used to determine the number the computer selected. The ABS function was used to determine the numerical distance (disregarding signs) from C to P1 and P2.

2.7 Arrays

Up to now the variables used in BASIC have been single letters (A,X,R) and single letters followed by a single digit (A1, B7, X3). Sometimes it is convenient to be able to use a collection of variables. This can be done by using a *subscripted variable*. Subscripted means "written below," as in $A_1, A_2, A_3, \ldots$; however, because of keyboard limitations, computer terminals use A(1), A(2), A(3), and so on.

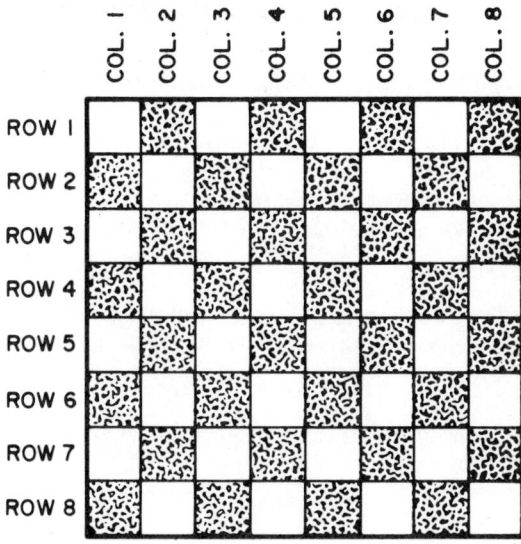

Fig. 2-6 Chessboard containing eight rows and eight columns

Subscripted variables are used to identify specific positions within an *array* of values. In BASIC there are two types of arrays: a one-dimensional array (called a *list*) and a two-dimensional array (called a *table*). An array is given a name, say X, and positions within this array are identified by subscripts. For example, in the list named X,

$X(1)$ is the first location
$X(2)$ is the second location
$X(3)$ is the third location
$X(4)$ is the fourth location

and so on.

An array name in BASIC must consist of a single alphabetic character. For example, A, M, R are valid array names, whereas A1, M7, and R2 are not.

A table is composed of horizontal *rows* and vertical *columns*. Therefore, each position in a table has two subscripts. The first subscript refers to the row number, the second to the column number. As a simple analogy, let's consider the familiar chessboard, a table containing 64 squares in eight rows and eight columns (see Fig. 2–6). Applying BASIC terminology, we will give the chessboard a name, C, and specify a few locations on it. Any location in Table C can be specified by $C(I,J)$, where I represents the row and J the column. Thus location $C(2,5)$ is the square in the second row, fifth column. Likewise, to specify the square in the first row, seventh column, we use the subscripted variable $C(1,7)$.

Now lets look at the classical chess problem known as the *Knight's Tour,* the sequence of moves in which the knight lands once on every square on the chessboard but on no square more than once. The knight, whose moves are limited to one specific pattern, is allowed to move to any square on the board which is two rows and one column or two columns and one row away from the square he is currently occupying.

If we name the chessboard K, we can specify any square by the subscripted variable $K(I,J)$ where I represents the row and J the column. Thus the square in the upper right corner of the chessboard is represented as K(1,8), that is, the square of Table K that is in the first row, eighth column.

The knight's entire tour of the chessboard can be represented in subscripted variable notation. Figure 2–7 shows the knight's starting position and his first six moves, and it suggests the remainder in the final box, where each position is numbered in sequence. Note that the subscripted variable is given for the knight's positions at the beginning, after each of the first six moves, and at the end. As an exercise, the reader should write the entire knight's tour in subscripted variable notation.

If you want to use subscripts that are greater than 10, you must "tell" the computer of this desire with a dimension (DIM) statement. For example,

$$10 \quad DIM \quad A(27)$$

informs the computer that you will need 27 memory locations labeled A(1), A(2), A(3), ..., A(27). The statement,

$$10 \quad DIM \quad X(20,40)$$

informs the computer that you will need 800 memory locations for a table named X, as follows: X(1,1), X(1,2), X(1,3), ..., X(20,40).

2.8 The RESTORE Statement

The BASIC language has a provision for using the same data in a program more than once. Thus, if a program had been written and the data inserted, we can send the computer back to the beginning of the data list by using a statement called RESTORE.

Once data has been entered, the computer reads the DATA statements in the order of their occurrence. By adding a RESTORE statement, the computer reverts to the first DATA statement in the program. For example, in the program,

```
10   READ A, B, C
20   LET S=A*A+B-3*C
30   PRINT S
40   RESTORE
50   LET X=A*A*A-B+C*C
60   PRINT X
70   DATA 10, 15, 17
80   END

RUN

64
1274
```

the computer reads A, B, and C (10, 15, and 17), executes the loop, resets an internal *pointer* to the beginning of the DATA statement, and then rereads A, B, and C.

The RESTORE statement permits the use of the same data values for different variables. For example,

```
10   READ A, B, C
       .
       .
       .
```

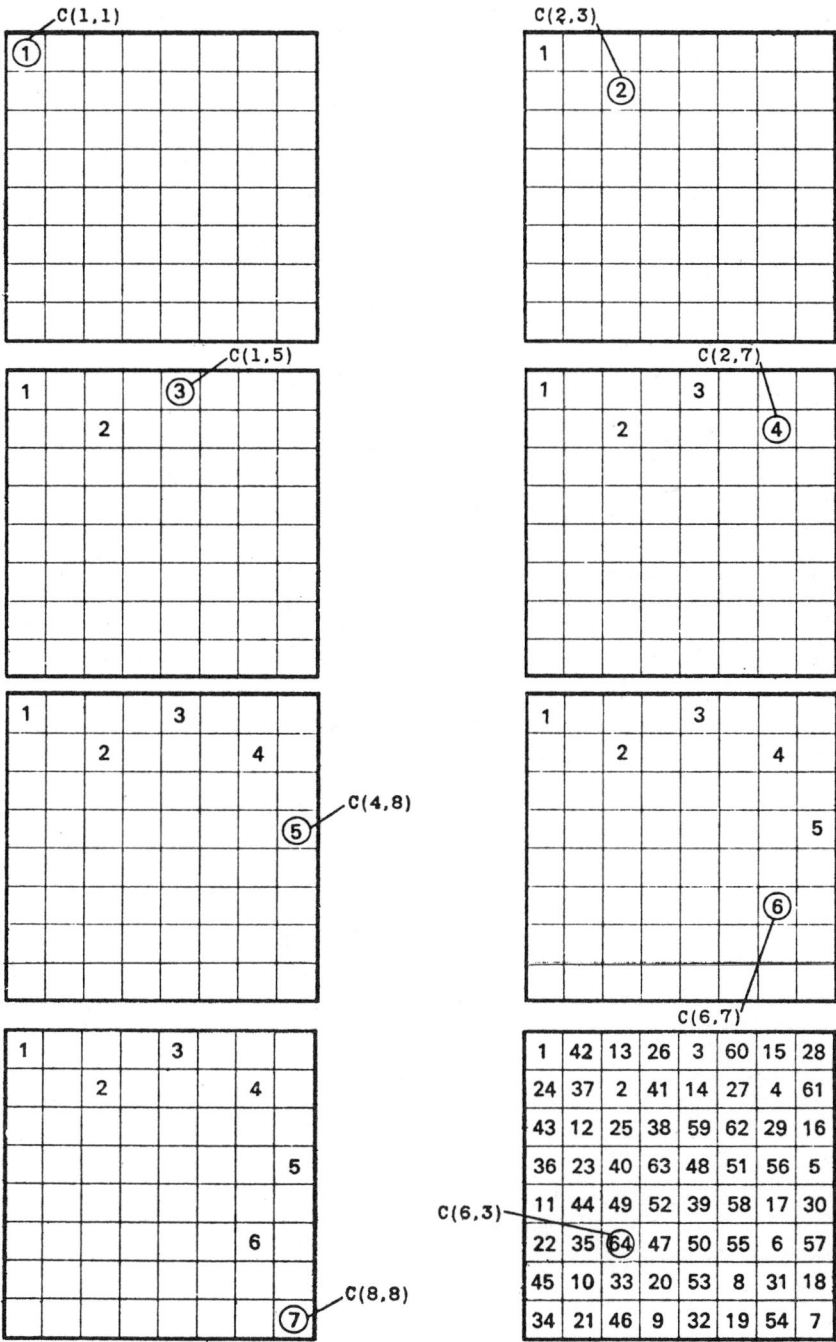

Fig. 2-7 Knight's Tour in subscripted variable notation

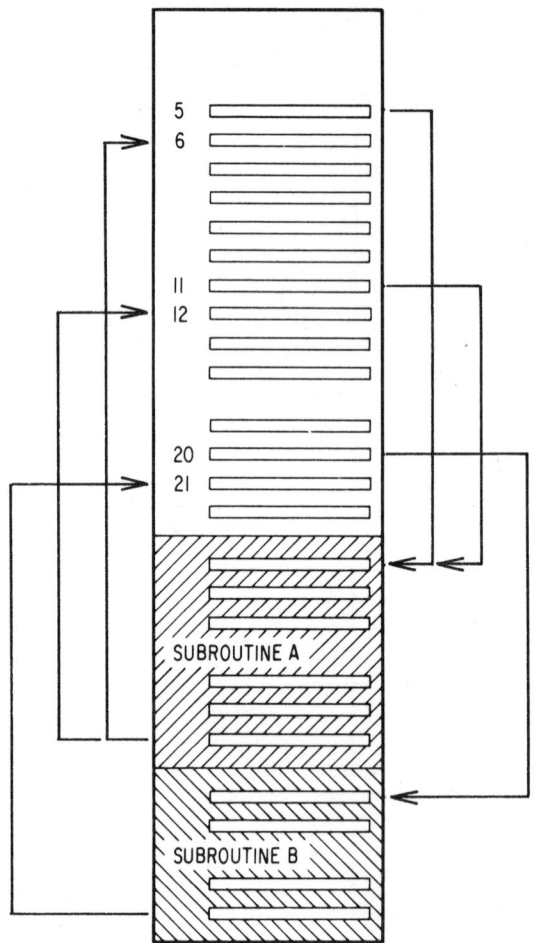

Fig. 2-8 Statements in a main program referencing two subroutines

```
50    RESTORE
60    READ X, Y, Z
         .
         .
         .
110   RESTORE
120   READ D, E, F
         .
         .
         .
180   DATA 27, 13, 64
```

TALKING IN BASIC

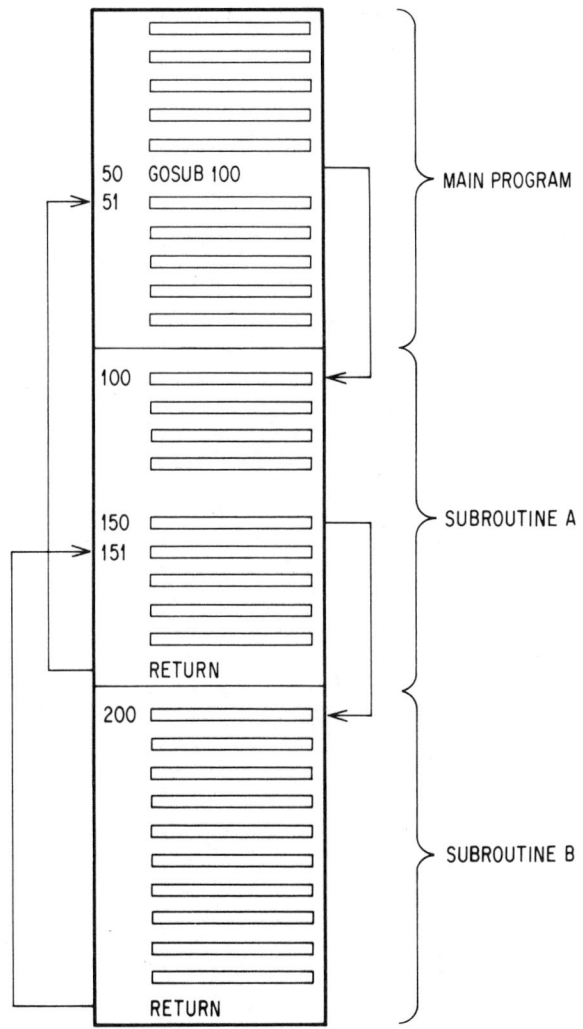

Fig. 2-9 Subroutine referencing another subroutine

assigns the three values in the DATA statement to the variables A, B, C, X, Y, Z, D, E, and F.

2.9 Subroutines

A *subroutine* is essentially an independent program, but it is written in such a way that it can be executed only when called by another statement. Subroutines, like functions, are used to perform tasks that are needed on more than one occasion. A subroutine call can be written at any place in a program; that is, at different times and/or in different locations, a *main program* may call upon a subroutine to perform a certain operation.

In Figure 2-8, statement 5 of the main program transfers control to subroutine A.

When all statements in subroutine A have been executed, control is returned to the main program, to statement 6, that is, which is the statement immediately following the calling statement. At statement 11, control again passes to subroutine A for the execution of all of its statements, and then control returns to the main program at statement 12. A similar series of events occurs between statements 20 and 21, but there, subroutine B is called. A subroutine may be called any number of times, and reentry to the main program at the proper point is automatically controlled by the calling statement. Subroutines offer a powerful means for accomplishing a very basic task in programming: the process of using the same set of statements repeatedly.

A subroutine in BASIC may consist of any number of statements, but its last one must be a RETURN statement.

The statement by which a BASIC subroutine is called has the general form

GOSUB ln

where ln represents the line number of the first statement in a subroutine.

A subroutine can also call another subroutine. Figure 2–9 illustrates a main program that calls a subroutine that, itself, calls another subroutine. In this example, when statement 50 is executed, program control is transferred to statement 100, the beginning of subroutine A. Statement 150 transfers control to statement 200. When execution of subroutine B is completed, control returns to subroutine A, statement 151, for the completion of Subroutine A, after which control returns to statement 51 in the main program.

2.10 Summary

This chapter contained only a brief introduction to the BASIC language. Hopefully, it contains enough information to point out to the reader the primary characteristics of the language. BASIC is ideally suited for writing game playing programs. A more complete description of BASIC may be found in any of the texts listed in the Bibliography.

chapter 3

IT'S GAME PLAYING TIME

In Chapters 1 and 2 we learned a little about computers and how to program them to play games. In the remainder of this book we will combine ideas from game playing and computer programming to do some interesting and fun things.

The number and variety of games is very large, certainly in the order of several thousand. Most people know the exact rules for relatively few games; nevertheless, it is usually easy to learn the rules of a new one. This chapter deals with several familiar games and recreations. To equip the computer to deal with these games, it is necessary to define the rules of the game, to develop a playing algorithm, and to furnish the computer with a program which will actually play the game.

3.1 Tossing a Coin

If a coin is perfectly balanced, then the probability of tossing a head is equal to the probability of tossing a tail. Hence, to simulate a coin-tossing game, we simply use the RND function and assign half the random numbers that can be generated to tails and the other half to heads. Therefore, exactly half of all random numbers will be in the range of 0 to 0.5 and could be regarded as representing heads. The other half will be in the range 0.5 to 1 and could be regarded as representing tails.

Let us write a program that will cause the computer to flip a coin a specified number of times. In the program below the computer flips 17 coins:

```
10   REM COIN TOSSING PROGRAM
20   PRINT "TYPE THE NUMBER OF COINS TO BE TOSSED";
30   INPUT S
40   PRINT
50   FOR N=1 TO S
60   LET R=RND(1)
70   IF R<.5 THEN 100
80   PRINT "TOSS";N;"IS A TAIL"
90   GOTO 110
100    PRINT "TOSS";N;"IW A HEAD"
110    NEXT N
120    END
```

```
RUN


TYPE THE NUMBER OF COINS TO BE TOSSED?17

TOSS 1      IS A HEAD
TOSS 2      IS A HEAD
TOSS 3      IS A HEAD
TOSS 4      IS A HEAD
TOSS 5      IS A TAIL
TOSS 6      IS A HEAD
TOSS 7      IS A HEAD
TOSS 8      IS A TAIL
TOSS 9      IS A TAIL
TOSS 10     IS A TAIL
TOSS 11     IS A TAIL
TOSS 12     IS A TAIL
TOSS 13     IS A TAIL
TOSS 14     IS A HEAD
TOSS 15     IS A TAIL
TOSS 16     IS A HEAD
TOSS 17     IS A TAIL
```

The following program causes the computer to flip a coin 15 times and also to count the number of tails and heads.

```
10    REM COIN TOSSING PROGRAM
20    LET T=0
30    LET H=0
40    FOR N=1 TO 15
50    LET R=RND(1)
60    IF R<.5 THEN 100
70    PRINT "TAIL"
80    LET T=T+1
90    GOTO 120
100   PRINT "HEAD"
110   LET H=H+1
120   NEXT N
130   PRINT "NUMBER OF TAILS =";T
140   PRINT "NUMBER OF HEADS =";H
150   END


RUN

HEAD
TAIL
TAIL
TAIL
TAIL
TAIL
HEAD
TAIL
TAIL
HEAD
HEAD
HEAD
TAIL
TAIL
TAIL
NUMBER OF TAILS = 10
NUMBER OF HEADS = 5
```

IT'S GAME PLAYING TIME

Both of these programs illustrate how a computer is used to toss a coin, where the order of heads and tails is random just as if you tossed a real coin. If you run either Coin Tossing Program several times, it is highly probable that the average number of tails will be approximately equal to the average number of heads. Using only a few samplings of random flips, the computer may not produce exactly a 50–50 split of heads and tails, just as such a split would not be guaranteed if the flips were performed by hand with a real coin. As in a real coin flipping situation, the more flips that are made, the more accurate will be the results.

As an exercise, the reader should run the Second Coin Tossing Program on the computer for 50, 100, 500, 1,000, and 5,000 flips (the reader will probably want to eliminate the printout on each flip to conserve printout time). The number of coins to be flipped is determined by the upper loop control limit in line number 40.

3.2 Rolling Dice

The rolling of one die is simulated in the following program and consists essentially of the generation of random integers from 1 to 6, inclusive:

```
10   REM ROLLING A DIE
20   PRINT "TYPE NUMBER OF TIMES"
30   PRINT "DIE IS TO BE ROLLED";
40   INPUT N
50   FOR X=1 TO N
60   LET R=INT(6*RND(1))+1
70   PRINT "ROLL";X;"IS A";R
80   NEXT X
90   END

RUN

TYPE NUMBER OF TIMES
DIE IS TO BE ROLLED?15
ROLL  1      IS A 2
ROLL  2      IS A 1
ROLL  3      IS A 3
ROLL  4      IS A 4
ROLL  5      IS A 1
ROLL  6      IS A 4
ROLL  7      IS A 2
ROLL  8      IS A 5
ROLL  9      IS A 5
ROLL 10      IS A 1
ROLL 11      IS A 6
ROLL 12      IS A 1
ROLL 13      IS A 6
ROLL 14      IS A 1
ROLL 15      IS A 1
```

The simulation of the rolling of two dice at a time is slightly more complicated. The possible results of this simulation are the integers from 2 to 12, inclusive, but they do not appear with equal probabilities. The following program simulates the rolling of two dice 18 times:

```
10   REM ROLLING TWO DICE
20   PRINT "TYPE NUMBER OF ROLLS TO BE MADE";
30   INPUT N
```

```
40   PRINT "FIRST DIE","SECOND DIE","TOTAL"
50   PRINT
60   FOR A=1 TO N
70   LET D1=INT(6*RND(1)+1)
80   LET D2=INT(6*RND(1)+1)
90   LET T=D1+D2
100  PRINT D1,D2,T
110  NEXT A
120  END
```

```
RUN

TYPE NUMBER OF ROLLS TO BE MADE? 18
```

FIRST DIE	SECOND DIE	TOTAL
4	4	8
6	4	10
2	6	8
4	2	6
2	1	3
3	2	5
4	1	5
6	4	10
3	4	7
2	2	4
6	3	9
3	5	8
3	6	9
2	5	7
4	6	10
2	3	5
1	2	3
1	6	7

Let us now examine a method of determining the percentage of times the throw of two dice will result in 7 or 11. One way to solve this problem is to actually roll a pair of dice 1,000 times and record the number of times the result is 7 or 11. It might be more interesting to obtain the result by observing a dice game in progress in a Las Vegas casino. An easier and faster way, however, is to have a computer simulate 1,000 rolls of the dice.

The following program simulates the event of rolling two dice 1,000 times. It also estimates the percentage of rolls of two dice which yield a 7 or 11.

```
10   REM DICE PROGRAM - SEVEN OR ELEVEN
20   LET S=0
30   FOR T=1 TO 1000
40   LET D=INT(6*RND(1))+1+INT(6*RND(1))+1
50   IF (D-7)*(D-11) <> 0 THEN 70
60   LET S=S+1
70   NEXT T
80   PRINT "PERCENTAGE OF ROLLS"
90   PRINT "WHICH ARE 7 OR 11 IS"S/10
99   END

RUN

PERCENTAGE OF ROLLS
WHICH ARE 7 OR 11 IS 22.3
```

IT'S GAME PLAYING TIME

The previous dice program computed a percentage of 22.3. The true answer is 22.2 percent (6/36 + 2/36 = 2/9). The problem of deciding how many times to simulate the event in order to get a good approximation to the true value is a difficult one. Ten times is obviously not enough, and one billion simulations would require too large an amount of computer time. One way to approach this problem would be to run the program four or five times with some fairly small number of simulations of the event. If the answers are all fairly close to each other, that is an indication that the number of simulations was sufficient. If the answers are quite different, then the number of simulations could be increased by a factor of ten if there is sufficient computer time available to execute the program. The dice program was run three more times with the following results: 21.5 percent, 22.1 percent, and 24.6 percent.

3.3. Mouse in a Maze

In Fig. 3-1 a mouse is put in a maze at the place labeled START, and he walks until he arrives at CHEESE. The maze, consisting of a pattern of horizontal and vertical paths, can be represented in array form as a rectangular table containing five rows and five columns (Fig. 3-2). The starting point is located at row 4, column 1, and the cheese at row 2, column 5.

The object of this simulation is to follow the mouse through the maze from the outset to the point at which he finds the cheese. A move, which is defined as a transfer from one position to some other position at a distance of one row or column, is determined by a random number from 1 to 4, each of which specifies the direction of the move, as follows:

1—right
2—left
3—up
4—down

A move is disregarded whenever the random number selected directs the mouse outside the boundaries of the maze. For example, the random number 2 would be disre-

Fig. 3-1 Maze

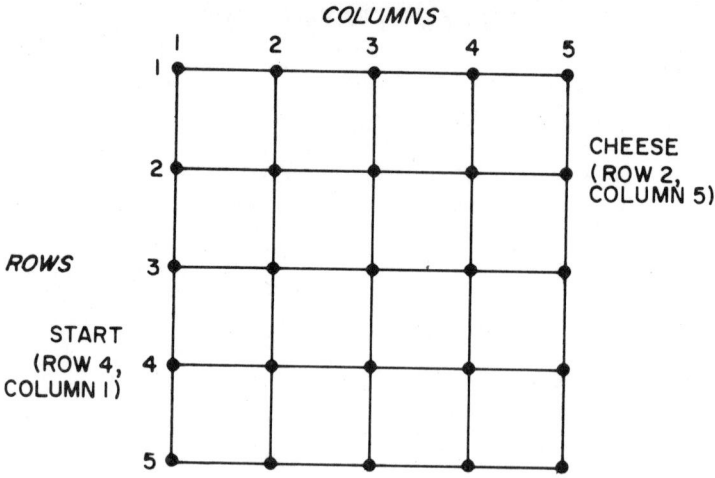

Fig. 3-2 Intersections of corridors of the maze

garded if generated as the first move of the mouse because a move can be made only up, down, or to the right at the starting position.

A flowchart that generates routes of an unspecified number of mice through the maze is shown in Fig. 3–3. The number of different mice that may tour the maze is an input to the following program:

```
55    REMARK MAZE PROBLEM
60    PRINT "TYPE THE NUMBER OF MICE THAT ARE TO ENTER THE MAZE";
65    INPUT M
70    LET N=1
75    PRINT
80    PRINT "MAZE TOUR --- MOUSE NUMBER";N
85    PRINT
90    PRINT "ROW","COLUMN"
95    PRINT
100   REMARK ESTABLISH ENTRY POINT
105   LET C=1
110   LET R=4
115   LET S=INT(4*RND(0)+1)
120   IF S <> 1 THEN 150
125   REMARK DETERMINE IF RIGHT MOVE IS VALID
130   LET C=C+1
135   IF C<6 THEN 245
140   LET C=C-1
145   GOTO 115
150   IF S <> 2 THEN 180
155   REMARK DETERMINE IF LEFT MOVE IS VALID
160   LET C=C-1
165   IF C <> 0 THEN 245
170   LET C=C+1
175   GOTO 115
180   IF S <> 3 THEN 220
185   REMARK DETERMINE IF UP MOVE IS VALID
190   LET R=R-1
195   IF R <> 0 THEN 245
200   LET R=R+1
210   GOTO 115
215   REMARK DETERMINE IF DOWN MOVE IS VALID
220   LET R=R+1
225   IF R<6 THEN 245
```

IT'S GAME PLAYING TIME

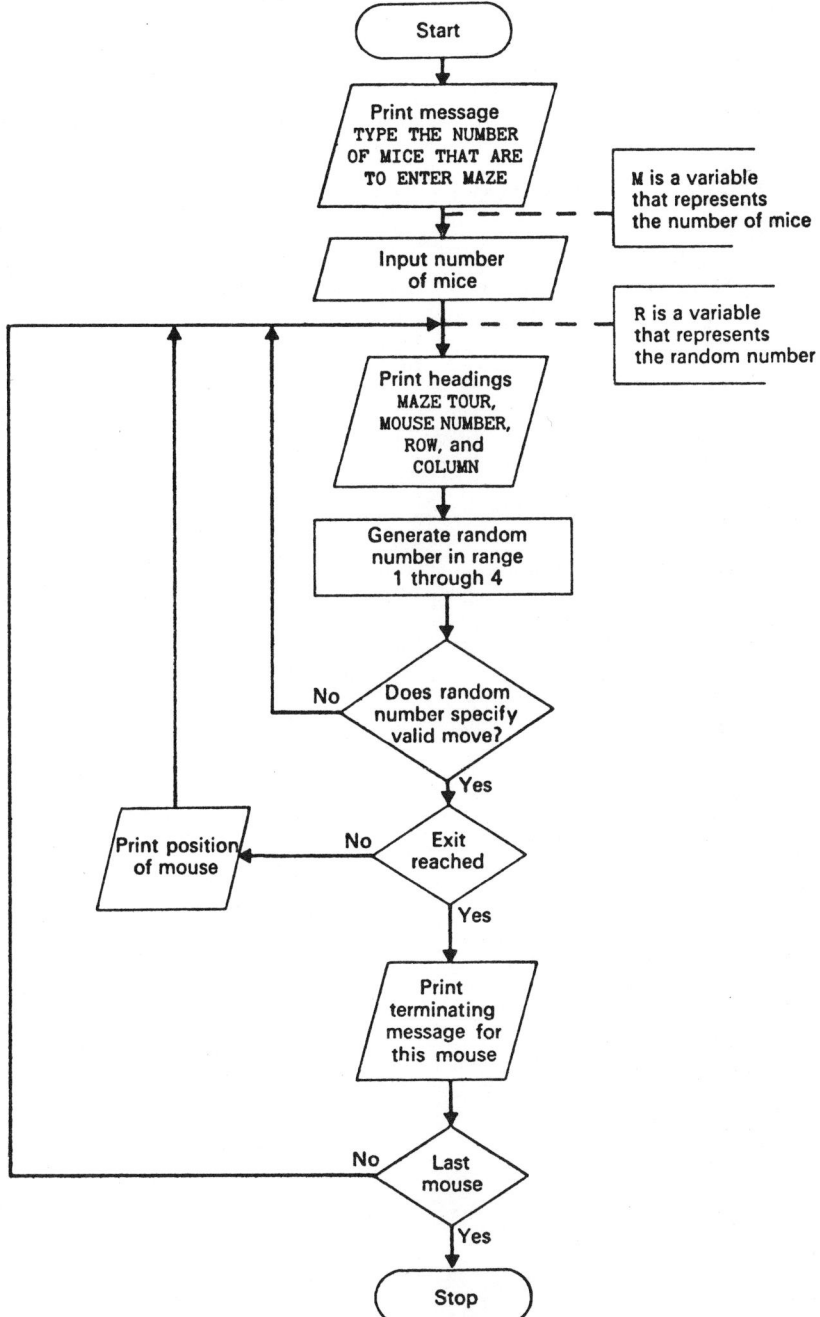

Fig. 3-3 Flowchart representing the simulation of the Mouse in the Maze

```
230   LET R=R-1
235   GOTO 115
240   REMARK DETERMINE IF MOUSE TOUR IS COMPLETE
245   IF C <> 5 THEN 260
250   IF R=2 THEN 270
255   REMARK PRINT POSITION OF MOUSE
260   PRINT R,C
265   GOTO 115
270   PRINT "END OF TOUR FOR MOUSE NUMBER";N
275   PRINT
280   PRINT
285   PRINT
290   REMARK DETERMINE IF THIS IS THE LAST MOUSE TOUR
295   IF N=M THEN 310
300   LET N=N+1
305   GOTO 75
310   END

RUN

TYPE THE NUMBER OF MICE THAT ARE TO ENTER THE MAZE? 1

MAZE TOUR --- MOUSE NUMBER 1
```

ROW	COLUMN
3	1
3	2
2	2
2	1
3	1
2	1
1	1
1	2
1	1
1	2
1	3
1	4
2	4
1	4
1	3
1	4
2	4
3	4
3	5
4	5
5	5
5	4
4	4
3	4
2	4
3	4
3	5
4	5
5	5
5	4
5	5
5	4
4	4
3	4
3	5

```
END OF TOUR FOR MOUSE NUMBER 1
```

The output of this program illustrates the path taken by one mouse. Perhaps the reader would like to execute this program using several mice. A discussion of how the program works follows.

55	Program name
60	Message to operator
65	Request for input of number of mice to enter the maze
70	Initialization of looping constant
75–95	Headings to be printed
100	Informative comment
105–110	Establishment of first values of maze indexes as entry point of maze
115	Evaluation of random number function
120–145	Determination of whether the random number generated is 1. If so, the column index C is increased by 1 and a check is made to see whether the index now specifies a position outside the maze. If so, the index is reduced by 1 and a new random number is generated. If the random number specifies a valid position within the boundary of the maze, program control is transferred to the statement at line number 245.
150–175	Determination of whether the random number generated is a 2 and whether the new column index specifies a valid position within the maze.
180–210	Determination of whether the random number generated is a 3 and whether the new row index specifies a valid position within the maze.
215–235	Determination of whether the new row index specifies a valid position within the maze.
240–250	Determination of whether maze indexes C and R indicate that the exit position of the maze has been reached. If so, program control is transferred to statement 270.
255–265	Printout of the current values of the maze indexes and transfer of control to statement 115, where a new random number is generated.
270	Printout of a terminating message for each mouse
275–285	Skipping of three lines in printout
290	Informative comment
295–305	A check to see whether all mice have entered the maze. If not, N is increased by 1 and program control is returned to statement 75, where a new maze tour is started by a new mouse.
310	Program terminating statement

3.4 Sam the Drunk

Assume that Sam, who is intoxicated beyond reason, is standing at the midpoint of a narrow bridge. The bridge, which is 40 feet long, spans a river containing alligators and piranha fish. Sam staggers first in one direction, then the other. It is unpredictable in which direction he will stagger next. However, he is a lucky drunk and every time he takes a step, it will be either toward the left bank of the river or toward the right bank. He will not fall off the bridge.

The following program simulates the staggering of Sam. The program assumes that the drunk takes steps of 1 foot each. A flowchart is shown in Fig. 3–4.

```
10   REM SAM THE DRUNK
20   LET D=20
30   LET N=0
40   LET N=N+1
50   LET X=RND(1)
60   IF X<.5 THEN 100
70   LET D=D+1
```

```
 80   IF D=40 THEN 130
 90   GOTO 40
100   LET D=D-1
110   IF D=0 THEN 150
120   GOTO 40
130   PRINT "SAM REACHES THE RIGHT BANK"
135   PRINT "AFTER";N;"STEPS"
140   GOTO 160
150   PRINT "SAM REACHES THE LEFT BANK"
155   PRINT "AFTER";N;"STEPS"
160   END

RUN


SAM REACHES THE LEFT BANK
AFTER 350    STEPS
```

Our run of the program resulted in Sam reaching the left bank after 356 steps. Perhaps the reader would like to execute this program on a computer. If you want to run the program over and over again until it is stopped manually, you could type

160   GO TO 20

This change will result in a printout similar to the one that follows.

```
SAM REACHES THE LEFT BANK AFTER 410 STEPS
SAM REACHES THE RIGHT BANK AFTER 382 STEPS
SAM REACHES THE RIGHT BANK AFTER 450 STEPS
                        •
                        •
                        •
```

Problems of this type are called *random walk* problems and are patterned after an old gambling problem.

Suppose a gambler tosses a fair coin repeatedly and wins a dollar every time it falls heads but loses a dollar every time it falls tails. A gain of a dollar is like one step to the right, and a loss of a dollar is like one step to the left. So the fluctuations in the net gain of the player are precisely the fluctuations of the distance of Sam from the center of the bridge when he stumbles in a symmetric, random walk in one direction. The fact that Sam is likely to spend much time on one side or the other is equivalent to the fact that either the gambler or his opponent is likely to be in the lead for long stretches of time. In fact, it is not unusual for the winner in such a game to be in the lead nearly all of the time. This fact is emphasized most dramatically by an example cited by the probabilist William Feller in one of his books: If the coin is tossed once a second for 365 days, there is 1 chance in 20 that the winner will be in the lead for more than 364 days and 10 hours.

One of the interesting questions asked about random walks is, "What is the probability that the subject will sooner or later return to its starting point?" The answer turns out to be 1.

3.5 Battle of Numbers

The game of Battle of Numbers starts with a pile of objects (usually coins, marbles, rocks, shells, sticks, etc.). You and your opponent (the computer) alternately remove at least one and at most L, where L is some previously established number greater than one. The player who removes the last object *loses*.

IT'S GAME PLAYING TIME

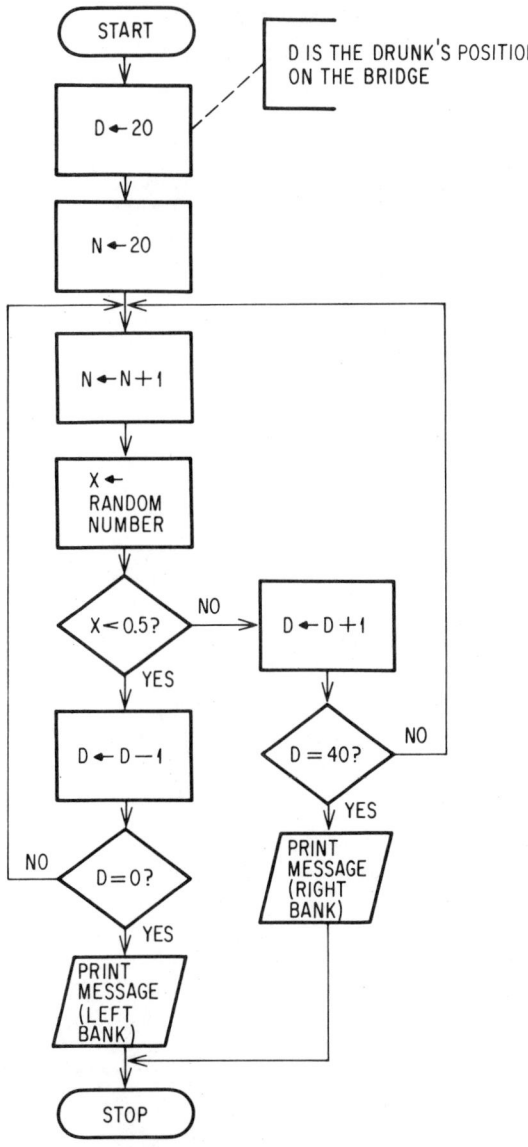

Fig. 3-4 Flowchart for "Sam the Drunk" simulation

As an example, suppose that the pile contains 15 objects, and each player must remove from 1 to 8 objects. If the first player removes 8, the second player will remove 6 and win. If the first player removes three, the second player can remove 4, and eventually win. In fact, the only first-player move that will guarantee a win is 5. Now the second player will remove something from 1 to 8. For any of these moves, the first player can win.

A flowchart for the Battle of Numbers is shown in Fig. 3–5. A program that plays the Battle of Numbers follows.

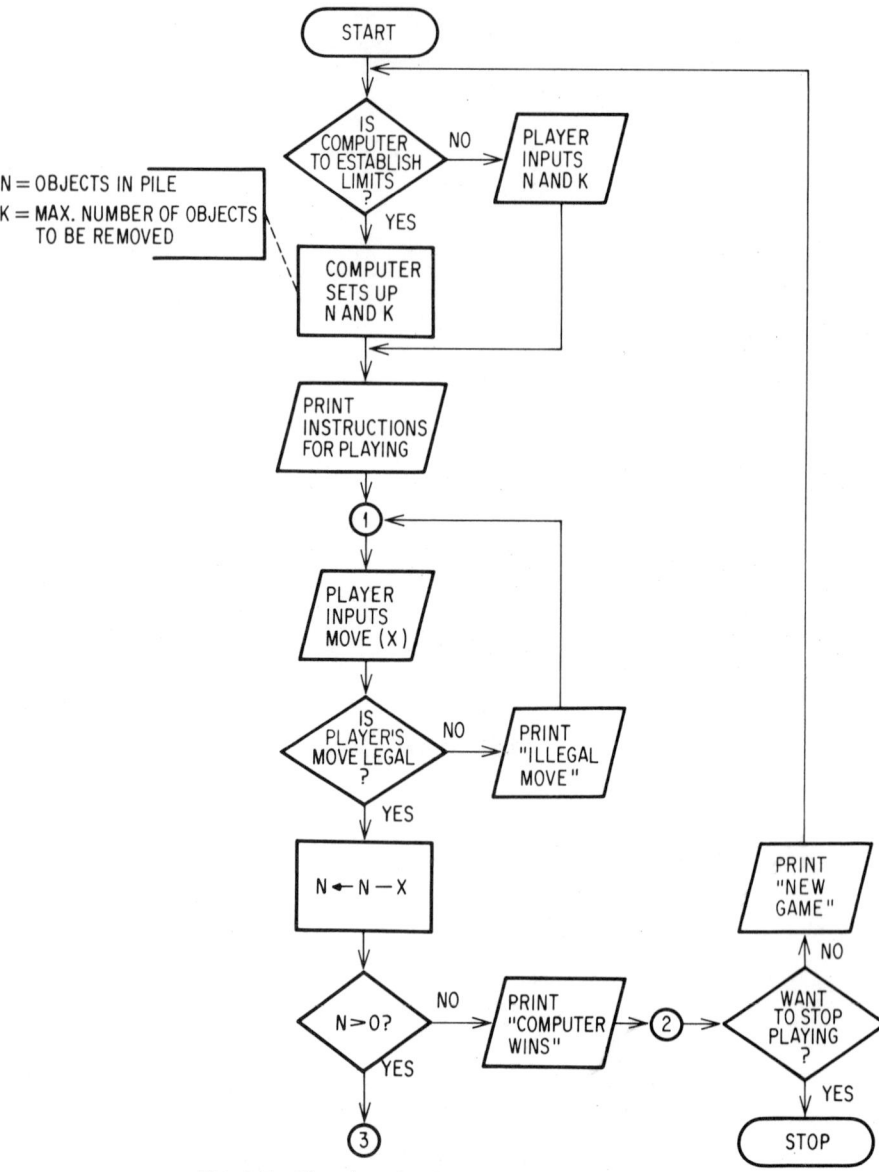

Fig. 3-5 Flowchart for the Battle of Numbers

```
10    REM BATTLE OF NUMBERS
20    PRINT "DO YOU WISH TO CHOSE LIMITS-(YES-1,NO-ANY NUMBER)";
30    INPUT L
40    IF L <> 1 THEN 100
50    PRINT "NUMBER OF OBJECTS IN PILE";
60    INPUT N
70    PRINT "MAXIMUM NUMBER OF OBJECTS TO BE REMOVED";
80    INPUT K
90    GOTO 120
```

IT'S GAME PLAYING TIME

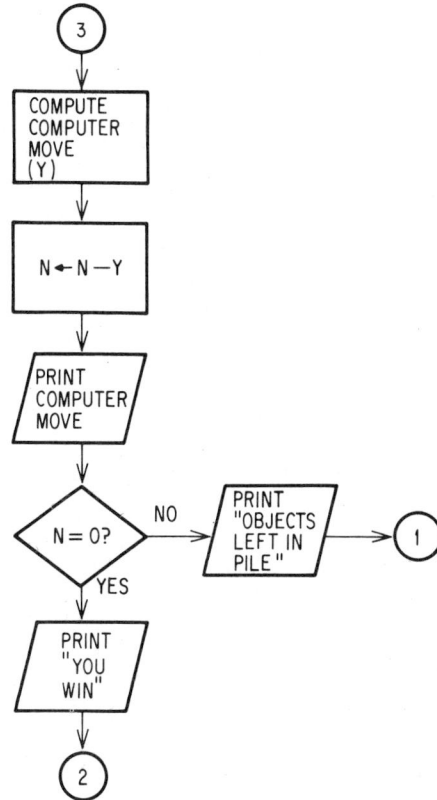

Fig. 3-5 Flowchart for the Battle of Numbers (cont'd)

```
100    LET N=20+INT(80*RND(1))
110    LET K=5+INT(10*RND(1))
120    PRINT "INSTRUCTIONS FOR PLAYING BATTLE OF NUMBERS"
130    PRINT "NUMBER OF OBJECTS IN PILE IS";N
140    PRINT "YOU MAY REMOVE FROM 1 TO";K;"OBJECTS"
150    PRINT "THE PLAYER WHO REMOVES THE LAST OBJECT LOSES"
160    REM HUMAN PLAYER'S MOVE
170    PRINT "YOUR MOVE";
180    INPUT X
190    IF X>K THEN 220
200    IF X<1 THEN 220
210    IF X <= 10 THEN 250
220    PRINT "ILLEGAL MOVE"
230    PRINT
240    GOTO 170
250    REM TEST FOR WIN
260    LET N=N-X
270    IF N>0 THEN 350
280    PRINT "**** COMPUTER WINS****"
290    PRINT
300    PRINT "DO YOU WANT TO STOP PLAYING-(YES-1,NO-ANYNUMBER)";
310    INPUT Z
320    IF Z=1 THEN 540
330    PRINT "NEW GAME"
340    GOTO 20
```

```
350   REM COMPUTER'S MOVE
360   LET Q=INT((N-1)/(K+1))
370   LET Y=N-1-Q*(K+1)
380   IF Y=0 THEN 460
390   LET N=N-Y
400   PRINT "COMPUTER MOVE";Y
410   IF N=0 THEN 520
420   PRINT "OBJECTS LEFT IN PILE-";N
430   PRINT
440   PRINT
450   GOTO 170
460   REM MAKE RANDOM MOVE
470   IF N>1 THEN 500
480   LET Y=1
490   GOTO 390
500   LET Y=1+INT(K*RND(1))
510   GOTO 390
520   PRINT "****YOU WIN****"
530   GOTO 290
540   END

RUN

DO YOU WISH TO CHOSE LIMITS-(YES-1,NO-ANY NUMBER)?1
NUMBER OF OBJECTS IN PILE?100
MAXIMUM NUMBER OF OBJECTS TO BE REMOVED?10
INSTRUCTIONS FOR PLAYING BATTLE OF NUMBERS
NUMBER OF OBJECTS IN PILE IS 100
YOU MAY REMOVE FROM 1 TO 10    OBJECTS
THE PLAYER WHO REMOVES THE LAST OBJECT LOSES
YOUR MOVE?1
COMPUTER MOVE 10
OBJECTS LEFT IN PILE- 89

YOUR MOVE?2
COMPUTER MOVE 9
OBJECTS LEFT IN PILE- 78

YOUR MOVE?3
COMPUTER MOVE 8
OBJECTS LEFT IN PILE- 67

YOUR MOVE?4
COMPUTER MOVE 7
OBJECTS LEFT IN PILE- 56

YOUR MOVE?5
COMPUTER MOVE 6
OBJECTS LEFT IN PILE- 45

YOUR MOVE?6
COMPUTER MOVE 5
OBJECTS LEFT IN PILE- 34

YOUR MOVE?7
COMPUTER MOVE 4
OBJECTS LEFT IN PILE- 23
```

IT'S GAME PLAYING TIME 45

```
YOUR MOVE?8
COMPUTER MOVE 3
OBJECTS LEFT IN PILE- 12

YOUR MOVE?9
COMPUTER MOVE 2
OBJECTS LEFT IN PILE- 1

YOUR MOVE?1
**** COMPUTER WINS****

DO YOU WANT TO STOP PLAYING-(YES-1,NO-ANYNUMBER)?6
NEW GAME
DO YOU WISH TO CHOSE LIMITS-(YES-1,NO-ANY NUMBER)?1
NUMBER OF OBJECTS IN PILE?27
MAXIMUM NUMBER OF OBJECTS TO BE REMOVED?5
INSTRUCTIONS FOR PLAYING BATTLE OF NUMBERS
NUMBER OF OBJECTS IN PILE IS 27
YOU MAY REMOVE FROM 1 TO 5      OBJECTS
THE PLAYER WHO REMOVES THE LAST OBJECT LOSES
YOUR MOVE?3
COMPUTER MOVE 5
OBJECTS LEFT IN PILE- 19

YOUR MOVE?5
COMPUTER MOVE 1
OBJECTS LEFT IN PILE- 13

YOUR MOVE?5
COMPUTER MOVE 1
OBJECTS LEFT IN PILE- 7

YOUR MOVE?1
COMPUTER MOVE 5
OBJECTS LEFT IN PILE- 1

YOUR MOVE?1
**** COMPUTER WINS****

DO YOU WANT TO STOP PLAYING-(YES-1,NO-ANYNUMBER)?1
```

This program allows the player to choose the number of objects in the pile as well as the maximum number of objects that can be removed at each turn. If the player chooses not to establish these values, the computer will do so.

The computer can be beaten only if the player makes the proper play on each move. The first move is critical. For example, consider a game using 27 objects where either 1, 2, 3, 4, or 5 objects can be removed at each turn. To win, add the lower and upper limit, 1 +5 = 6. The multiples of 6 are 6, 12, 18, 24, 30, 36, ... Notice that 24 is the closest multiple of 6 less than 27. Add 1 to 24 and make sure the computer takes its turn with one more than a multiple of 6 available each time. Once the first move has been made, simply take enough to make the computer's choice and your choice total 6. The magic numbers for this game would then be 25, 19, 13, and 7. If the computer has that many left on its turn, it will lose if you make your total and its total add to 6.

```
             START WITH 27 OBJECTS

             YOUR MOVE—2
             COMPUTER MOVE—5
             OBJECTS LEFT IN PILE—20

             YOUR MOVE—1
             COMPUTER MOVE—3
             OBJECTS LEFT IN PILE—16

             YOUR MOVE—3
             COMPUTER MOVE—5
             OBJECTS LEFT IN PILE—8

             YOUR MOVE—1
             COMPUTER MOVE—5
             OBJECTS LEFT IN PILE—2

             YOUR MOVE—1
             COMPUTER MOVE—1

             ——YOU WIN——
```

3.6 Dealing a Poker Hand

When playing Poker a regular deck of 52 cards is used. Cards rank in importance from Ace as the high card, down through King, Queen, Jack, ten, and onward down to two, the low card. An exception is the use of the Ace as low card in a straight or straight flush, as 5, 4, 3, 2, Ace.

The sequence of importance in a Poker game is based on five cards. Hands are listed below in order of declining importance. In a Poker game, the owner of the highest group is the winner.

Royal Flush: Five cards in numerical sequence of the same suit, the Ace being the high card.

Straight Flush: Five cards in numerical sequence of the same suit.

Four-of-a-Kind: Four of the same number or four face cards the same.

Full-House: Three of one number or of the same face card, and two other cards of their own identical number or of the same face card.

Flush: Five cards of the same suit, not in numerical sequence.

Straight: Five cards in numerical sequence, regardless of suit.

Three-of-a-Kind: Three cards of the same value. The other cards held are ignored.

Two Pairs: Two cards of one number, and two more of another number, as two 5s and two Queens. Remaining card(s) are ignored.

One Pair: Two cards of one number. Other cards held are disregarded.

No Pair: The high card wins if nobody has at least one pair.

Let us now discuss the simulation of dealing a five card poker hand. The program must be able to deal several cards from a standard deck. For our purpose let us think of the cards, in some standard order, as being numbered from 0 through 51, as follows:

IT'S GAME PLAYING TIME

CLUB (2—Ace)	0—12
DIAMOND (2—Ace)	13—25
HEART (2—Ace)	26—38
SPADE (2—Ace)	39—51

The program first sets up the deck, then deals, interprets, and prints the values of five cards. A flowchart is shown in Fig. 3–6, and the program follows.

```
100    REM DEALING A POKER HAND
110    REM SET UP DECK
120    DIM L[52]
130    FOR I=1 TO 52
140    LET L[I]=I
150    NEXT I
160    REM DEAL 5 CARDS
170    FOR C=1 TO 5
180    REM DEAL ONE CARD
190    LET I=INT(52*RND(0))+1
200    LET X=L[I]
210    IF X<0 THEN 190
220    LET L[I]=-1
230    REM PRINT ONE CARD
240    LET S=INT(X/13)
250    LET V=X-13*S
260    IF S>0 THEN 290
270    PRINT "CLUB     ";
280    GOTO 360
290    IF S>1 THEN 320
300    PRINT "DIAMOND  ";
310    GOTO 360
320    IF S>2 THEN 350
330    PRINT "HEART    ";
340    GOTO 360
350    PRINT "SPADE    ";
360    IF V>8 THEN 390
370    PRINT V+2
380    GOTO 490
390    IF V>9 THEN 420
400    PRINT "JACK"
410    GOTO 490
420    IF V>10 THEN 450
430    PRINT "QUEEN"
440    GOTO 490
450    IF V>11 THEN 480
460    PRINT "KING"
470    GOTO 490
480    PRINT "ACE"
490    NEXT C
500    END
```

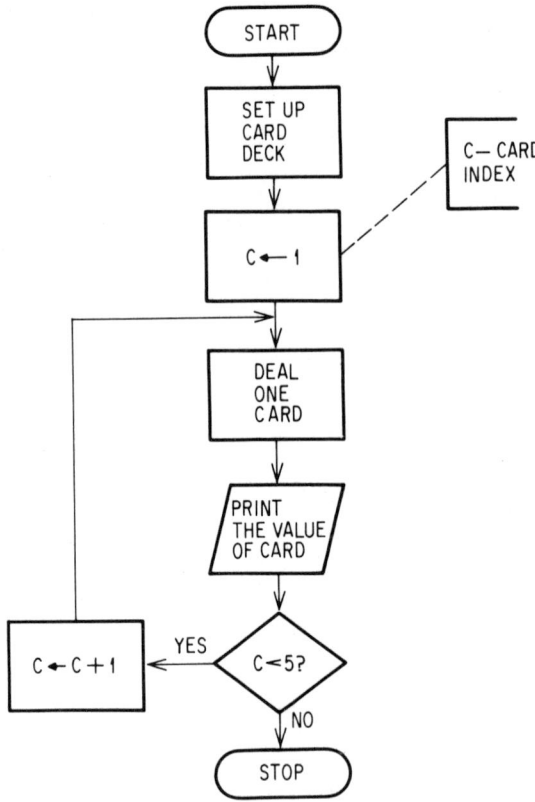

Fig. 3-6 Flowchart for dealing a Poker hand

```
RUN

DIAMOND  KING
SPADE    9
SPADE    JACK
HEART    4
SPADE    3
```

The frequency of poker hands is shown in the following table:

Hand	Frequency
Five of a kind	0
Royal Flush	4
Straight flush	36
Four of a kind	624
Full house	3,744
Flush	5,108
Straight	10,200
Three of a kind	54,912

Two pairs	123,552
One pair	1,098,240
No pair	1,302,540
Total combinations	2,598,960

These are the chances of being dealt such combinations in the original five cards. The exact odds against a particular hand are determined by deducting the number of combinations from the total combinations, then dividing the larger number by the smaller. For example, the odds against being dealt three of a kind are 2,598,960 minus 54,912, or 2,544,048, divided by 54,912, or about 46 to 1.

3.7 Fox and Geese

Fox and Geese is one of the simplest games played on a checkerboard. One can learn the game readily, but it is a tricky little game of skill. It is related to checkers and played on the black squares of a checkerboard. Place the counters as shown in Fig. 3-7, with the four geese in one row on the black squares. The fox is placed on any square in the row on the opposite side of the board.

Play is on the black squares only. Neither the fox nor the geese can jump. No men are removed from the board. The fox moves forward or backward one square at a time. The geese move forward only one square at a time. The object of the game for the fox player is to break through the line of geese. Once he has done that, he has won the game no matter where the breakthrough occurs on the board.

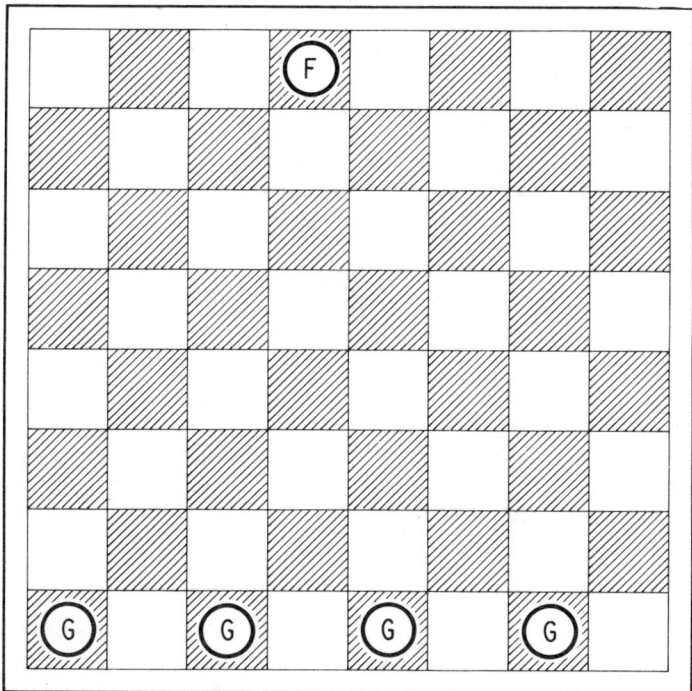

Fig. 3-7 Original position of counters for Fox and Geese

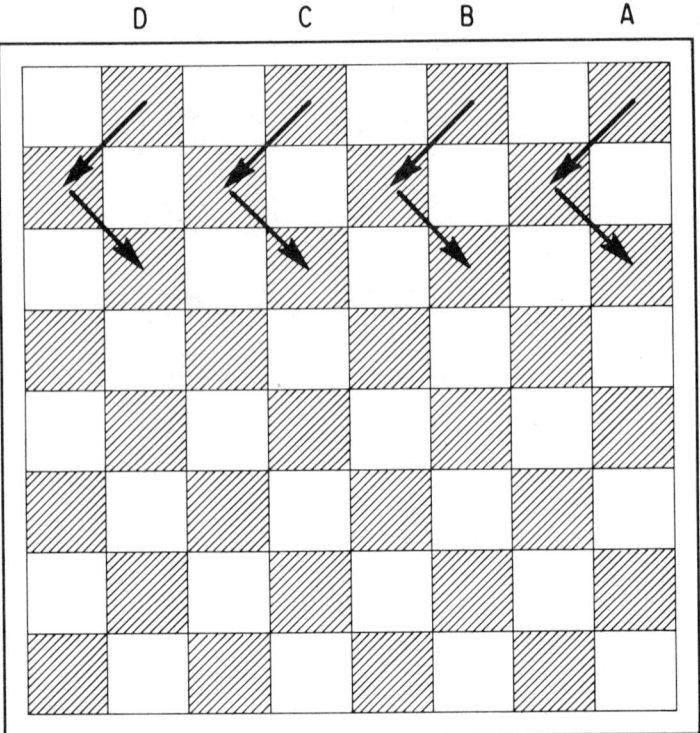

Fig. 3-8 Moves in Fox and Geese

The object for the geese is to pen the fox up in a corner so that he cannot move. If the geese are successful in doing this, they win the game.

The geese usually have the first move. Although at first glance one might think that the geese don't have a chance to win, with careful play they can win. The fox must play an offensive game pushing into the line of geese, retreating only when necessary. The geese must play a defensive game, always wary lest the fox find a hole to slip through.

Part of the algorithm to play this game is to play the geese in the order A,B,C,D,D,C,B,A,A,B,C,D,D, etc., following the arrows shown in Fig. 3–8.

The fox will attempt to frustrate this ordered advance by blocking. When he does so, there will be a goose (A or D) furthest from him. This goose (A or D) must now move toward the fox. Such a move may result in the goose crossing over and changing places with another goose (B or C). However, the geese A, B(C,D) are not allowed to cross from the right (left) half of the board to the left (right) half. It is left to the reader to develop an algorithm for playing this game.

3.8 Tac Tix

Tac Tix is played on a 5 by 5 grid. At the start of a game, twenty-five markers are placed in the 25 cells of the grid, as shown in Fig. 3–9.

The game is played between you and your opponent (the computer), alternately removing markers according to the following rules:

IT'S GAME PLAYING TIME

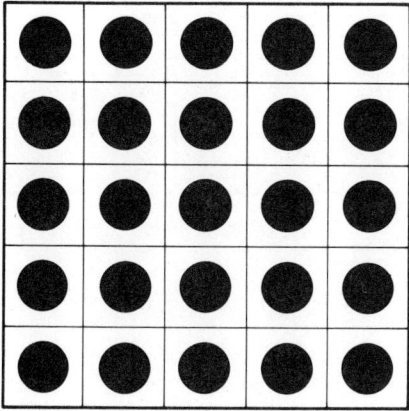

Fig. 3-9 Tac Tix grid

1. At least one marker must be taken during a turn.
2. At any one turn, a player may take as many markers as he wishes from any one row or column provided that the markers are in adjacent cells.
3. The player who removes the last marker *wins*.

A simplified game played on a 3 by 3 board is shown in Fig. 3–10. In this game, player 2 wins on his second move.

Can you devise a winning strategy and write a program for this game?

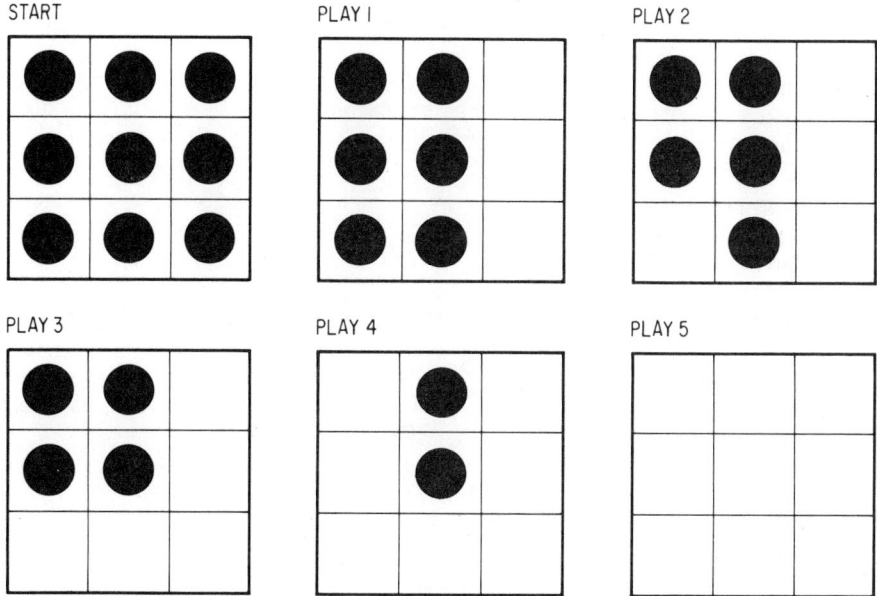

Fig. 3-10 Simplified Tac Tix game

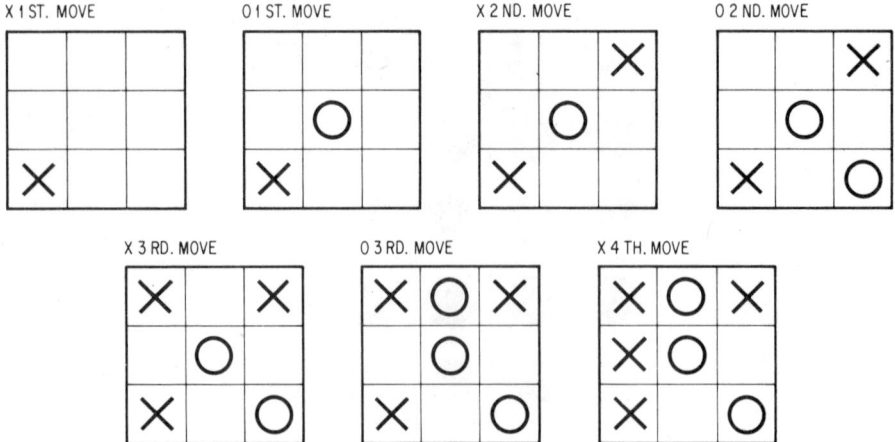

Fig. 3-11 Game of Tic-Tac-Toe

3.9 Tic-Tac-Toe

Tic-Tac-Toe is played using the following rules. One player uses an X marker and the second player (or computer) uses an 0 marker. The playing board consists of a square divided into nine smaller squares, and the object of the player is to get three of his own markers in a straight line. Plays are made on the board in alternate moves. The moves of a typical game may be represented as shown in Fig. 3–11. In this example, the player using marker X wins the game in his fourth move.

When playing Tic-Tac-Toe, the following strategies should be employed.

1. If you move first, take the center square.

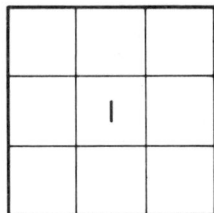

2. If you move second, take the center square if it is unoccupied.

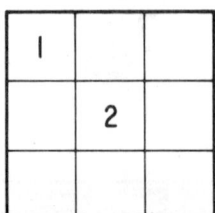

IT'S GAME PLAYING TIME

3. If you move second, take a corner square if the center is occupied.

2		2
	1	
2		2

4. Subsequently, play to block two in a row by your opponent, or play to win.

These rules cover most of the playing situations that can occur. There are, of course, other possible strategies; for instance, it is not necessary to take the center square in order to force a draw. But the above rules are simple and can easily be expressed in a computer algorithm.

Our program uses a Tic-Tac-Toe board numbered as follows:

```
1 2 3
8 9 4
7 6 5
```

In our example, the computer will move first and always take the center position. This tactic places the computer on the offensive and continually forces the player to defend against two in a row. Thus, the computer program must merely check to see if the player's move properly defends; if it does not, the computer completes his three in a row and wins. The algorithm used in the program will allow the player to tie but not beat the computer. A program is shown below.

```
100   PRINT "TIC TAC TOE PROGRAM"
110   PRINT "THE GAME BOARD IS NUMBERED THUS:"
120   PRINT "1   2   3"
130   PRINT "8   9   4"
140   PRINT "7   6   5"
150   PRINT
180   DEF FNM(X)=X-8*INT((X-1)/8)
200   GOTO 210
210   PRINT
220   PRINT
230   LET A=9
240   LET M=A
250   GOSUB 650
260   LET P=M
270   LET B=FNM(P+1)
280   LET M=B
290   GOSUB 650
300   LET Q=M
310   IF Q=FNM(B+4) THEN 360
320   LET C=FNM(B+4)
330   LET M=C
340   GOSUB 700
350   GOTO 730
360   LET C=FNM(B+2)
370   LET M=C
380   GOSUB 650
390   LET R=M
```

```
400    IF R=FNM(C+4) THEN 450
410    LET D=FNM(C+4)
420    LET M=D
430    GOSUB 700
440    GOTO 730
450    IF P/2 <> INT(P/2) THEN 500
460    LET D=FNM(C+7)
470    LET M=D
480    GOSUB 700
490    GOTO 730
500    LET D=FNM(C+3)
510    LET M=D
520    GOSUB 650
530    LET S=M
540    IF S=FNM(D+4) THEN 590
550    LET E=FNM(D+4)
560    LET M=E
570    GOSUB 700
580    GOTO 730
590    LET E=FNM(D+6)
600    LET M=E
610    GOSUB 700
620    PRINT "THE GAME IS A DRAW"
630    GOTO 210
650    GOSUB 700
660    PRINT "YOUR MOVE";
670    INPUT M
680    RETURN
700    PRINT "COMPUTER MOVES ";M
710    RETURN
730    PRINT "AND WINS"
740    GOTO 210
750    END

RUN

TIC TAC TOE PROGRAM
THE GAME BOARD IS NUMBERED THUS:
1   2   3
8   9   4
7   6   5


COMPUTER MOVES   9
YOUR MOVE?5
COMPUTER MOVES   6
YOUR MOVE?2
COMPUTER MOVES   8
YOUR MOVE?4
COMPUTER MOVES   3
YOUR MOVE?7
COMPUTER MOVES   1
THE GAME IS A DRAW


COMPUTER MOVES   9
YOUR MOVE?1
COMPUTER MOVES   2
YOUR MOVE?6
COMPUTER MOVES   4
YOUR MOVE?7
COMPUTER MOVES   8
AND WINS
```

IT'S GAME PLAYING TIME

Tic-Tac-Toe is a game where the program author can become quite creative. There are many printer or typewriter formats that may be used, and if the author is imaginative, he can make the game output more interesting by producing appropriate messages at key game points. For example, the following game printouts illustrate an interesting format with comments.

```
         I'LL PLAY BLINDFOLDED

         BOARD  YOUR PLAY    MY PLAY

         1 2 3
         4 5 6
         7 8 9     5           3

         1 2 M
         4 Y 6
         7 8 9     7           4

         1 2 M
         M Y 6
         Y 8 9     8           2

         1 M M
         M Y 6
         Y Y Y     9

         1 M M
         M Y 6
         Y Y Y       GIVE THAT MAN A CIGAR

         I'M LEARNING

         BOARD  YOUR PLAY    MY PLAY

         1 2 3
         4 5 6
         7 8 9     5           3

         1 2 M
         4 Y 6
         7 8 9     7           4

         1 2 M
         M Y 6
         Y 8 9     8           9

         1 2 M
         M Y 6
         Y Y M     9 THAT'S MINE
                   2

         1 Y M
         M Y 6
         Y Y M       GIVE THAT MAN A CIGAR

         I'M ON TO YOUR DIRTY TRICKS

         BOARD  YOUR PLAY    MY PLAY

         1 2 3
         4 5 6
         7 8 9     1           5
```

```
        Y 2 3
        4 M 6
        7 8 9       9            3

        Y 2 M
        4 M 6
        7 8 Y       7            8

        Y 2 M
        4 M 6
        Y M Y       4

        Y 2 M
        Y M 6
        Y M Y       FIRE THE PROGRAMMER
```

The game of Tic-Tac-Toe has been completely analyzed, and a variety of computers have been programmed to play an unbeatable game. These computers use algorithms that will allow a person to tie (draw) or loose but never win. Another interesting method for developing a playing strategy uses *heuristics*, which is the only way more complicated games, such as chess and checkers, can be approached. A Tic-Tac-Toe program using heuristics attempts to obtain a good, but not necessarily perfect, strategy. In such a program, the results of previous games are *remembered* and used in future decision making-processes. Several such programs have been developed.

3.10 Go-Moko

Go-Moko is an Oriental game played by two players (or one person and a computer) on a board of intersecting lines (19 left-to-right lines, 19 top-to-bottom lines, 361 intersections). Each player has 180 markers; one player uses white markers, the other, black. Players alternate moves, placing a marker on an intersection of the board. The object is to obtain five adjacent markers in a row either vertically, horizontally, or diagonally. The player who does this wins the game. Figure 3–12 shows a game of Go-Moko where the player with white markers wins at the eighteenth move.

For computer play, the reader may wish to use a smaller board. A 7 by 7 line board is the smallest that can be used for a meaningful game.

3.11 Knight's Tour

Let us now look at the classical chessboard problem known as the *Knight's Tour*, a sequence of moves in which the knight lands once on every square of the chessboard but on no square more than once. The knight, whose moves are limited to one specific pattern, is allowed to move to any square on the board which is two rows and one column or two columns and one row away from the square he is currently occupying. In other words, the knight can make any of the eight moves shown in Fig. 3–13 but no others. Several knight's tours of the chessboard are shown in Fig. 3–14.

An interesting question is this: Suppose that we were to make random knight's moves starting at some position on the board, what is the likelihood of accidentally discovering a knight's tour (a random move is one selected at random from the available moves). The probability of obtaining a knight's tour by using random moves is very small indeed; however, it does make an interesting programming exercise.

The following program simulates the moves of the knight and attempts to complete a tour of the chessboard. The program carries out a series of knight's moves until no further move is possible. It then prints out the final position and the length of the series. This program attempted thirty games without finding a complete tour.

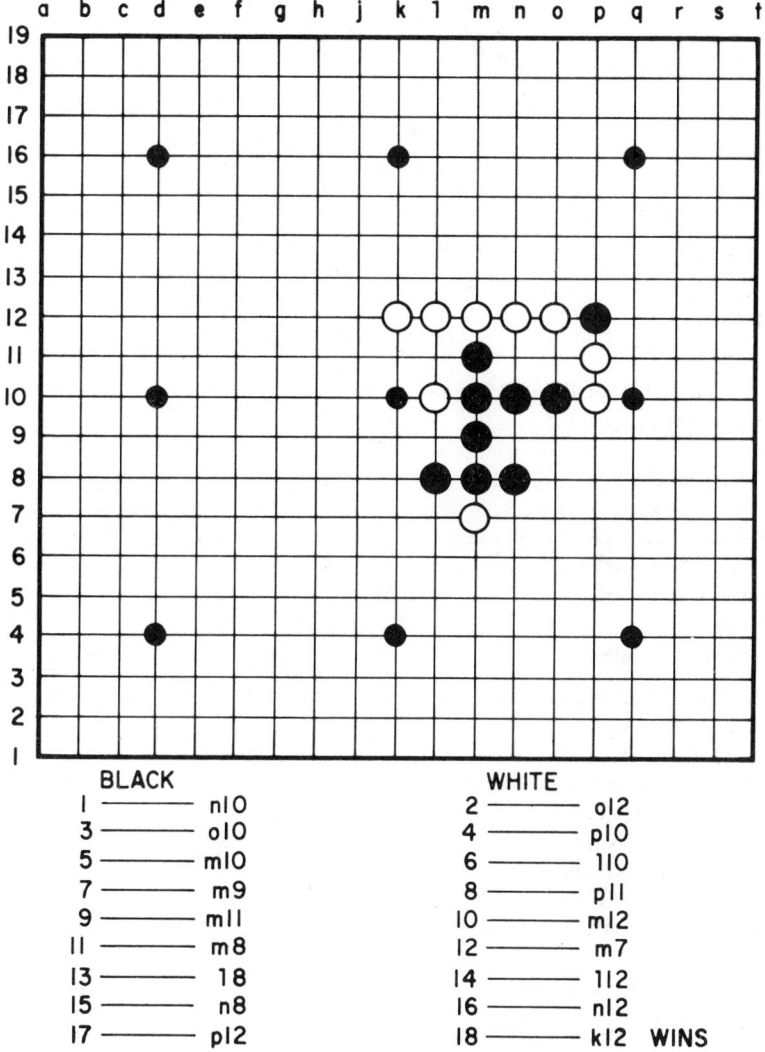

BLACK			WHITE		
1	———	n10	2	———	o12
3	———	o10	4	———	p10
5	———	m10	6	———	l10
7	———	m9	8	———	p11
9	———	m11	10	———	m12
11	———	m8	12	———	m7
13	———	l8	14	———	l12
15	———	n8	16	———	n12
17	———	p12	18	———	k12 WINS

Fig. 3-12 Go-Moko game

```
10    REM THIS PROGRAM CARRIES OUT A SERIES OF KNIGHT'S MOVES
20    REM UNTIL NO FURTHER MOVE IS POSSIBLE.  IT THEN PRINTS
30    REM OUT THE FINAL POSITION AND THE LENGTH OF THE SERIES.
40    LET Z=1
50    REM WE READ IN THE INITIAL PLACEMENT OF THE KNIGHT
60    READ I0,J0
70    PRINT "ROW","COLUMN","NUMBER OF MOVES"
80    REM WE ZERO THE BOARD AND INITIALIZE
90    FOR I=1 TO 8
100     FOR J=1 TO 8
110       LET B[I,J]=0
120     NEXT J
130   NEXT I
140   LET I=I0
150   LET J=J0
160   LET M=1
```

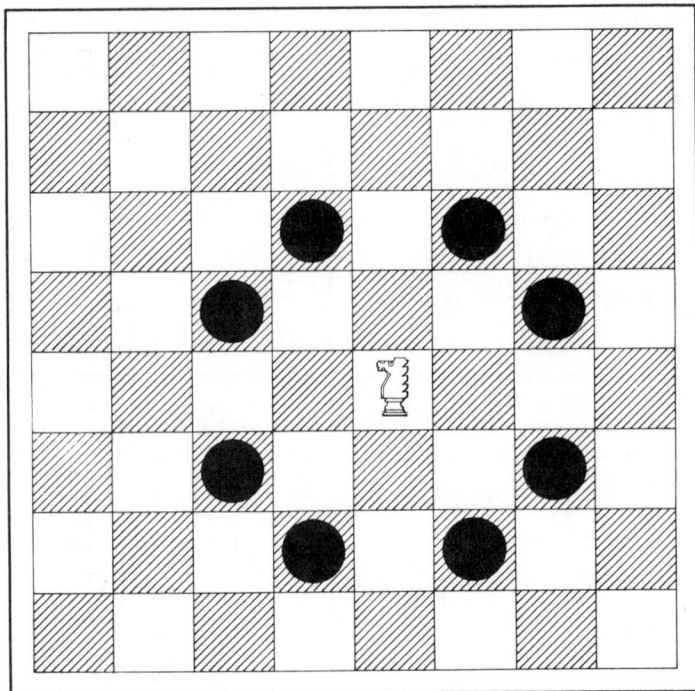

Fig. 3-13 Moves permitted a Knight

```
170    LET B[I,J]=-1
180    REM WE NOW START THE SERIES OF MOVES
190    LET C1=9
200    LET C=0
210    FOR I1=I-2 TO I+2
220    IF I1=I THEN 360
230    IF ABS(I1-4.5)>4 THEN 360
240    LET D1=3-ABS(I1-I)
250    FOR J1=J-D1 TO J+D1 STEP 2*D1
260    IF ABS(J1-4.5)>4 THEN 350
270    IF B[I1,J1]<0 THEN 350
280    LET C=C+1
290    IF C <> C1 THEN 350
300    LET I=I1
310    LET J=J1
320    LET B[I,J]=-1
330    LET M=M+1
340    GOTO 190
350    NEXT J1
360    NEXT I1
370    IF C=0 THEN 410
380    REM WE NOW SELECT A RANDOM INTERGER TO SELECT A MOVE
390    LET C1=INT(RND(Z)*C+1)
400    GOTO 200
410    REM WE HAVE GONE AS FAR AS WE CAN
420    PRINT I,J,M
430    IF Z >= 30 THEN 480
440    LET Z=Z+1
450    GOTO 90
460    REM THE DATA FOR THE STARTING POSITION
470    DATA 1,1
480    END
```

IT'S GAME PLAYING TIME 59

28	61	16	5	30	57	18	7
15	4	29	56	17	6	31	54
60	27	62	51	58	55	8	19
3	14	59	48	39	50	53	32
26	41	38	63	52	47	20	9
13	2	25	40	49	64	33	46
42	37	12	23	44	35	10	21
1	24	43	36	11	22	45	34

64	23	52	39	62	5	50	37
41	28	63	24	51	38	61	4
22	53	40	27	6	3	36	49
29	42	25	2	17	14	9	60
54	21	16	13	26	7	48	35
43	30	1	18	15	10	59	8
20	55	32	45	12	57	34	47
31	44	19	56	33	46	11	58

47	10	23	64	49	2	59	6
22	63	48	9	60	5	50	3
11	46	61	24	1	52	7	58
62	21	12	45	8	57	4	51
19	36	25	40	13	44	53	30
26	39	20	33	56	29	14	43
35	18	37	28	41	16	31	54
38	27	34	17	32	55	42	15

35	40	47	44	61	8	15	12
46	43	36	41	14	11	62	9
39	34	45	48	7	60	13	16
50	55	42	37	22	17	10	63
33	38	49	54	59	6	23	18
56	51	28	31	26	21	64	3
29	32	53	58	5	2	19	24
52	57	30	27	20	25	4	1

Fig. 3-14 Knight's Tours

RUN

ROW	COLUMN	NUMBER OF MOVES
1	4	40
8	7	28
3	1	37
2	4	47
2	8	23
8	8	27
1	3	25
1	6	40
1	5	43
8	1	22
8	2	21
8	2	55
4	2	37
2	1	36
8	8	39
8	1	34
8	1	34
8	1	52
8	1	40
1	3	45
5	1	35
8	8	29

1	6	20
2	1	42
2	2	39
1	2	26
2	8	37
3	8	38
2	4	49
6	1	34

3.12 Sharky, the Card Player

Sharky has been playing cards since he was ten years old. His favorite game is described here. Draw two cards from the deck of 52 cards. If at *least one* card is a diamond you win $1.00. If *neither* card is a diamond, you lose $1.00. Play the game with Sharky 100, 200, 300, 400, 500,..., 1,000 times and determine your wins and losses for each 100 games.

The following program uses random numbers to form the card deck, as shown below:

Diamonds:	1 through 13
Spades:	14 through 26
Clubs:	27 through 39
Hearts:	40 through 52

```
100    REM SHARKY - THE CARD PLAYER
110    LET W=0
120    LET L=0
130    PRINT "GAMES WINS  LOS  YOUR MONEY"
140    PRINT
150    FOR G=1 TO 900
160    LET X=INT(52*RND(1))+1
170    LET Y=INT(52*RND(1))+1
180    IF X>13 AND Y>13 THEN 210
190    LET W=W+1
200    GOTO 220
210    LET L=L+1
220    IF G/100 <> INT(G/100) THEN 240
230    PRINT G;W;L;W-L
240    NEXT G
250    END

RUN

GAMES WINS  LOS  YOUR MONEY

 100   44   56    -12
 200   85  115    -30
 300  136  164    -28
 400  181  219    -38
 500  220  280    -60
 600  263  337    -74
 700  301  399    -98
 800  353  447    -94
 900  397  503   -106
```

Can you determine why you did not beat Sharky at this game?

chapter 4

NUMBER RECREATIONS

Introduction

Any book on games and mathematical recreations must eventually come to number amusements. From early days, people have been interested in numbers and their interesting properties, often attaching mystical importance to them. The study of these numbers and properties forms a branch of mathematics called "number theory." If you are a puzzle enthusiast, you can probably recall many puzzles which depend for their interest upon properties of numbers, and if you have solved any of these puzzles, you have already been initiated into some of the elements of number theory.

However this field of mathematics does not consist entirely of puzzles, games, and mathematical tricks, for it has many practical applications in engineering and physics and many uses in proving theorems in other fields of mathematics. An engineer who designs a gear train must use a form of number theory, and so must a physicist who undertakes to explain the interactions between atoms and radiation.

As a simple introduction into the field of number recreations, try baffling your nonmathematical friends with the following mathematical trick. Tell your friend to follow these instructions:
 1. Think of a number
 2. Add 3 to this number
 3. Multiply your answer by 2
 4. Subtract 4 from your answer
 5. Divide by 2
 6. Subtract the number with which you started.

If your friend carries out these instructions carefully, the answer will always be 1, regardless of the number your friend started with. We can explain why this trick works by using algebraic symbols, as shown below.
 1. Think of a number: x
 2. Add 3: $x + 3$

3. Multiply by 2:	$2x + 6$
4. Subtract 4:	$2x + 2$
5. Divide by 2:	$x + 1$
6. Subtract the original number, x:	$(x + 1) - x = 1$

Try to make up a similar trick of your own.

4.1 Guess the Number

This is a game between two players and a computer. The players are asked to guess which number between 1 and 100 the computer has randomly picked. Ten points is given to the player who is closer. The game ends when either player reaches a score of 50.

A flowchart is shown in Fig. 4–1, and the program follows.

```
10    REM GUESS THE NUMBER
20    LET C1=0
30    LET C2=0
40    PRINT "EACH PLAYER SHOULD CHOSE A NUMBER BETWEEN 1 AND 100."
50    PRINT "PLAYER 1";
60    INPUT P1
70    PRINT "PLAYER 2";
80    INPUT P2
90    LET X=INT(100*RND(0)+1)
100   PRINT "THE COMPUTER HAS CHOSEN"; X
110   IF ABS(X-P1) <> ABS(X-P2) THEN 140
120   PRINT "TIE - NO CHANGE IN SCORE"
130   GOTO 40
140   IF ABS(X-P1)<ABS(X-P2) THEN 210
150   LET C2=C2+10
160   PRINT "PLAYER 2 WAS CLOSER"
170   PRINT "SCORE: PLAYER 1 HAS"; C1; "POINTS - PLAYER 2 HAS"; C2; "POINTS"
180   IF C2<50 THEN 50
190   PRINT "PLAYER 2 WINS GAME"
200   GOTO 260
210   LET C1=C1+10
220   PRINT "PLAYER 1 WAS CLOSER"
230   PRINT "SCORE: PLAYER 1 HAS"; C1; "POINTS - PLAYER 2 HAS"; C2; "POINTS"
240   IF C1<50 THEN 50
250   PRINT "PLAYER 1 WINS GAME"
260   END

RUN

EACH PLAYER SHOULD CHOSE A NUMBER BETWEEN 1 AND 100.
PLAYER 1?43
PLAYER 2?67
THE COMPUTER HAS CHOSEN 55
TIE - NO CHANGE IN SCORE
EACH PLAYER SHOULD CHOSE A NUMBER BETWEEN 1 AND 100.
PLAYER 1?24
PLAYER 2?12
THE COMPUTER HAS CHOSEN 66
PLAYER 1 WAS CLOSER
SCORE: PLAYER 1 HAS 10    POINTS - PLAYER 2 HAS 0    POINTS
PLAYER 1?67
PLAYER 2?76
THE COMPUTER HAS CHOSEN 56
PLAYER 1 WAS CLOSER
SCORE: PLAYER 1 HAS 20    POINTS - PLAYER 2 HAS 0    POINTS
PLAYER 1?1
PLAYER 2?2
```

NUMBER RECREATIONS

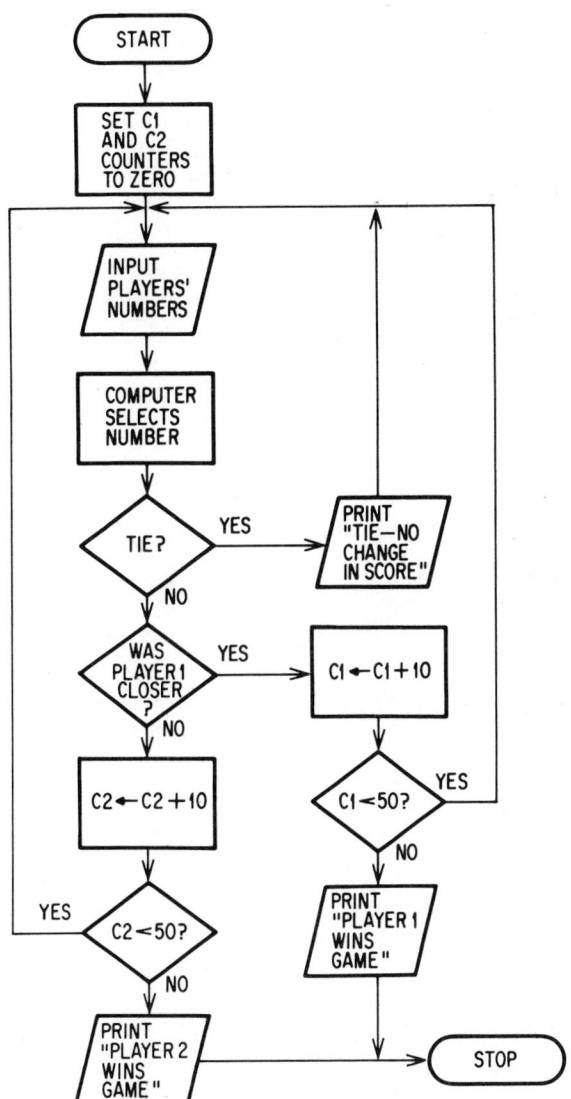

Fig. 4-1 Guess the Number

```
THE COMPUTER HAS CHOSEN 9
PLAYER 2 WAS CLOSER
SCORE: PLAYER 1 HAS 20     POINTS - PLAYER 2 HAS 10    POINTS
PLAYER 1?99
PLAYER 2?98
THE COMPUTER HAS CHOSEN 73
PLAYER 2 WAS CLOSER
SCORE: PLAYER 1 HAS 20     POINTS - PLAYER 2 HAS 20    POINTS
PLAYER 1?45
PLAYER 2?55
THE COMPUTER HAS CHOSEN 62
```

```
PLAYER 2 WAS CLOSER
SCORE: PLAYER 1 HAS 20    POINTS - PLAYER 2 HAS 30    POINTS
PLAYER 1?67
PLAYER 2?66
THE COMPUTER HAS CHOSEN 2
PLAYER 2 WAS CLOSER
SCORE: PLAYER 1 HAS 20    POINTS - PLAYER 2 HAS 40    POINTS
PLAYER 1?2
PLAYER 2?1
THE COMPUTER HAS CHOSEN 77
PLAYER 1 WAS CLOSER
SCORE: PLAYER 1 HAS 30    POINTS - PLAYER 2 HAS 40    POINTS
PLAYER 1?99
PLAYER 2?100
THE COMPUTER HAS CHOSEN 44
PLAYER 1 WAS CLOSER
SCORE: PLAYER 1 HAS 40    POINTS - PLAYER 2 HAS 40    POINTS
PLAYER 1?25
PLAYER 2?75
THE COMPUTER HAS CHOSEN 27
PLAYER 1 WAS CLOSER
SCORE: PLAYER 1 HAS 50    POINTS - PLAYER 2 HAS 40    POINTS
PLAYER 1 WINS GAME
```

4.2 Prime Numbers

A positive number greater than 1 is called a *prime number* (or *prime*) if it has no positive divisors other than itself and 1. The following twenty-five numbers make up all the primes less than 100: 2, 3, 5, 7, 11, 13, 17, 19, 23, 29, 31, 37, 41, 43, 47, 53, 59, 61, 67, 71, 73, 79, 83, 89, and 97.

The prime numbers are useful in analyzing problems concerning divisibility and interesting in themselves because of some of the special properties which they possess as a class. These properties have fascinated mathematicians and others since ancient times.

The discovery of the small prime numbers can be accomplished very conveniently by means of a simple procedure first used by a Greek scholar named Eratosthenes. First we write down all the numbers 1, 2, 3, . . . , as far as we care to go. We then strike out all those we know are *not* primes, and those that are left constitute our table of primes. First every even number goes out, except 2 itself. Next we cross out all multiples of 3, except 3 itself. Four can be ignored, since it is already crossed out. Five is next; we cross out all multiples of 5, except 5 itself. We next cross out all multiples of 7, and then all remaining numbers must be primes.

Also, it is not necessary to test for primes greater than $\sqrt{N}$ since they would have been discovered during the division by primes smaller than $\sqrt{N}$.

```
  2    3    4̸    5    6̸    7    8̸
  9̸   1̸0̸  11   1̸2̸  13   1̸4̸  1̸5̸
 1̸6̸  17   1̸8̸  19   2̸0̸  2̸1̸  2̸2̸
 23   2̸4̸  2̸5̸  2̸6̸  2̸7̸  2̸8̸  29
 3̸0̸  31   3̸2̸  3̸3̸  34   3̸5̸  3̸6̸
 37   3̸8̸  3̸9̸  4̸0̸  41   4̸2̸  43
 4̸4̸  4̸5̸  4̸6̸  47   4̸8̸  4̸9̸  5̸0̸
 5̸1̸  5̸2̸  53   5̸4̸  5̸5̸  5̸6̸  5̸7̸
 5̸8̸  5̸9̸  6̸0̸  61   6̸2̸  6̸3̸  64
 6̸5̸  66   67   6̸8̸  6̸9̸  7̸0̸  71
 7̸2̸  73   7̸4̸  7̸5̸  7̸6̸  7̸7̸  7̸8̸
```

NUMBER RECREATIONS

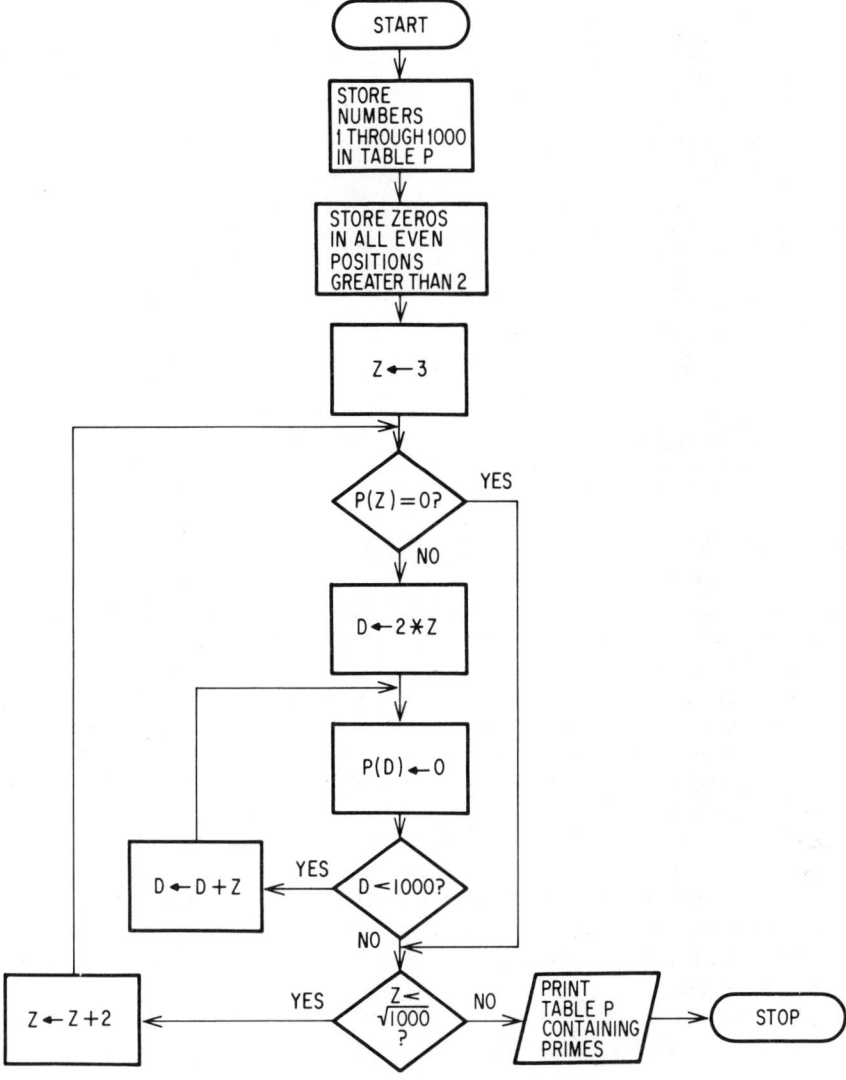

Fig. 4-2 Flowchart for generating Prime Numbers by the Sieve of Eratosthenes

$$79 \quad \cancel{80} \quad \cancel{81} \quad \cancel{82} \quad 83 \quad \cancel{84} \quad \cancel{85}$$
$$\cancel{86} \quad \cancel{87} \quad \cancel{88} \quad 89 \quad \cancel{90} \quad \cancel{91} \quad \cancel{92}$$
$$\cancel{93} \quad \cancel{94} \quad \cancel{95} \quad \cancel{96} \quad 97 \quad \cancel{98} \quad \cancel{99}$$

This procedure for finding prime numbers is called the "Sieve of Eratosthenes." Figure 4–2 is a flowchart of a procedure that will find all primes less than 1,000 by means of the Sieve of Eratosthenes. A program to do this follows.

```
100 REM SIEVE OF ERATOSTHENES
110 DIM N[1000],P[200]
120 FOR I=2 TO 1000
130 LET N[I]=0
140 NEXT I
150 LET K=0
160 FOR P=2 TO 1000
170 IF N[P] <> 0 THEN 240
180 LET K=K+1
190 LET P[K]=P
200 IF P>SQR(1000) THEN 240
210 FOR I=P TO 1000 STEP P
220 LET N[I]=-1
230 NEXT I
240 NEXT P
250 REM PRINT PRIME NUMBERS
260 LET C=1
270 FOR I=1 TO K
280 PRINT P[I];
290 LET C=C+1
300 IF C <= 7 THEN 330
310 PRINT
320 LET C=1
330 NEXT I
340 END
RUN
```

2	3	5	7	11	13	17
19	23	29	31	37	41	43
47	53	59	61	67	71	73
79	83	89	97	101	103	107
109	113	127	131	137	139	149
151	157	163	167	173	179	181
191	193	197	199	211	223	227
229	233	239	241	251	257	263
269	271	277	281	283	293	307
311	313	317	331	337	347	349
353	359	367	373	379	383	389
397	401	409	419	421	431	433
439	443	449	457	461	463	467
479	487	491	499	503	509	521
523	541	547	557	563	569	571
577	587	593	599	601	607	613
617	619	631	641	643	647	653
659	661	673	677	683	691	701
709	719	727	733	739	743	751
757	761	769	773	787	797	809
811	821	823	827	829	839	853
857	859	863	877	881	883	887
907	911	919	929	937	941	947
953	967	971	977	983	991	997

Since we know immediately and automatically that 2 is the only even prime number, a better way to generate primes would be to examine only the odd numbers, starting with 3, and divide each succeeding odd number up to some final desired value by all the primes we have found. A flowchart of a procedure to do this is shown in Fig. 4-3, and a program follows.

```
10 REM PRIME NUMBER GENERATOR
20 DIM A[400]
30 PRINT "PRIME NUMBERS"
```

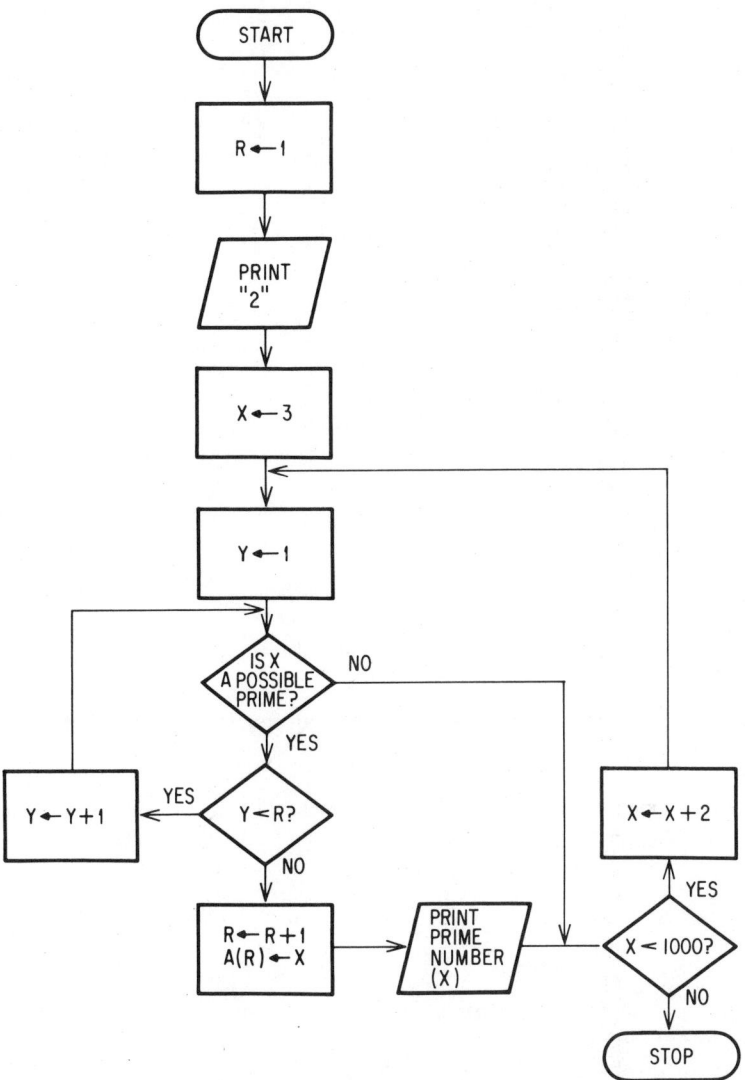

Fig. 4-3 Prime Number generator

```
40   LET R=1
50   LET A[1]=2
60   FOR X=3 TO 400 STEP 2
70   FOR Y=1 TO R
80   IF INT(X/A[Y])*A[Y]=X THEN 130
90   NEXT Y
100  LET R=R+1
110  LET A[R]=X
120  PRINT X;
130  NEXT X
140  END
```

RUN

PRIME NUMBERS
```
  3    5    7   11   13   17   19   23   29   31   37   41
 43   47   53   59   61   67   71   73   79   83   89   97
101  103  107  109  113  127  131  137  139  149  151  157
163  167  173  179  181  191  193  197  199  211  223  227
229  233  239  241  251  257  263  269  271  277  281  283
293  307  311  313  317  331  337  347  349  353  359  367
373  379  383  389  397
```

4.3 Chinese Remainder Theorem

Prime numbers occur in many types of mathematical recreation. One is the Chinese Remainder Theorem, which is used in an old mind reading trick when the huckster asks someone in the audience to think of a number between one and 30. Then his spiel goes: "Don't tell me the number, but divide the number by two and give me the remainder, next divide the number by three and give me the remainder, and last, divide the number by five, and give me the remainder." When the huckster has the three remainders he is able to calculate the original number.

Take the number 12, for example:

$$12/2=6, \text{ remainder } 0$$
$$12/3=4, \text{ remainder } 0$$
$$12/5=2, \text{ remainder } 2$$

Given these three remainders, it is easy to figure out the original number since there is only one number less than 30 with these three remainders. Try it for yourself. Note that the three divisors are relatively prime (no common factors within the range $2 \times 3 \times 5 = 30$).

The following program uses the Chinese Remainder Theorem and has the computer play the part of the huckster. In this program, 5, 7, and 9 are used for the divisors (Range $=5 \times 7 \times 9 = 315$).

```
100   REM CHINESE REMAINDER THEOREM
101   PRINT "I WANT YOU TO THINK OF A NUMBER"
102   PRINT "LESS THAN 316.  WRITE THIS NUMBER"
103   PRINT "DOWN AND DIVIDE BY 5.  NOW GIVE ME"
104   PRINT "THE REMAINDER LEFT OVER";
110   INPUT R5
111   PRINT
120   PRINT "NOW DIVIDE YOUR ORGINAL NUMBER BY"
121   PRINT "7 AND GIVE ME THIS REMAINDER";
130   INPUT R7
131   PRINT
140   PRINT "NOW DIVIDE YOUR ORGINAL NUMBER BY"
141   PRINT "9 AND GIVE ME THIS REMAINDER";
150   INPUT R9
151   PRINT
160   REM CALCULATE NUMBER
170   LET A=126*R5+225*R7+280*R9
180   LET X=A-INT(A/315)*315
190   PRINT
200   PRINT "I AM HAPPY TO TELL YOU THAT YOUR"
201   PRINT "NUMBER CHOSEN WAS";X
210   END
```

```
RUN

             I WANT YOU TO THINK OF A NUMBER
             LESS THAN 316. WRITE THIS NUMBER
             DOWN AND DIVIDE BY 5. NOW GIVE ME
             THE REMAINDER LEFT OVER?1

             NOW DIVIDE YOUR ORGINAL NUMBER BY
             7 AND GIVE ME THIS REMAINDER?5

             NOW DIVIDE YOUR ORGINAL NUMBER BY
             9 AND GIVE ME THIS REMAINDER?2

             I AM HAPPY TO TELL YOU THAT YOUR
             NUMBER CHOSEN WAS 236
```

In the output example, the number 236 was chosen. The algorithm for calculating the number is:

$$X = (126 \times R5 + 225 \times R7 + 280 \times R9) \bmod 315$$
$$X = (126 \times 1 + 225 \times 5 + 280 \times 2) \bmod 315$$
$$X = (1811) \bmod 315$$
$$X = 236$$

X is the number. R5 is the remainder when X is divided by 5, R7 is the remainder when X is divided by 7, and R9 is the remainder when X is divided by 9. Mod 315 indicates remainder arithmetic where the parenthesized quantity is divided by 315, but the result is the remainder and not the quotient.

The algorithm in the program is not exactly of this form since BASIC does not have a modulus function.* However, BASIC does have an INTEGER function, and this is used in the program (line number 180) to do the remainder arithmetic.

4.4 Perfect Numbers

The number 6 has a curious property. By adding the divisors of 6, a sum equal to the number itself is found:

$$3 + 2 + 1 = 6$$

This is also true of the number 28:

$$14 + 7 + 4 + 2 + 1 = 28$$

Such numbers are called *perfect*. A formula for generating perfect numbers is

$$2^{n-1}(2^n - 1)$$

in which the factor $2^n - 1$ must be a *prime number*. For many years only 12 perfect numbers were known, namely those computed by setting n equal to 2, 3, 5, 7, 13, 17, 19, 31, 61, 89, 107, 127, 521, 607, 1279, 2203, and 2281 in the previous formula.

n	$2^{n-1}(2^n - 1)$
2	6

---

*Some versions of the BASIC language include a library function to perform modulus arithmetic.

3	28
5	496
7	8128
13	33,550,336
17	8,589,869,056
•	•
•	•
•	•

In recent years, computers have been used to generate very large perfect numbers. No one knows whether or not an odd number can be perfect! None has been found, yet no one has proved they do not exist. Several interesting facts exist about perfect numbers. Every even perfect number must end in either 28 or 6. Another interesting fact is that the sum of the reciprocals of all the divisors of an even perfect number must equal 2. For example, the perfect number 6 has divisors 1, 2, 3, and 6, and their reciprocals total 1 + (1/2) + (1/3) + (1/6) = 2.

The following BASIC program computes the first two perfect numbers. If you have a lot of computer time available, perhaps you would like to modify this program to generate the third perfect number.

```
10  REM PERFECT NUMBERS
15  FOR N=2 TO 100
20  LET S=0
30  FOR D=1 TO N/2
40  IF INT(N/D) <> N/D THEN 60
50  LET S=S+D
60  NEXT D
70  IF S <> N THEN 90
80  PRINT N;"IS A PERFECT NUMBER"
90  NEXT N
99  END
```

4.5 Fibonacci Numbers

A man bought a pair of rabbits and bred them. The pair produced one pair of young after one month, and a second pair after the second month. They then stopped breeding. Each new pair also produced two more pairs in the same way and then stopped breeding. How many new pairs of rabbits did the man get each month?

To answer this question, let us write down in a line the number of pairs in each generation. First write the number 1 for the single pair he started with. Next we write the number 1 for the pair they produced after a month.

The next month both pairs had young, so the next number is 2. We now have three numbers in a line: 1, 1, 2. Each number represents a new generation. Now the first generation stopped producing. The second generation (1 pair) produced 1 pair. The third generation (2 pairs) produced 2 pairs. So the next number we write is 1 + 2, or 3. Now the second generation stopped producing. The third generation (2 pairs) produced 2 pairs. The fourth generation (3 pairs) produced 34 pairs. So the next number we write is 2 + 3, or 5.

Each month, only the last two generations produce, so we can get the next number and all succeeding numbers by adding the last two numbers in the line (see Fig. 4–4.) The numbers we get in this way are called *Fibonacci numbers*. The first twelve of them are: 1, 1, 2, 3, 5, 8, 13, 21, 34, 55, 89, 144. They have interesting properties and keep popping up in many places in nature.

NUMBER RECREATIONS

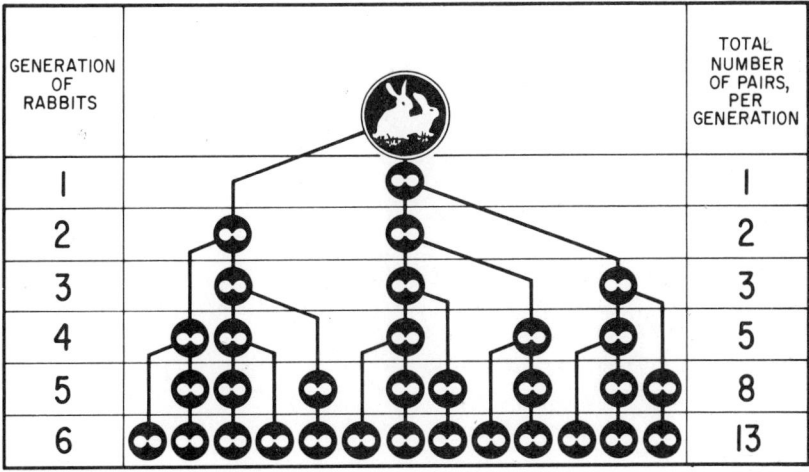

Fig. 4-4 Rabbits and generations

The Fibonacci numbers are such that, after the first two, every number in the sequence equals the sum of the two previous numbers:

$$F_n = F_{n-1} + F_{n-2}$$

Suppose a tree grows according to the following, not unrealistic, formula. Each old branch (including the trunk) puts out one new branch per year; each new branch grows through the next year without branching, after which it qualifies as an old branch. The growth is represented schematically in Fig. 4–5. The number of branches after n years is equal to F_n.

Figure 4–6 presents a flowchart of a procedure that will compute Fibonacci numbers, and a program that computes and prints 22 of these numbers follows.

```
100   REM FIBØNACCI NUMBERS
110   DIM F[24]
120   PRINT "FIBØNACCI NUMBERS"
130   PRINT
140   LET F[1]=1
150   LET F[2]=1
160   FØR N=1 TØ 22
170   LET F[N+2]=F[N+1]+F[N]
180   NEXT N
190   REM PRINT 22 FIBØNACCI NUMBERS
200   FØR X=1 TØ 22
210   PRINT F[X]
220   NEXT X
230   END

RUN

FIBØNACCI NUMBERS

 1
 1
 2
 3
 5
 8
```

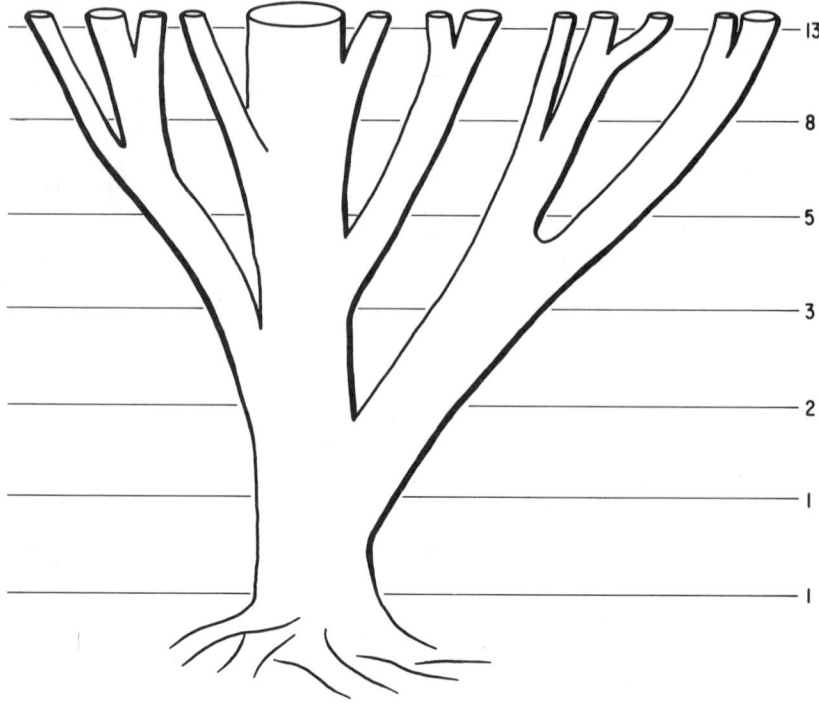

Fig. 4-5 The Fibonacci tree

```
    13
    21
    34
    55
    89
   144
   233
   377
   610
   987
  1597
  2584
  4181
  6765
 10946
 17711
```

4.6 Amicable Numbers

Once there was a king who thought of himself as quite a mathematician. He told a prisoner, "Give me a problem to solve. You may go free until I solve it. But as soon as I have the answer, off comes your head!" Now the prisoner was rather clever himself. Here is the problem he gave the king. The numbers 220 and 284 are called *amicable numbers*. The sum of the proper divisors of 220 equal 284:

$$1 + 2 + 4 + 5 + 10 + 11 + 20 + 22 + 44 + 55 + 110 = 284$$

and the sum of the proper divisors of 284 equals 220:

NUMBER RECREATIONS

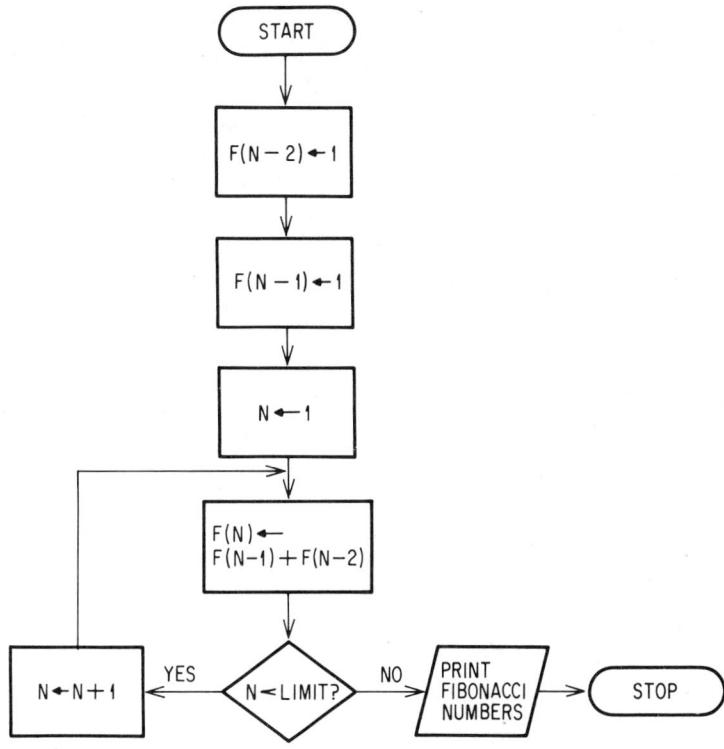

Fig. 4-6 Flowchart for generating Fibonacci numbers

$$1 + 2 + 4 + 71 + 142 = 220$$

Find the next pair of amicable numbers! The story goes that the prisoner went free and finally died of old age. The king never solved the problem.

There are about 400 amicable pairs of numbers known, of which some are:

220 and 284 (the smallest pair)
1184 and 1210
2620 and 2924
6232 and 6368
10,744 and 10,856
17,296 and 18,416
9,363,584 and 9,437,056
111,448,537,712 and 118,853,793,424

Several methods are available for finding amicable pairs. One common method is the following. Let

$$a = (3)(2^x) - 1$$
$$b = (3)(2^{x-1}) - 1$$
$$c = (9)(2^{2x-1}) - 1$$

If x is greater than 1, and a, b, and c are all primes, then $2^x ab$ and $2^x c$ constitute an amicable pair of numbers. For example, if x = 4, then a = 47, b = 23, and c = 1,151, which are all primes. Then,

$$(2^4)(47)(23) = 17,296$$

and

$$(2^4)(1151) = 18,416$$

Too bad the king didn't have a computer. He could have written the following program to produce the next pair of amicable numbers.

```
100    REM AMICABLE NUMBERS
110    FOR A=1 TO 7000
120    LET S=0
130    FOR D=1 TO A/2
140    IF A/D <> INT(A/D) THEN 160
150    LET S=S+D
160    NEXT D
170    IF S <= A THEN 260
180    LET B=S
190    LET T=0
200    FOR F=1 TO B/2
210    IF B/F <> INT(B/F) THEN 230
220    LET T=T+F
230    NEXT F
240    IF T <> A THEN 260
250    PRINT A;"AND";B;"ARE AMICABLE NUMBERS"
260    NEXT A
270    END
```

4.7 Mind-Reading Tricks

The ability of a "mind reader" to determine a number selected by someone in his audience is of the nature of a paradox to most people. Contained in this section are a few examples of tricks of this sort. They are all based upon fairly simple mathematical operations. The reader may wish to let the computer become the "mind reader" by programming one or more of the examples.

Trick 1 The mind reader (computer) asks a person in his audience to think of a number, multiply it by 5, add 6, multiply by 4, add 9, multiply by 5, and state the result. The person chooses the number 12, calculates successively 60, 66, 264, 273, 1,365, and announces the last number. The mind reader (computer) subtracts 165 from the result, gets 1,200, knocks off the two zeros, and informs the person that 12 was the number that he thought of.

The trick is easily seen if put in mathematical symbols. If the number chosen is a, then the successive operations yield

$$5a$$
$$5a + 6$$
$$20a + 24$$
$$20a + 33$$
$$100a + 165$$

When the mind reader (computer) is told this number, it is evident that he can determine a if he subtracts 165 and divides by 100.

NUMBER RECREATIONS

Trick 2   If the mind reader (computer) desires to tell a person the result without asking any questions, he must so arrange the various operations that the original number thought of drops out. Here is an example in which three unknown numbers are introduced and done away with.

The mind reader (computer) says: Think of a number. Add 10. Multiply by 2. Add the amount of change in your pocket. Multiply by 4. Add 20. Add 4 times your age in years. Divide by 2. Subtract twice the amount of change in your pocket. Subtract 10. Divide by 2. Subtract your age in years. Divide by 2. Subtract the original number you thought of.

The person, who chooses the number 7, has 30 cents in his pocket, and is 20 years old, thinks: 7, 17, 34, 64, 256, 276, 356, 178, 118, 108, 54, 34, 17, 10. The mind reader (computer) says your result is 10, is it not? The person replies, Right!

In this case, if we denote the person's original number by a, the amount of change in his pocket by b, and his age in years by c, the successive operations give

$$a$$
$$a + 10$$
$$2a + 20$$
$$2a + 20 + b$$
$$8a + 80 + 4b$$
$$8a + 100 + 4b + 4c$$
$$4a + 50 + 2b + 2c$$
$$4a + 50 + 2c$$
$$4a + 40 + 2c$$
$$2a + 20 + c$$
$$2a + 20$$
$$a + 10$$
$$10$$

Problems of this type can be set up in a wide variety of ways.

Trick 3   Many tricks of the kind we are discussing are based upon the principle of positional notation. Consider the following. The mind reader (computer) says: Throw three dice and note the three numbers which appear. Operate on these numbers as follows: Multiply the number on the first die by 2, add 5, multiply by 5, add the number on the second die, multiply by 10, add the number on the third die, and state the result.

The person throws a 2, a 3, and a 4, and thinks: 4, 9, 45, 48, 480, 484. He gives the answer: 484. The mind reader (computer) subtracts 250 and gets 234. He then states that the numbers thrown were 2, 3, 4.

Trick 4   The mind reader (computer) says: Choose any *prime number* greater than 3, square it, add 17, divide by 12, and remember the remainder.

The person thinks: 11, 121, 138, 11 6/12, 6. The mind reader (computer) states that the remainder is 6.

Here use is made of the fact that *any prime number greater than 3 is of the form: 6n±1, where n is a whole number*. (The symbol ± means plus *or* minus.) Its square is then of the form $36n^2 \pm 12n + 1$. This number, when divided by 12, leaves a remainder of 1. Now the mind reader (computer) had the person add 17, which, divided by 12, leaves a remainder of 5. The final remainder must thus be 1 + 5, or 6.

The mind reader (computer) can vary this trick by asking a person to add a number whose remainder, in dividing by 12, is, say, k. Then the final remainder will always turn out to be 1 + k.

4.8 Square Numbers

Numbers like 4, 9, 16, 25, 36, and the like, are called square numbers because

$$2^2 = 4$$
$$3^2 = 9$$
$$4^2 = 16$$
$$5^2 = 25$$
$$6^2 = 36$$

and so on.

Certain pairs of numbers when added together give a square number and when subtracted also give a square number, for example, the numbers 8 and 17.

$$8 + 17 = 25 \text{ (a square number)}$$
$$17 - 8 = 9 \text{ (a square number)}$$

The following program finds all the pairs of numbers less than 100 which give a square number when added and when subtracted.

```
100    REM SQUARE NUMBERS
110    PRINT " N       P       N+P     P-N"
120    PRINT
130    FOR N=1 TO 100
140    FOR P=N+1 TO 100
150    IF SQR(N+P) <> INT(SQR(N+P)) THEN 180
160    IF SQR(P-N) <> INT(SQR(P-N)) THEN 180
170    PRINT N;P;N+P;P-N
180    NEXT P
190    NEXT N
200    END

RUN
```

N	P	N+P	P-N
4	5	9	1
6	10	16	4
8	17	25	9
10	26	36	16
12	13	25	1
12	37	49	25
14	50	64	36
16	20	36	4
16	65	81	49
18	82	100	64
20	29	49	9
24	25	49	1
24	40	64	16
28	53	81	25
30	34	64	4
32	68	100	36
36	45	81	9
36	85	121	49
40	41	81	1
42	58	100	16
48	52	100	4

48	73	121	25
54	90	144	36
56	65	121	9
60	61	121	1
64	80	144	16
70	74	144	4
72	97	169	25
80	89	169	9
84	85	169	1
96	100	196	4

4.9 Armstrong Numbers

One hundred fifty three is an interesting number because

$$153 = 1^3 + 5^3 + 3^3$$

Numbers such as this are called *Armstrong numbers*. Any n-digit number is an Armstrong number if the sum of the nth power of the digits is equal to the original number.

The following program finds three other three-digit numbers like 153. Perhaps the reader would be interested in writing a similar program to find Armstrong numbers for any n digits.

```
100 REM ARMSTRONG NUMBERS
110 FOR N=100 TO 999
120 LET A=INT(N/100)
130 LET B=INT(N/10)-10*A
140 LET C=N-100*A-10*B
150 IF N<>A*A*A+B*B*B+C*C*C THEN 190
160 PRINT "ARMSTRONG NUMBER";N
170 PRINT "EQUALS";A*A*A;"+";B*B*B;"+";C*C*C
180 PRINT
190 NEXT N
200 END

RUN

ARMSTRONG NUMBER 153
EQUALS 1     + 125   + 27

ARMSTRONG NUMBER 370
EQUALS 27    + 343   + 0

ARMSTRONG NUMBER 371
EQUALS 27    + 343   + 1

ARMSTRONG NUMBER 407
EQUALS 64    + 0     + 343
```

chapter 5

GAMBLING GAMES

Introduction

Although many people think of gambling games as being used only for the winning and losing of money, computer simulations of gambling games can also serve serious purposes. For example, mathematicians use games like Blackjack in order to analyze money management and game playing strategies in detail. Simulations (programs that imitate something) of slot machines provide excellent techniques for studying the operation of complex machines and complex ideas.

The rules for playing gambling games are often easy to learn. Such games offer ideal problems for students just learning to develop algorithms and programs for computer processing. This chapter deals with seven gambling games, namely slot machines, Blackjack, Roulette, Craps, Keno, Baccarat, and the Wheel of Fortune. The gambling information contained in this chapter is purely informational and is certainly not intended to encourage gambling.

5.1 Slot Machines

Several years ago a $1 slot machine at a Las Vegas casino paid off two $5,000 jackpots in as many days. The chances of something like that happening are close to 1 in 1,000,000. Most people that play the slot machines loose all their gambling money in a relatively short period of time.

Slot machines are beautiful pieces of machinery perfectly maintained and precision manufactured. Each machine contains between 300 and 1,400 parts. These machines are set to win for their owners. Any person who plays them for any other purpose than boredom or to get rid of loose change in his pocket needs his head examined.

Every time the arm is pulled, three wheels are set rotating. Pasted to the rim of each wheel is a strip of paper on which are printed pictures of bells, plums, cherries, bars, oranges, or the like. The wheels spin until a retarder brings them to a stop, lining up certain combinations of pictures. A typical payoff for various combinations is shown in Fig. 5–1.

GAMBLING GAMES

PAYOFF TABLE	
COMBINATION	PAYOFF (NICKELS)
▨ ▨ ▨	200
BAR BAR ▨	100
🔔 🔔 🔔	18
🔔 🔔 ▨	18
♣ ♣ ♣	14
♣ ♣ ▨	14
○ ○ ○	10
○ ○ ▨	10
🍒 🍒 —	5
🍒 — —	2

Fig. 5-1 Payoff table for slot machines

    The number of picture combinations possible is 8,000. You multiply the number of pictures on the first wheel by the number on the second wheel, by the number on the third wheel (20 × 20 × 20 = 8,000) to get all possible combinations.

    As the wheels spin, players get excited because it seems they are coming so close to a win. But let's now take a look at what's printed on those spinning wheels. Every other symbol on the third reel of this particular slot machine is a lemon (see Fig. 5–2), which doesn't figure in any of the payoffs. If each of the machine's 8,000 possible combinations

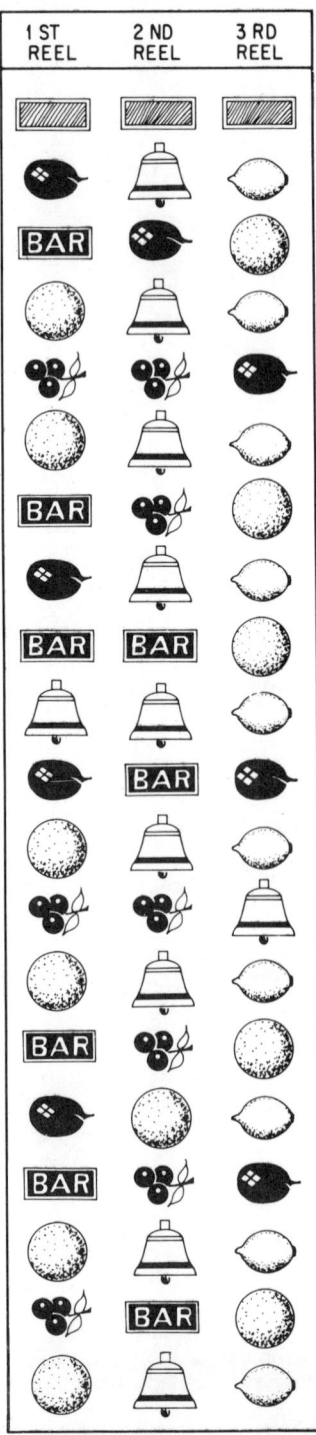

Fig. 5-2 How the house makes its percentage with slot machines

GAMBLING GAMES

comes up once, the total payout will be 6,708 nickels. The machine keeps 1,292 nickels for the house percentage of 16.1 percent.

Rather than gamble with a slot machine, let us "gamble" with a computer. The computer's typewriter (or CRT keyboard/display device) is used as the "slot machine," a typewriter (or CRT keyboard) input is the "handle," and, instead of figures showing behind the "windows," the typewriter (or CRT display) outputs three words representing the figures.

There are only three winning payoffs in this slot machine:

BAR	BAR	BAR	pays $3.00
ORANGE	ORANGE	ORANGE	pays $3.00
CHERRY	CHERRY	CHERRY	pays $3.00

It is a 50-cent machine. A bar, an orange, or a cherry appears in each window each time you put money in the machine and pull the imaginary handle. If all three figures are the same, you win $3.00; otherwise you lose your 50 cents.

The following program and program run illustrate gambling with a simulated slot machine. A flowchart is shown in Fig. 5-3.

```
10   REM SLOT MACHINE
20   PRINT "THIS IS A SIMULATED $.50 SLOT MACHINE"
30   PRINT "WINNING COMBINATIONS ARE"
40   PRINT "3 BARS    3 ORANGES    3 CHERRIES"
45   PRINT "WINNING PAYOFF IS $3.00."
50   PRINT "HOW MANY 50 CENT PIECES DO YOU"
55   PRINT "WANT TO PLAY";
60   INPUT M
70   LET M=M*.5
80   PRINT "YOU START WITH $";M
90   PRINT "DO YOU WISH TO PLAY"
95   PRINT "(TYPE 1 FOR YES -- 0 FOR NO)",
100  INPUT A
110  IF A=0 THEN 430
115  REM COUNTERS FOR BARS,ORANGES,CHERRIES
120  LET B=0
130  LET O=0
140  LET C=0
145  REM DETERMINE 3 FIGURES
150  FOR I=1 TO 3
160  LET N=INT(3*RND(1))+1
165  IF N=2 THEN 210
170  IF N=3 THEN 240
180  PRINT "----BAR----"
190  LET B=B+1
200  GOTO 260
210  PRINT "---ORANGE---"
220  LET O=O+1
230  GOTO 260
240  PRINT "---CHERRY---"
250  LET C=C+1
260  NEXT I
265  REM DETERMINE IF PLAYER WON
270  IF B=3 THEN 350
280  IF O=3 THEN 350
290  IF C=3 THEN 350
295  REM
300  PRINT "   TOO BAD --- YOU LOST"
305  REM SUBTRACT 50 CENTS FROM M
310  LET M=M-.5
320  PRINT
325  REM CHECK TO SEE IF PLAYER HAS ANY MONEY LEFT
```

```
330   IF M=0 THEN 400
340   GØTØ 380
350   PRINT " LUCKY --- YØU WØN $3.00"
360   LET M=M+3
370   PRINT
380   PRINT "YØU NØW HAVE $";M
390   GØTØ 90
400   PRINT "YØU HAVE LØST ALL YØUR MØNEY"
410   PRINT
420   GØTØ 440
430   PRINT "YØU ARE A WISE PERSØN"
440   END
RUN

THIS IS A SIMULATED $.50 SLØT MACHINE
WINNING CØMBINATIØNS ARE
3 BARS     3 ØRANGES     3 CHERRIES
WINNING PAYØFF IS $3.00.
HØW MANY 50 CENT PIECES DØ YØU
WANT TØ PLAY?2
YØU START WITH $ 1
DØ YØU WISH TØ PLAY
(TYPE 1 FØR YES -- 0 FØR NØ)   ?1
----BAR----
---CHERRY---
----BAR----
   TØØ BAD --- YØU LØST

YØU NØW HAVE $ .5
DØ YØU WISH TØ PLAY
(TYPE 1 FØR YES -- 0 FØR NØ)   ?1
---CHERRY---
---CHERRY---
---CHERRY---
 LUCKY --- YØU WØN $3.00

YØU NØW HAVE $ 3.5
DØ YØU WISH TØ PLAY
(TYPE 1 FØR YES -- 0 FØR NØ)   ?1
----BAR----
----BAR----
---CHERRY---
   TØØ BAD --- YØU LØST

YØU NØW HAVE $ 3
DØ YØU WISH TØ PLAY
(TYPE 1 FØR YES -- 0 FØR NØ)   ?0
YØU ARE A WISE PERSØN
```

5.2 Blackjack

One of the most popular casino gambling games is Blackjack, sometimes called 21.* In this game the value of the cards is as marked, that is, the two has a value of 2, the three has a value of 3, etc. King, Queen, and Jack count 10. The Ace counts as 11 or, if the player chooses, as one.

The dealer deals two cards, face down, to each player and two cards to himself, one face down and the other face up. The object of the game is to have your cards total 21, or as near to 21 as possible. If your cards total more than 21, you have gone "busted." If your first two cards are an Ace and a ten, you have a "blackjack" and will win one and a half to one. You cannot lose, but if the dealer should also get a blackjack, it is a stand-off.

*The French know it as *Vingt-et-un* and the English call it Van John.

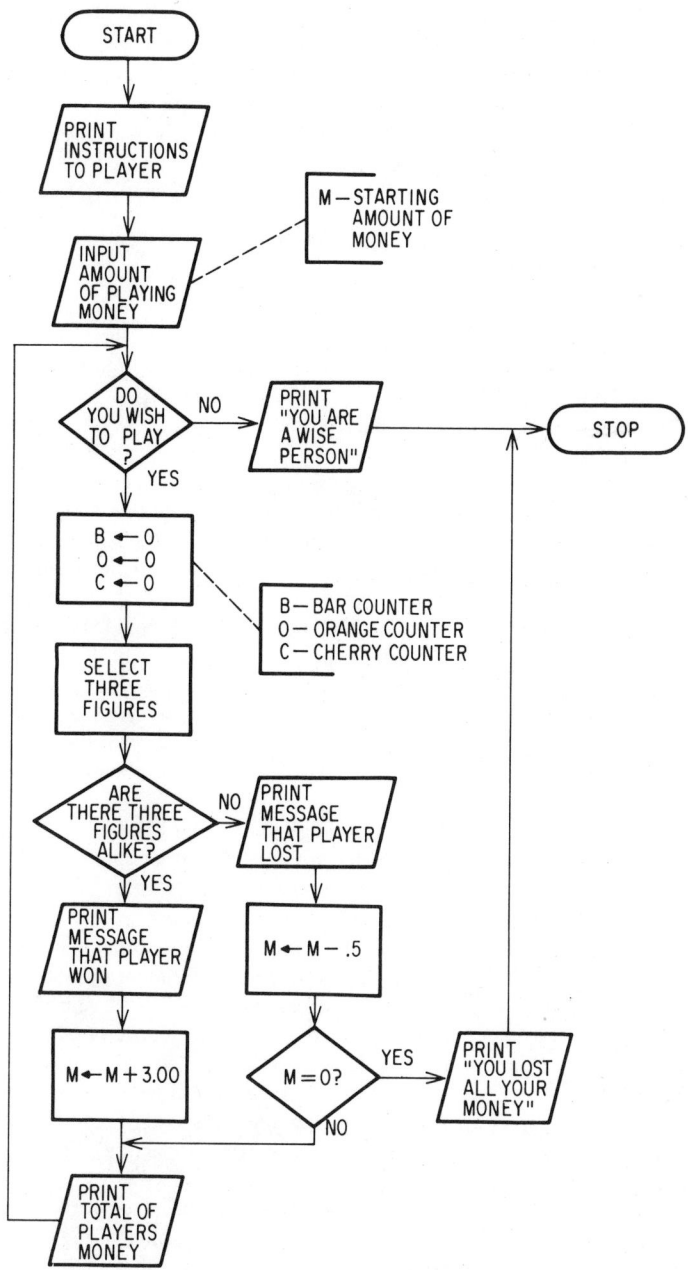

Fig. 5-3 Flowchart for simulated slot machine play

If you feel the total of your first two cards can beat the dealer's total, you "stand pat" and do not draw additional cards. If you feel that the dealer has cards that can beat your total, you may ask for additional cards, one at a time. This is called a "hit."

If your first two cards are a pair, you may "split" them. Turn them both up and bet the same amount of your original bet on both hands. You may take as many hits on each as you want but must finish one hand before going on to the other. If you split a pair of Aces, you may take only one hit on each Ace. With your first two cards, you may also elect to "double down." Generally, this is done when your first two cards total either ten or eleven. Turn your cards up, double your bet, and you'll be allowed only one hit.

Any time the dealer deals himself an Ace for his "up" card, you may insure your hand against the possibility that his hole card is a face card, which would give him an automatic blackjack. To insure, you place an amount equal to one-half of your bet on the "insurance line." If the dealer does have a blackjack, you do not lose, even though he has your hand beat, and you keep your bet and your insurance money. If he does not have a blackjack, he takes your insurance money and play continues in the normal fashion.

After each player is satisfied, the dealer exposes his down card. If his two cards total 16 or less, he must hit until he reaches 17. He cannot hit after he reaches 17 or over. If your total is closer to 21 than the dealer's, you win even money for your bet. If the dealer busts, you also win.

Blackjack is the one casino gambling game that requires judgment and skill to play well; however, anyone can get the basic idea and play passably in a few minutes.

Up until a few years ago, not even professional gamblers knew much about the game or its strategy. In recent years, however, several mathematicians have, with the aid of computers, tested Blackjack playing theories.

Professor Edward O. Thorp in his book *Beat The Dealer* made the gambling world take notice when he explained how to beat the game of Blackjack. Thorp's method was based on card-counting and betting heavily when the cards remaining in the deck favored the player. *The Casino Gamblers Guide* by Dr. Allan Wilson, *The Theory of Gambling and Statistical Logic* by Richard A. Epstein, and *Playing Blackjack As a Business* by Lawrence Revere also contain Blackjack strategies that were obtained with the use of computers.

Card counting is the most effective strategy for playing Blackjack. When the dealer begins a new hand without shuffling after the completion of the previous hand, the composition of the deck is different from the standard deck or decks he began with. This condition changes the probabilities of the hand totals which are possible on the next deal. By counting the discards after each hand, the player can exploit these situations in which he has a greater opportunity of winning by increasing the amount of his wager. He can also improve his playing strategy according to the remaining cards. Card counting is an effective playing strategy since it can reduce the casino advantage to a minimum.

A person who counts the cards is known to the gambling casino as a "counter." Blackjack dealers are always on alert to detect "counters." If they suspect you of being a counter, they will attempt to distract your counting by speeding up the game, loudly riffling the cards, or by talking. If you are a consistent winner, they may even bar you from playing Blackjack in their casino.

The basic strategy for playing Blackjack has been determined by several mathematicians. While these experts differ slightly on some points of the play, they are in surprisingly close agreement on the player's basic strategy. If the reader desires to learn more about the various Blackjack strategies, it is suggested that he read one or more of the books by Thorp, Wilson, Epstein or Revere (see Bibliography).

The following basic strategy can be used to play a good game of Blackjack. In a single deck game in which the dealer must hit 16 and stand on 17, and the player is not allowed to double down after he has split a pair, the player's strategy should usually be:

Always stand on all hands with a count of 17 or more except a soft 17 and a soft 18.*
Stand on a count of 13 through 16 if dealer's up card is 2 through 6, but draw if dealer's card is 7 through 10 or an Ace. Stand on a count of 12 if the dealer's up card is a 4, 5, or 6. Otherwise, draw a card. Always hit a soft hand of 17 or less. Hit a soft 18 only if the dealer's face-up card has a count of 9 or 10.

Always split a pair of Aces or eights. Never split a pair of face cards, 10s, or 5s. Split a pair of twos, threes, or sixes if dealer has 2 through 7 face up; with any other face-up card, hit. Split a pair of 7s if the dealer has 2 through 8 face up. Split a pair of nines if the dealer has 2 through 6, 8, or 9, face-up. Split fours if the dealer up card is a 5.

Always double down with a count of 11. Double down with a count of 10 except when the dealer's face-up card is a 10 or Ace. Double down with 9 only when the dealer has a low face-up card, 2 to 6.

How might a computer program be written to play Blackjack? Let's say you want to play against the computer (which serves as the dealer). First, the program should instruct the computer to set up the deck, shuffle it, and deal itself a card face up. Then it should deal you two cards. After printing the value of your two cards, the computer should ask you (via an appropriate message) if you want another card. You could let a "0" indicate that you wish to stand pat, and a "1" or non-zero number to indicate that you want a hit. Of course, the decisions about cards dealt to the dealer are built into the program logic.

The Blackjack program should be written in such a manner that it prints instructions to the player and directs all of the player's entries on the terminal. For example, the terminal messages should be descriptive and should help the player make his entries at appropriate times. The following printout illustrates the play of six games of Blackjack. The player wins four hands; the computer wins two.

```
THE RULES FOR THE GAME ARE AS FOLLOWS:        Instructions to player
1. BLACKJACK PAYS DOUBLE.
2. PAIRS MAY NOT BE SPLIT.
3. DEALER HITS 16, STANDS ON 17.
4. TIES ARE REPLAYED.
GOOD LUCK

YOU HAVE Q OF SPADES, 2 OF HEARTS.            Game 1: Player wins
DEALER SHOWS Q OF HEARTS
HIT?  YES 6 OF DIAMONDS
HIT?  NO
DEALER HAS 7 OF HEARTS, Q OF HEARTS
DEALER'S SCORE IS 17. YOUR SCORE IS 18.
YOU WIN THIS ONE.

YOU HAVE 8 OF SPADES, K OF CLUBS.             Game 2: Computer wins
DEALER SHOWS A OF HEARTS
HIT?  NO
DEALER HAS 10 OF HEARTS, A OF HEARTS
DEALER'S SCORE IS 21. YOUR SCORE IS 18.
DEALER TAKES THIS ONE.

YOU HAVE J OF CLUBS, 8 OF SPADES.             Game 3: Player wins
DEALER SHOWS THREE OF HEARTS
HIT?  NO
DEALER HAS J OF HEARTS, 3 OF HEARTS
4 OF DIAMONDS
DEALER'S SCORE IS 17. YOUR SCORE IS 18.
YOU WIN THIS ONE.
```

*A "soft" hand contains an Ace as one of the cards.

```
                                                              Game 4: Player wins
YOU HAVE 10 OF SPADES, 5 OF DIAMONDS.
DEALER SHOWS 4 OF HEARTS
HIT?   YES 4 OF SPADES
HIT?   NO
DEALER HAS 3 OF SPADES, 4 OF HEARTS
J OF DIAMONDS
DEALER'S SCORE IS 17.  YOUR SCORE IS 19.
YOU WIN THIS ONE.

                                                              Game 5: Computer wins
YOU HAVE 5 OF CLUBS, 8 OF HEARTS.
DEALER SHOWS 2 OF HEARTS
HIT?   YES 2 OF SPADES
HIT?   YES A OF CLUBS
HIT?   NO
DEALER HAS 5 OF HEARTS, 2 OF HEARTS
5 OF SPADES
2 OF CLUBS
6 OF CLUBS
DEALER'S SCORE IS 20.  YOUR SCORE IS 16.
DEALER TAKES THIS ONE.
```

A program to play Blackjack follows.

```
10     REM -- BLACKJACK GAME
20     REM -- PRINT INSTRUCTIONS TO PLAYER
30     PRINT "THIS IS A GAME OF BLACKJACK.  YOU WILL"
40     PRINT "BE PLAYING AGAINST THE HOUSE.  EACH TIME"
50     PRINT "THE DEALER ASKS YOU IF YOU WANT ANOTHER"
60     PRINT "CARD, PLEASE RESPOND WITH A 1 IF YOU DO."
70     PRINT "0 IF YOU DO NOT."
80     PRINT "THE RULES ARE AS FOLLOWS:"
90     PRINT "  1.  EACH CARD HAS POINTS EQUAL TO ITS FACE"
100    PRINT "      VALUE.  JACKS, QUEENS, KINGS = 10."
110    PRINT "      ACES MAY EQUAL 1 OR 11."
120    PRINT "  2.  YOU WIN IF YOUR POINTS TOTAL"
130    PRINT "      MORE THAN THE HOUSE BUT <= 21."
140    PRINT "  3.  INITIALLY, YOU MAY SEE ONE CARD DRAWN"
150    PRINT "      BY THE HOUSE."
160    PRINT
170    REM -- INITIALIZE
180    DIM D[52],F[8],R[8,8]
190    FOR I=1 TO 8
200    FOR J=1 TO 8
210    LET R[I,J]=0
220    NEXT J
230    NEXT I
240    REM -- SET UP DECK
250    GOSUB 780
260    REM -- DEAL A CARD TO HOUSE. P=1
270    LET P=1
280    GOSUB 910
290    PRINT "HOUSE CARD IS A";
300    GOSUB 990
310    PRINT
320    REM -- DEAL TWO CARDS TO PLAYER. P=2
330    LET P=2
340    FOR I=1 TO 2
350    GOSUB 910
360    PRINT "YOUR CARD IS A";
370    GOSUB 990
380    NEXT I
390    PRINT
400    PRINT "DO YOU WANT ANOTHER CARD ";
410    INPUT A
420    IF A=0 THEN 470
```

GAMBLING GAMES

```
430   GOSUB 910
440   PRINT "YOUR NEXT CARD IS A";
450   GOSUB 990
460   GOTO 390
470   REM -- PLAYER QUITS.  COMPUTE FINAL SCORE
480   GOSUB 1220
490   PRINT "YOU STAND PAT.  TOTAL POINTS = ";F[P]
500   PRINT
510   IF F[P]>21 THEN 170
520   REM -- HOUSE DRAWS AGAIN
530   REM -- STRATEGY FOR HOUSE:
540   REM -- STAND PAT AT 17.  (ACES = 11)
550   LET P=1
560   GOSUB 910
570   PRINT "NEXT HOUSE CARD IS A";
580   GOSUB 990
590   REM -- CHECK POINTS SO FAR
600   IF R[P,2]<17 THEN 560
610   REM -- HOUSE STANDS PAT.  COMPUTE FINAL SCORE
620   GOSUB 1220
630   PRINT "HOUSE STANDS PAT.  TOTAL POINTS = ";F[P]
640   REM -- DETERMINE WINNER
650   IF F[1]=21 THEN 700
660   IF F[1]>21 THEN 680
670   IF F[1] >= F[2] THEN 700
680   PRINT "CONGRATULATIONS.  YOU JUST WON."
690   GOTO 710
700   PRINT "SORRY, THE HOUSE WON."
710   PRINT
720   PRINT "IF YOU WOULD LIKE TO PLAY AGAIN,"
730   PRINT "INPUT A 1.  IF NOT, INPUT A 0 ";
740   INPUT Z
750   PRINT
760   IF Z=1 THEN 170
770   GOTO 1290
780   REM -- CREATE DECK OF CARDS
790   REM -- LIST D CONTAINS FACE VALUE OF EACH CARD
800   REM -- N IS INITIALIZED TO 52: THE NUMBER OF
810   REM -- CARDS IN DECK
820   LET N9=0
830   FOR I=1 TO 4
840   FOR J=1 TO 13
850   LET N9=N9+1
860   LET D[N9]=J
870   NEXT J
880   NEXT I
890   LET N=52
900   RETURN
910   REM -- DRAW A CARD
920   REM -- C IS THE CARD DRAWN
930   REM -- N IS THE NUMBER OF UNDRAWN CARDS IN DECK
940   LET K=INT(1+(RND(0)*N))
950   LET C=D[K]
960   LET D[K]=D[N]
970   LET N=N-1
980   RETURN
990   REM -- PRINT VALUE OF CARD DRAWN AND ADD TO
1000  REM -- TOTAL POINTS
1010  REM -- R(P,1) IS POINTS WITH ACES = 1
1020  REM -- R(P,2) IS POINTS WITH ACES = 11
1030  IF C>10 THEN 1120
1040  LET R[P,1]=R[P,1]+C
1050  IF C=1 THEN 1090
1060  LET R[P,2]=R[P,2]+C
1070  PRINT C
1080  RETURN
```

GAME PLAYING WITH BASIC

```
1090    PRINT "N ACE"
1100    LET R[P,2]=R[P,2]+11
1110    RETURN
1120    IF C>11 THEN 1150
1130    PRINT " JACK"
1140    GOTO 1190
1150    IF C>12 THEN 1180
1160    PRINT " QUEEN"
1170    GOTO 1190
1180    PRINT " KING"
1190    LET R[P,1]=R[P,1]+10
1200    LET R[P,2]=R[P,2]+10
1210    RETURN
1220    REM -- COMPUTE FINAL SCORE: F[P]
1230    IF R[P,1]=R[P,2] THEN 1270
1240    IF R[P,2]>21 THEN 1270
1250    LET F[P]=R[P,2]
1260    RETURN
1270    LET F[P]=R[P,1]
1280    RETURN
1290    END

RUN

THIS IS A GAME OF BLACKJACK.  YOU WILL
BE PLAYING AGAINST THE HOUSE.   EACH TIME
THE DEALER ASKS YOU IF YOU WANT ANOTHER
CARD, PLEASE RESPOND WITH A 1 IF YOU DO.
0 IF YOU DO NOT.
THE RULES ARE AS FOLLOWS:
    1.  EACH CARD HAS POINTS EQUAL TO ITS FACE
        VALUE.  JACKS, QUEENS, KINGS = 10.
        ACES MAY EQUAL 1 OR 11.
    2.  YOU WIN IF YOUR POINTS TOTAL
        MORE THAN THE HOUSE BUT <= 21.
    3.  INITIALLY, YOU MAY SEE ONE CARD DRAWN
        BY THE HOUSE.

HOUSE CARD IS A 2

YOUR CARD IS A JACK
YOUR CARD IS A 8

DO YOU WANT ANOTHER CARD ?0
YOU STAND PAT.  TOTAL POINTS =  18

NEXT HOUSE CARD IS A 4
NEXT HOUSE CARD IS A KING
NEXT HOUSE CARD IS A 5
HOUSE STANDS PAT.  TOTAL POINTS =  21
SORRY, THE HOUSE WON.

IF YOU WOULD LIKE TO PLAY AGAIN,
INPUT A 1.  IF NOT, INPUT A 0 ?1

HOUSE CARD IS A 4

YOUR CARD IS A 2
YOUR CARD IS A 9

DO YOU WANT ANOTHER CARD ?1
YOUR NEXT CARD IS A 8

DO YOU WANT ANOTHER CARD ?0
YOU STAND PAT.  TOTAL POINTS =  19
```

```
NEXT HOUSE CARD IS A 8
NEXT HOUSE CARD IS AN ACE
HOUSE STANDS PAT.  TOTAL POINTS =  13
CONGRATULATIONS.  YOU JUST WON.

IF YOU WOULD LIKE TO PLAY AGAIN,
INPUT A 1.  IF NOT, INPUT A 0 ?0
```

5.3 Roulette

Roulette is a popular game in gambling casinos throughout the world. Figure 5–4 illustrates the wheel and layout used in the game.

Roulette is played by betting against a bank. The bank offers odds on any bet, based generally on the proper calculations for a wheel with 36 sectors. Since the wheel has 38 sectors (counting the zero and double zero) designed to be all equally likely to receive the little ball, the bank pays slightly less than the true odds. On all bets the casino advantage is 5.26 percent. There is one exception, and that is a bet on 0, 00, 1, 2, and 3, a five way bet in which the casino advantage is 7 34/38 percent.

Bets are placed on a layout similar to the one shown in Figure 5–4. This layout is painted on a green cloth. The layout consists of a series of alternating black and red squares numbered 1 through 36. It is divided into three groups: first dozen, second dozen, and third dozen. Another grouping is any number between 1 and 18 or between 19 and 36. There are spaces for betting red or black; odd or even. A player may also bet on numbers running horizontally: from 3 to 36, 2 to 35, 1 to 34. One may also place a wager on 0 and 00.

There are many ways to place bets at Roulette. In "one number" or "straight" bets, a chip or chips is placed on a single number, on red or black, on odd or even, or any one of the numbered groups. In "partial" bets, a player's bet is split on a combination of numbers.

By placing chips in various prescribed positions on the layout, a player can bet on one or more numbers or combinations of numbers. If the player wins, he will be paid off at the following odds:

> SINGLE NUMBERS pay 35 to 1
> DOUBLE NUMBERS pay 17 to 1
> THREE NUMBERS pay 11 to 1
> FOUR NUMBERS pay 8 to 1
> FIVE NUMBERS pay 8 to 1
> SIX NUMBERS pay 5 to 1
> COLUMNS pay 2 to 1
> HIGH OR LOW pay even
> RED OR BLACK pay even
> ODD OR EVEN pay even
> 1 TO 18 or 19 TO 36 pays even

The roulette bets are as follows:

1. *A Single Number, or Straight Bet:* A player may place a bet on any single number, including zero and double zero, by placing his chips on the chosen number. If that number appears, he will be paid 35 times the money he wagered.

2. *A Two Number, or Split Bet:* Any two numbers can be bet by placing chips on

GAME PLAYING WITH BASIC

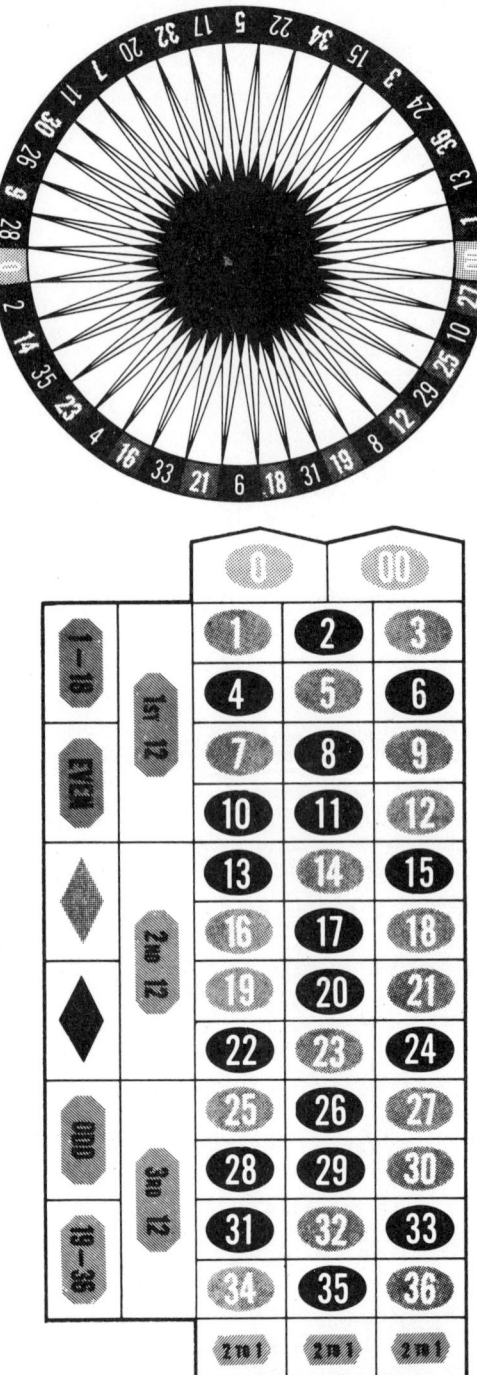

Fig. 5-4 Roulette wheel and table layout

the line separating them, and if either of these numbers appear, the player will be paid 17 chips for each chip wagered.

3. *A Three Number, or Street Bet:* A bet may be made either on the numbers 0, 00, and 2, or, more usually, on any three numbers on the layout by placing the chip on the line separating the numbers from the dozens. The payoff is 11 to 1.

4. *A Four Number, or Square Bet:* Any four numbers may be bet by placing a chip or chips at the intersection point of any four numbers on the layout. The winning payoff is 8 to 1.

5. *A Five Number, or House Special Bet:* There is only one way to bet on five numbers by the placement of one chip. This bet is on the numbers 0, 00, 1, 2, and 3 and is made by placing a chip on the line that separates the 0, 00 and the 1, 2, 3. The payoff of this bet is 6 to 1; however, the house percentage is 7 34/38 percent on this bet. Needless to say, this is the poorest of all Roulette bets.

6. *A Six Number, or Line Bet:* A chip placed on the intersection of the line separating any two rows and either outside vertical line constitutes a bet made on the six numbers of those two rows. The player will collect five chips for each one bet on a winning number. The numbers 4, 5, 6, 7, 8, and 9 are an example of a six number bet.

7. *A Column Bet:* The Roulette layout has three columns of 12 numbers. They are composed of the following numbers:

   Column 1:   1, 4, 7, 10, 13, 16, 19, 22, 25, 28, 31, 34
   Column 2:   2, 5, 8, 11, 14, 17, 20, 23, 26, 29, 32, 35
   Column 3:   3, 6, 9, 12, 15, 18, 21, 24, 27, 30, 33, 36

A column bet is made by placing a chip or chips in the space at the bottom of the selected column. If any one of the numbers comes up, the player will collect at 2 to 1 odds.

8. *A Dozen Bet:* The layout is divided into three squares of 12 numbers: first twelve (or first dozen), second twelve (or second dozen), third twelve (or third dozen). A bet placed in one of the squares labeled first 12, second 12, or third 12 will be paid at 2 to 1 odds whenever a number of that dozen comes up.

9. *High-Low Bet:* A bet placed in the area marked 1-18 will win if a number in that range appears. Likewise a bet placed on 19–36 would win only if the number lies in the range from 19 to 36. This bet pays one to one, even money.

10. *Red-Black Bet.* A bet placed on red will win if one of the following numbers comes up: 1, 3, 5, 7, 9, 12, 14, 16, 18, 19, 21, 23, 25, 27, 30, 32, 34, 36. A wager placed on black will win if any one of the following numbers appears: 2, 4, 6, 8, 10, 11, 13, 15, 17, 20, 22, 24, 26, 28, 29, 31, 33, 35. This is an even money bet.

11. *Even-Odd Bet:* A bet placed on even will win if any of the following numbers comes up: 2, 4, 6, 8, 10, 12, 14, 16, 18, 20, 22, 24, 26, 28, 30, 32, 34, 36. Likewise, a bet placed on odd will win only if one of the following number appears: 1, 3, 5, 7, 9, 11, 13, 15, 17, 19, 21, 23, 25, 27, 29, 31, 33, 35. All even-odd bets will be paid off at one-to-one odds.

Suppose a gambler enters a casino in Reno, Nevada with $1,000. He plays Roulette and bets $1.00 each time on red. Assuming that each bet takes one minute, how much money would the gambler have after one hour of play? The following program simulates a one-hour gambling session in which the gambler bets $1.00 each minute on red.

```
100    REM   ROULETTE PLAY SIMULATION
110    LET M=1000
120    FOR T=1 TO 60
```

```
130   REM   PLACE BET
140   LET M=M-1
150   RESTORE
160   REM   SPIN WHEEL
170   REM   SIMULATE SPIN OF ROULETTE WHEEL
180   LET R=INT(38*RND(0))+1
190   FOR I=1 TO 18
200   READ N
210   IF R=N THEN 250
220   NEXT I
230   GOTO 260
240   REM   PAY OFF
250   LET M=M+2
260   NEXT T
270   PRINT "GAMBLER HAS $";M;"LEFT"
280   DATA 1,3,5,7,9,12,14,16,18,19,21,23,25,27,30,32,34,36
290   END

RUN

GAMBLER HAS $ 992   LEFT
```

5.4 Craps

Craps is played with two dice on a crap table. The mechanics of Craps is simple. When a die is rolled, each of its six sides has a equal chance of being on top when the die stops rolling. Since the sides of the die bear the numbers from one through six, each of those numbers should, over an extended period, come up once in six rolls. When you add a second die, any number from 2 through 12 may be rolled. There are 6 × 6 or 36 ways of arriving at these 11 totals. Basically, that's what Craps is all about, the appearance at certain times of certain numbers from 2 through 12. Figure 5–5 is a chart showing the 36 possible combinations, how many of them will produce each number from 2 through 12, and what the mathematical probability is for any number's appearance.

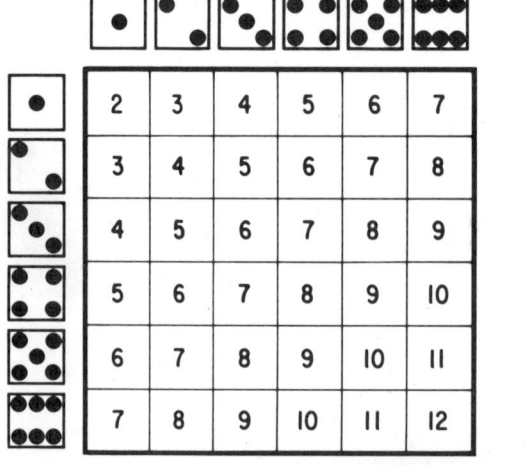

Fig. 5-5 Thirty-six possible combinations of two dice along with the mathematical probability of any number's appearance

GAMBLING GAMES

Since both 2 and 12 can be rolled in only one way and 3 can be rolled in only two ways, four rolls out of 36 should produce *craps*. In other words, if the dice follow the mathematical pattern, you should throw craps once in every nine rolls.

The 11 is a two-way number, so it should appear once in 18 rolls. The 4 and 10 are three-way numbers, so each should appear once in 12 rolls. Four-way numbers are 5 and 9, and percentages indicate that each should turn up in one roll out of nine. The 6 and 8 are five-way numbers and should show once in approximately seven throws.

Seven is the most important number. Six of the 36 possible combinations arrive at 7, so mathematical probability indicates that once out of every six times you roll the dice, they should come up with a seven.

The game is played on a green felt layout similar to that shown in Figure 5–6. The player rolling the dice is called the "shooter." His first roll of the dice is called the "come-out roll."

If his first roll is a 7 or 11, he wins. If his first roll is a 2, 3, or 12 he loses. If his first roll is a 4, 5, 6, 8, 9, or 10, then this number is called the shooter's "point."

If he rolls a point on his first roll, then he must continue rolling until he either rolls his point again or rolls a 7. If he makes his point, he wins. If he rolls a 7 before he makes his point, he loses.

After every decision, the next roll is a new come-out roll, and the play continues as before. The shooter keeps the dice until he "sevens-out"; then the dice pass to the player on his left.

The following program simulates a Craps game. A flowchart is shown in Figure 5–7. The program uses the previous rules of play which are implemented in line numbers 260 through 420. The simulation of 20 games is shown in the program output.

```
100   REM CRAPS SIMULATION
110   PRINT "THIS PROGRAM SIMULATES CRAPS"
120   PRINT "THE COMPUTER ROLLS THE DICE"
130   PRINT "IF THE SUM OF THE DICE IS 7 OR 11 - YOU WIN"
140   PRINT "IF THE SUM OF THE DICE IS 2,3,OR 12 - THE COMPUTER WINS"
150   PRINT "IF YOU MAKE YOUR POINT BEFORE"
160   PRINT "A 7 IS ROLLED - YOU WIN"
170   PRINT "IF YOU ROLL A 7 BEFORE MAKING"
180   PRINT "YOUR POINT - THE COMPUTER WINS"
190   PRINT
200   PRINT "HOW MANY TIMES DO YOU WANT THE"
210   PRINT "COMPUTER TO ROLL THE DICE";
220   INPUT N
230   FOR X=1 TO N
235   PRINT
240   GOSUB 450
250   REM DOES DICE TOTAL 2 OR 3
260   IF D<4 THEN 410
270   IF D=12 THEN 410
280   IF D=7 THEN 390
290   IF D=11 THEN 390
300   LET H=D
310   GOSUB 450
320   IF D=H THEN 350
330   IF D=7 THEN 370
340   GOTO 310
350   PRINT "YOU WIN - YOU MADE YOUR POINT"
360   GOTO 420
370   PRINT "YOU LOSE - YOU DIDN'T MAKE YOUR POINT"
380   GOTO 420
390   PRINT "YOU WIN ON THE FIRST ROLL"
400   GOTO 420
410   PRINT "YOU LOSE ON THE FIRST ROLL"
```

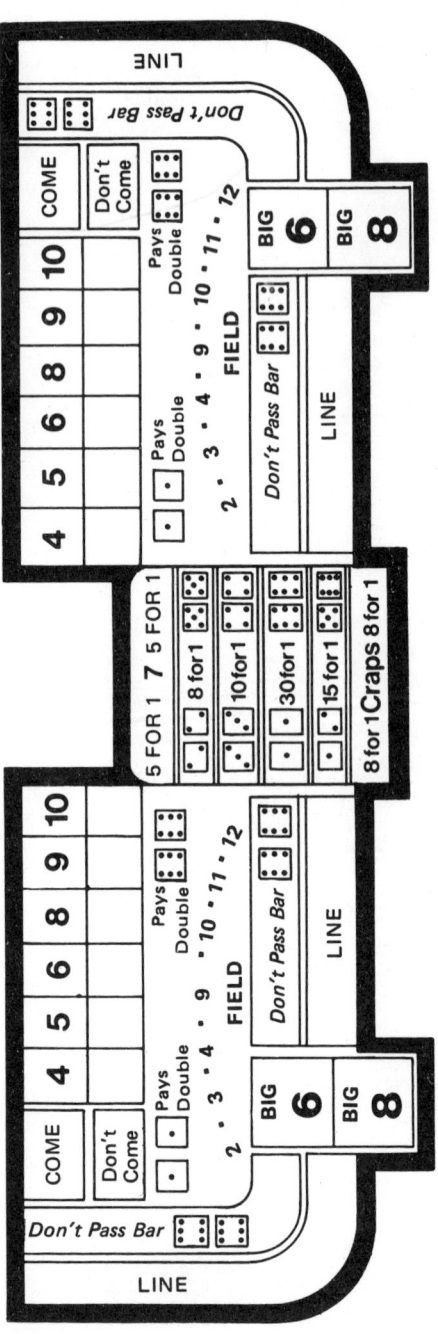

Fig. 5-6 A typical Craps table layout

GAMBLING GAMES

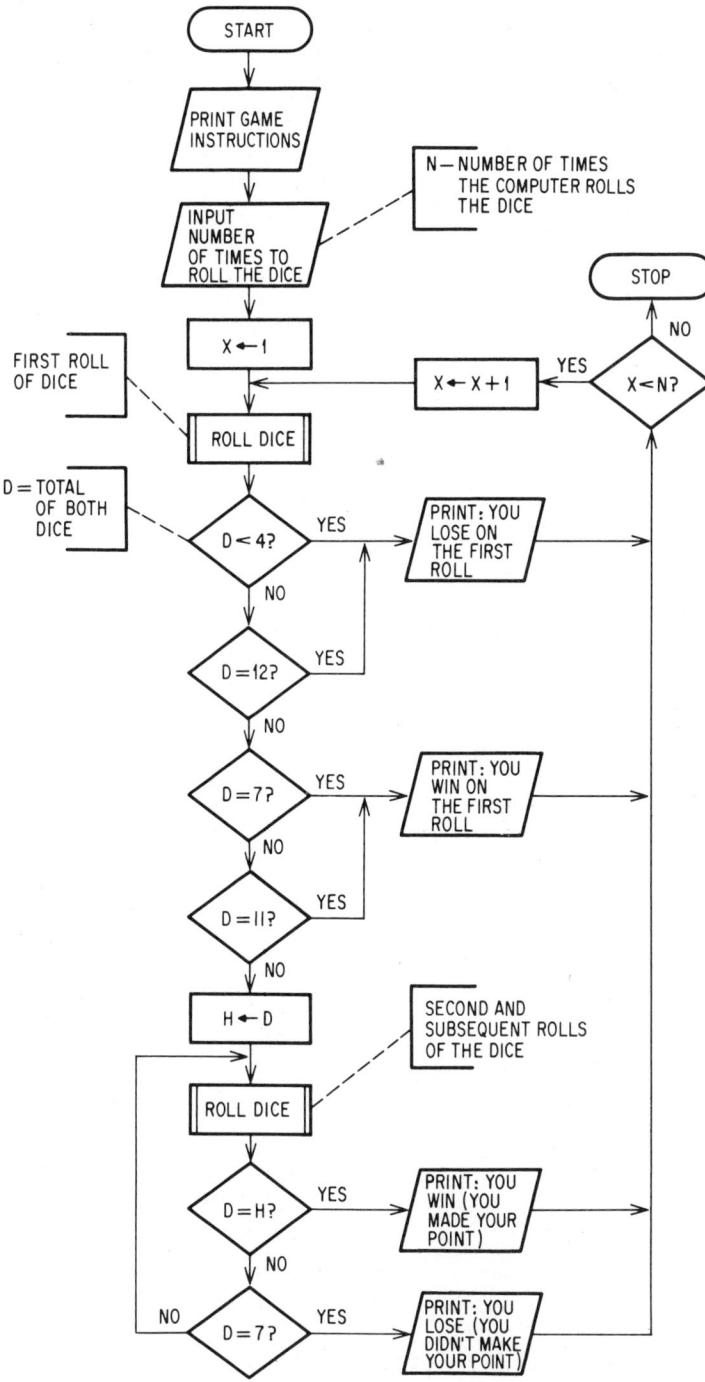

Fig. 5-7 Flowchart of Craps simulation

```
420   NEXT X
430   GOTO 500
440   REM SUBROUTINE WHICH ROLLS DICE
450   LET D1=INT(6*RND(0)+1)
460   LET D2=INT(6*RND(0)+1)
470   LET D=D1+D2
480   PRINT "DIE 1 =";D1;"DIE 2 =";D2
490   RETURN
500   END

RUN

THIS PROGRAM SIMULATES CRAPS
THE COMPUTER ROLLS THE DICE
IF THE SUM OF THE DICE IS 7 OR 11 - YOU WIN
IF THE SUM OF THE DICE IS 2,3,OR 12 - THE COMPUTER WINS
IF YOU MAKE YOUR POINT BEFORE
A 7 IS ROLLED - YOU WIN
IF YOU ROLL A 7 BEFORE MAKING
YOUR POINT - THE COMPUTER WINS

HOW MANY TIMES DO YOU WANT THE
COMPUTER TO ROLL THE DICE?20

DIE 1 = 4     DIE 2 = 2
DIE 1 = 3     DIE 2 = 1
DIE 1 = 3     DIE 2 = 2
DIE 1 = 2     DIE 2 = 6
DIE 1 = 5     DIE 2 = 4
DIE 1 = 5     DIE 2 = 3
DIE 1 = 1     DIE 2 = 1
DIE 1 = 1     DIE 2 = 6
YOU LOSE - YOU DIDN'T MAKE YOUR POINT

DIE 1 = 5     DIE 2 = 5
DIE 1 = 3     DIE 2 = 1
DIE 1 = 3     DIE 2 = 4
YOU LOSE - YOU DIDN'T MAKE YOUR POINT

DIE 1 = 2     DIE 2 = 6
DIE 1 = 3     DIE 2 = 4
YOU LOSE - YOU DIDN'T MAKE YOUR POINT

DIE 1 = 1     DIE 2 = 2
YOU LOSE ON THE FIRST ROLL

DIE 1 = 5     DIE 2 = 6
YOU WIN ON THE FIRST ROLL

DIE 1 = 5     DIE 2 = 1
DIE 1 = 4     DIE 2 = 1
DIE 1 = 1     DIE 2 = 5
YOU WIN - YOU MADE YOUR POINT

DIE 1 = 1     DIE 2 = 2
YOU LOSE ON THE FIRST ROLL

DIE 1 = 3     DIE 2 = 1
DIE 1 = 2     DIE 2 = 5
YOU LOSE - YOU DIDN'T MAKE YOUR POINT

DIE 1 = 3     DIE 2 = 3
DIE 1 = 3     DIE 2 = 4
YOU LOSE - YOU DIDN'T MAKE YOUR POINT

DIE 1 = 4     DIE 2 = 3
YOU WIN ON THE FIRST ROLL
```

GAMBLING GAMES

```
DIE 1 = 5     DIE 2 = 2
YOU WIN ON THE FIRST ROLL

DIE 1 = 3     DIE 2 = 4
YOU WIN ON THE FIRST ROLL

DIE 1 = 6     DIE 2 = 4
DIE 1 = 6     DIE 2 = 5
DIE 1 = 6     DIE 2 = 3
DIE 1 = 2     DIE 2 = 3
DIE 1 = 4     DIE 2 = 6
YOU WIN - YOU MADE YOUR POINT

DIE 1 = 4     DIE 2 = 1
DIE 1 = 3     DIE 2 = 6
DIE 1 = 2     DIE 2 = 6
DIE 1 = 3     DIE 2 = 1
DIE 1 = 4     DIE 2 = 5
DIE 1 = 3     DIE 2 = 3
DIE 1 = 6     DIE 2 = 5
DIE 1 = 6     DIE 2 = 5
DIE 1 = 3     DIE 2 = 3
DIE 1 = 2     DIE 2 = 4
DIE 1 = 3     DIE 2 = 5
DIE 1 = 1     DIE 2 = 4
YOU WIN - YOU MADE YOUR POINT

DIE 1 = 2     DIE 2 = 4
DIE 1 = 5     DIE 2 = 6
DIE 1 = 5     DIE 2 = 3
DIE 1 = 3     DIE 2 = 5
DIE 1 = 1     DIE 2 = 4
DIE 1 = 3     DIE 2 = 4
YOU LOSE - YOU DIDN'T MAKE YOUR POINT

DIE 1 = 1     DIE 2 = 4
DIE 1 = 3     DIE 2 = 3
DIE 1 = 2     DIE 2 = 5
YOU LOSE - YOU DIDN'T MAKE YOUR POINT

DIE 1 = 4     DIE 2 = 6
DIE 1 = 2     DIE 2 = 1
DIE 1 = 6     DIE 2 = 3
DIE 1 = 5     DIE 2 = 4
DIE 1 = 1     DIE 2 = 1
DIE 1 = 6     DIE 2 = 1
YOU LOSE - YOU DIDN'T MAKE YOUR POINT

DIE 1 = 2     DIE 2 = 3
DIE 1 = 4     DIE 2 = 6
DIE 1 = 3     DIE 2 = 6
DIE 1 = 2     DIE 2 = 6
DIE 1 = 4     DIE 2 = 6
DIE 1 = 2     DIE 2 = 1
DIE 1 = 4     DIE 2 = 4
DIE 1 = 3     DIE 2 = 1
DIE 1 = 6     DIE 2 = 1
YOU LOSE - YOU DIDN'T MAKE YOUR POINT

DIE 1 = 4     DIE 2 = 2
DIE 1 = 5     DIE 2 = 5
DIE 1 = 3     DIE 2 = 3
YOU WIN - YOU MADE YOUR POINT

DIE 1 = 5     DIE 2 = 1
DIE 1 = 4     DIE 2 = 1
DIE 1 = 5     DIE 2 = 2
YOU LOSE - YOU DIDN'T MAKE YOUR POINT
```

5.5 Keno

Keno, the oldest game of chance known to man, is of Chinese origin and dates back to the time before Christ. Legend states that the game was used as a national lottery by the Chinese and its revenues were used to finance one of the wonders of the world, the Great Wall of China. The game was brought to America during the early Western days by Chinese coolies. Today, virtually the same game is played in modern casinos.

Keno is played with a cage containing eighty numbered balls. A Keno dealer draws 20 of the balls, one at a time, and calls out each number as it is drawn. Before the game starts, each player marks the numbers he wishes to play on a Keno ticket (see Fig. 5–8). If

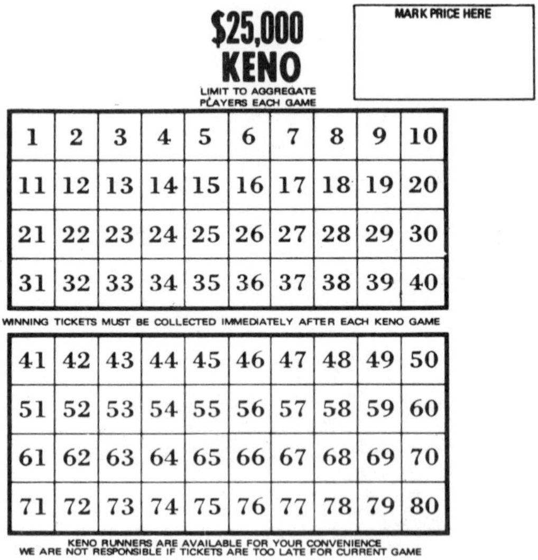

$25,000
KENO
LIMIT TO AGGREGATE
PLAYERS EACH GAME

MARK PRICE HERE

1	2	3	4	5	6	7	8	9	10
11	12	13	14	15	16	17	18	19	20
21	22	23	24	25	26	27	28	29	30
31	32	33	34	35	36	37	38	39	40

WINNING TICKETS MUST BE COLLECTED IMMEDIATELY AFTER EACH KENO GAME

41	42	43	44	45	46	47	48	49	50
51	52	53	54	55	56	57	58	59	60
61	62	63	64	65	66	67	68	69	70
71	72	73	74	75	76	77	78	79	80

KENO RUNNERS ARE AVAILABLE FOR YOUR CONVENIENCE
WE ARE NOT RESPONSIBLE IF TICKETS ARE TOO LATE FOR CURRENT GAME

Fig. 5-8 A typical Keno ticket

several of the numbers he has marked on his ticket match the numbers drawn, he wins according to the following payoff table:

Winning Spots	*70¢ Ticket Pays*	*$1.40 Ticket Pays*	*$7.00 Ticket Pays*
5	2.30	4.60	23.00
6	30.00	60.00	300.00
7	200.00	400.00	2,000.00
8	2,800.00	5,600.00	25,000.00
9	12,500.00	25,000.00	25,000.00

For example, select the nine numbers as shown in Figure 5–9. The amount that you bet is marked on the upper right corner of the ticket ($1.40 in our example). If five or more of the numbers you have selected on your ticket are drawn, you have a winner.

5 numbers: You win $4.60

GAMBLING GAMES

Fig. 5-9 A $1.40 Keno ticket with marked numbers: 13, 16, 19, 33, 39, 46, 53, 68, and 76

6 numbers:	You win $60.00
7 numbers:	You win $400.00
8 numbers:	You win $5,600.00
9 numbers:	You win $25,000.00

Keno has the highest house percentage and slowest rate of play of any casino game. Still the promised $25,000 payoff attracts a lot of players. The author would never advise the reader to play Keno in a casino, but he will invite him or her to write a program to simulate the game on a computer.

5.6 Baccarat

The object of Baccarat (pronounced Baa-caa-rah) is to bet that the one of two sides will achieve a score closer to 9 than the other side.

The game is actually a contest between two *hands* (each person playing the game does not receive cards, but rather each player bets that one of the two hands will win). One hand is called the "Banker's side," whereas the other hand is called the "Player's side." It is possible for all players to bet on the same side. The casino pays the winners and collects from the losers.

Baccarat is played with eight regular decks of cards, shuffled together, and dealt from a box called a "shoe." One card is dealt to the player's side; the next to the banker's side. A second card is then dealt to each. After each side receives two cards, if the rules dictate, a third card will be dealt.

All cards are counted at face value with picture cards valued at 10 and aces valued at 1. The score for either side is determined by adding the cards, for example, $8 + 9 = 17$ or $9 + 6 + 8 = 23$. From the total value, the digit on the right is the final value of the hand. For example: $8 + 9 = 17$, and the 7 wins; $9 + 6 + 8 = 23$, and the 3 loses. The side with 9, or closest to 9, as we have said, wins.

If either side has a value of 8 or 9 on the first two cards (called a "natural"), the other side cannot take a third card. The natural wins. If one side has a natural 8 and the other side a natural 9, the natural 9 wins. If both sides have the same card value for a hand, it is a tie and there is no winner. A tie hand is called a "push" or "standoff."

The Banker's side has a slight mathematical advantage; therefore, any money won playing the Banker's side is taxed 5 percent by the casino (called the "commission").

Neither the casino nor the player has a choice as to whether or not to draw a third card. The casino dealer (called a "croupier") calling the cards will instruct that cards be dealt according to the following rules.

Rules

PLAYER'S SIDE

1-2-3-4-5-10	Draws a card
6-7	Stands
8-9	Natural. Banker cannot draw.

BANKER'S SIDE

Having	Draws When Giving	Does Not Draw When Giving
3	1-2-3-4-5-6-7-9-10	8
4	2-3-4-5-6-7	1-8-9-10
5	4-5-6-7	1-2-3-8-9-10
6	6-7	1-2-3-4-5-8-9-10
7	Stands	
8-9	Natural. Player cannot draw.	

Pictures and Tens Do Not Count

If Player Takes No Card, Banker Stands On 6

The Player's side *must* draw a third card if the value of the initial two cards is 5 or less (5, 4, 3, 2, 1, or 0). The Player *cannot* draw a third card if the value of the initial two cards is 6 or more (6, 7, 8, or 9).

The Banker's side *must* draw a third card if the value of the initial two cards is 2 or less (2, 1, or 0). The Banker's side *cannot* draw a third card if the value of the initial two cards is 7 or more (7, 8, or 9).

When the value of the Banker's initial two cards is 3, 4, 5, or 6, the value of the third card taken by the Player's side determines whether or not the Banker's side must take a third card. If the Player's side does not take a third card, the Banker's side stands on 6 or more and draws on 5 or less. When the value of the Banker's initial two cards is 3 and the third card taken by the Player's side is an 8, the Banker's side cannot draw a third card.

When the value of the Banker's initial two cards is 4 and the third card taken by the Player's side is a 1, 8, 9, or 10, the Banker's side cannot draw a third card. When the value of the Banker's initial two cards is 5 and the third card taken by the Player's side is a 1, 2, 3, 8, 9, or 10, the Banker's side cannot draw a third card.

When the value of the Banker's initial two cards is 6 and the third card taken by the Player's side is a 1, 2, 3, 4, 5, 8, 9, or 10, the Banker's side cannot draw a third card.

Write a program to play Baccarat.

5.7 Wheel of Fortune

The Wheel of Fortune is a giant wheel with a diameter of about 5 feet. The rim of the wheel is divided into 50 sections. In 48 of these sections is paper money in denominations of $1, $2, $5, $10, and $20. The remaining two sections contain a Joker and a Flag. The Wheel of Fortune layout, which consists of seven corresponding numbers and symbols, is used by the players for placing bets.

The wheel is spun and players bet that it will come to rest with the pointer at a specified money denomination. The payoffs are as follows:

1. A player will win even money if he bet on $1 and the pointer stopped at the $1 bill.
2. A player will win $2 if he bet on $2 and the pointer stopped at the $2 bill.
3. If the wheel stops at the $5 bill, the player will collect $5 if he bet on that value.
4. If the wheel stops at the $10 bill, the player will win $10 if he has bet on that denomination.
5. If the wheel stops at the $20 bill, the player will win $20 if he was betting on that value.
6. The Joker and Flag pay off at 40 to 1 odds, and a player betting on either symbol will collect $40 if the wheel stops there.

On most wheels there are 22 $1 bills, 14 $2 bills, seven $5 bills, three $10 bills, two $20 bills, one Joker, and one Flag. With this in mind, write a program to simulate play at the Wheel of Fortune.

chapter 6

PUZZLES

Introduction

This chapter deals with five popular puzzles, namely Tower of Hanoi, the Colored Cube Puzzle, the 15 Puzzle, Pentominoes, and Buried Treasure.

6.1 Tower of Hanoi

This puzzle was invented by the French mathematician, Edouard Lucas, in the nineteenth century. It consists of a number of discs (see Fig. 6–1) of various diameters on a peg, with the largest on the bottom and the smallest on the top. The puzzle is to transfer the set of discs to one of the other two pegs, moving one disc at a time and never placing a disc on top of a smaller one. The aim is to do this in the least possible number of moves. The number of moves required can be shown to equal $2^n - 1$ where n is the number of discs in use. Each extra disc introduced into the puzzle thus essentially doubles the number of movements required to accomplish the goal.

Fig. 6-1 The Tower of Hanoi

PUZZLES

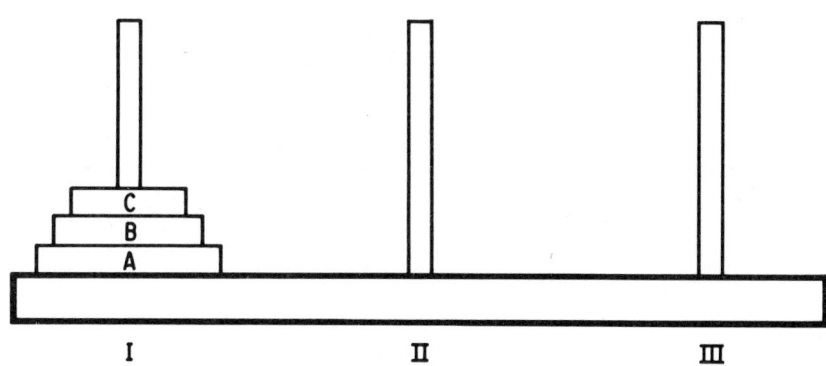

Fig. 6-2 A three-disc Tower of Hanoi requires seven transfers to move the disks to Peg III

A tower with three discs requires $2^3 - 1$ or seven transfers. For example, suppose the pegs are numbered I, II, and III, and the discs lettered A, B, and C, as shown in Fig. 6-2. A, B, and C proceed as follows: C to III, B to II, C to II, A to III, C to I, B to III, and C to III. A puzzle with five discs will require $2^5 - 1$ or 31 moves. Moving six discs takes 63 moves; moving seven discs takes 127 moves; moving eight discs takes 255 moves, etc. A tower with 12 discs requires 4,095 separate moves. A 20-disc tower would require 1,048,575 moves. A 64-disc tower would require 18,446,744,073,709,551,615 moves! Even a computer that could simulate one million moves per second would take more than 500,000 years to do a computer simulation of one such game.

The following program can be used to determine the number of moves required for a specific number of discs.

```
100  REM TOWER OF HANOI
110  PRINT "TOWER OF HANOI"
120  PRINT
130  PRINT "NUMBER OF DISCS";
140  INPUT D
150  FOR X=1 TO D
160  LET N=2↑X-1
170  NEXT X
180  PRINT D;"DISCS REQUIRES";N;"MOVES"
190  END
RUN

TOWER OF HANOI

NUMBER OF DISCS?18
 18   DISCS REQUIRES 262143.   MOVES
```

The input to this program is the number of discs. The output from the program is the number of moves that it will take to move the discs from one peg to another.

There is a way of letting numbers tell you how to make the right moves. Let us consider a four-disc game. In your mind, number the discs from 1 to 4 according to size, from the smallest to the largest. Also, number the moves in the game from first to last, using the numbers from 1 to 15. Write down the numbers of the moves in *the binary scale,* as you proceed from each move to the next. To find out what disc to transfer at each move, and where to place it, look at the binary-scale number that belongs to that move. Count the digits from the *right* until you reach the first digit that is a 1. The number of digits you counted tells you which disc to move. For example, if the first 1 from the right is the third digit, then you move the third disc. Now you have to find out where to place it. If there are no other digits to the left of the first 1, then you place the disc on the peg that has no discs on it. If there are other digits to the left of the first 1, you count digits from the right again until you reach the second 1. The number of digits you count this time identifies a larger disc that was moved before. You must decide whether to put the disc you are moving on top of this larger disc, or not on it, in which case you put it on the peg where the larger disc isn't. To decide this question, you count the number of zeros between the first 1 from the right and the second 1 from the right. If there are no zeros between them, or an even number of zeros between them, you put the disc that you are moving *on* the disc that the second 1 refers to. If the number of zeros between them is odd, you do *not* put the disc on it.

Here are the numbers from 1 to 15, written in the binary scale. Alongside them are the instructions they give for the required 15 moves:

1	Move disc 1
10	Move disc 2
11	Move disc 1 on disc 2
100	Move disc 3
101	Do not place disc 1 on disc 3
110	Place disc 2 on disc 3
111	Place disc 1 on disc 2
1000	Move disc 4
1001	Place disc 1 on disc 4
1010	Do not place disc 2 on disc 4
1011	Place disc 1 on disc 2
1100	Place disc 3 on disc 4
1101	Do not place disc 1 on disc 3
1110	Place disc 2 on disc 3
1111	Place disc 1 on disc 2

Perhaps the reader would be interested in writing a program which will print a list of instructions for placement of the discs. The program printout could appear as follows:

```
        TOWER OF HANOI, FOUR-DISC GAME

        MOVE DISK 1 FROM POLE 1 TO POLE 2
        MOVE DISK 2 FROM POLE 1 TO POLE 3
        MOVE DISK 1 FROM POLE 2 TO POLE 3
        MOVE DISK 3 FROM POLE 1 TO POLE 2
        MOVE DISK 1 FROM POLE 3 TO POLE 1
        MOVE DISK 2 FROM POLE 3 TO POLE 2
        MOVE DISK 1 FROM POLE 1 TO POLE 2
        MOVE DISC 4 FROM POLE 1 TO POLE 3
        MOVE DISK 1 FROM POLE 2 TO POLE 3
        MOVE DISK 2 FROM POLE 2 TO POLE 1
        MOVE DISK 1 FROM POLE 3 TO POLE 1
        MOVE DISK 3 FROM POLE 2 TO POLE 3
        MOVE DISK 1 FROM POLE 1 TO POLE 2
        MOVE DISK 2 FROM POLE 1 TO POLE 3
        MOVE DISK 1 FROM POLE 2 TO POLE 3
```

The story accompanying the original puzzle told how it was a simplified version of a votive object at one of the temples of Benares. In the Tower of Brahma rests a brass plate in which are fixed three diamond needles, each a cubit high and as thick as the body of a bee. On one of these needles God had placed sixty-four discs of pure gold, the largest disc resting on the brass plate, and the others getting smaller and smaller up to the one on top. Day and night unceasingly the priests transfer the discs from one diamond needle to another according to the fixed and immutable laws of Brahma, which require that the priest on duty must not move more than one disc at a time and that he must place this disc on a needle so that there is no smaller disc beneath it. When the sixty-four discs shall have been thus transferred from the needle on which at the creation God placed them to one of the other needles, tower, temple, and Brahmins alike will crumble into dust, and with a thunder-clap the world will vanish. This world's end prophecy is one of the most optimistic on record! If the priests were able to move one disc every second, day and night, it would take them over 500,000 million years to complete their task!

6.2 The Colored Cubes Puzzle

This puzzle consists of four cubes, each painted to show faces of four different colors (blue, green, red, white), the colors of two faces being repeats. The problem is to arrange them in a block so that each of the four long sides of the block is of the same color (see Fig. 6–3).

The arrangement of colors for each cube is not chosen at random but in such a way that there will be only one correct solution to the puzzle. It is not easy to solve, the probability of finding the solution by chance being less than 1 in 40,000. The first cube selected would have 1 chance in 3 of being correctly placed, as it is only necessary to ensure that the correct pair of opposite faces (there is a choice of 3) does not appear on the

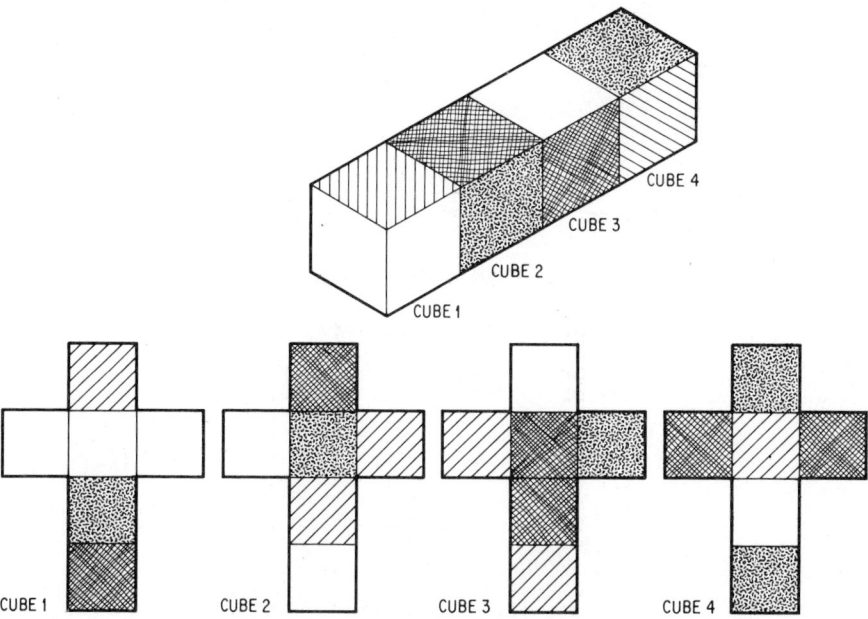

Fig. 6-3 The Colored Cubes problem and its solution

long sides of the block. The chances of correctly placing each of the other cubes, however, is 1 in 24 since each cube can be "resting" on any one of six faces and for each of these positions can be "facing" in four different ways relative to the first cube for a total of twenty-four positions.

To solve the puzzle, first take the cube which has three like faces, placing this so that two of these faces will not appear on any long side of the block. Next, select the cube that has two faces of the same color as the three in the first cube. It will also have two faces of a second color. Place this cube so that four different faces of it appear on the long sides. The third cube will be that with two faces of the second color; this is placed so that one of those faces is hidden and two faces of a third color both appear on the long sides. The last cube will have two opposite faces of the third color, neither of which must appear on the long sides. The cubes now merely have to be rotated about the axis of the block until the solution appears.

Write a program that solves the colored cubes problem. A printout of your program could be as follows:

COLORED CUBES PUZZLE

SIDE ORDER: LEFT, RIGHT, FRONT, BACK, TOP, BOTTOM

1 = BLUE, 2 = GREEN, 3 = RED, 4 = WHITE

```
2 2 1 4 1 3
3 3 2 3 4 1
4 3 3 1 2 4
1 4 4 2 3 2
```

6.3 The 15 Puzzle

This puzzle was invented many years ago by Sam Loyd (1841–1911), the great American innovator of puzzles. Known then as the *14–15 Puzzle,* it consisted of fifteen numbered squares in a box with four units to a side, leaving one empty square so that the numbers could be moved about in the box. In its original form (Fig. 6–4) all the pieces were in

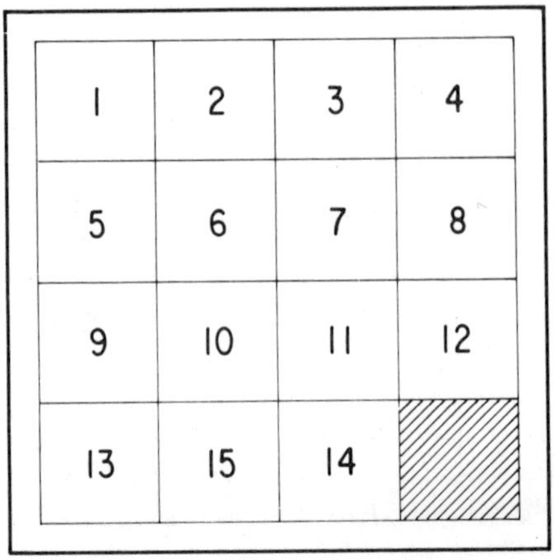

Fig. 6-4 Original 15 Puzzle

PUZZLES

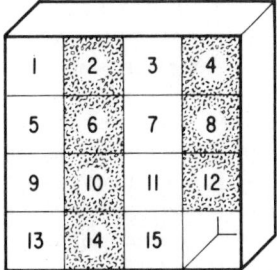

Fig. 6-5 Current arrangement of the 15 Puzzle

order except the 14 and 15 pieces, which were reversed. The problem was to slide the squares around in the box without lifting them out until all the numbers were in order and the empty space back in the bottom right-hand corner. Loyd offered a substantial reward for the first person to solve this puzzle; his money was quite safe, however, as it could not be solved. In the new arrangement of the puzzle, there are 10,461,394,944,000 possible ways the 15 numbers can be correctly arranged in 16 positions. There are also 10,461,394,944,000 impossible number arrangements.

Rather than get involved with the derivation of the method of determining whether a specific number arrangement is possible or not, I will simply state the method. In the normal position of the current 15 puzzle, shown in Fig. 6–5, every number block appears in its proper numerical order (that is, no number precedes a number smaller than itself). The order of the numbers will change when a new number arrangement exists. By recording how many times a number precedes one smaller than itself, and whether this value is odd or even, one can determine if the new number configuration is possible or impossible to achieve. The following steps describe this method in detail.

1. Let N be a number in position A (see Fig. 6–6) of the array to be achieved. Count how many numbers smaller than N are in positions higher lettered than A. Count the blank as 16.

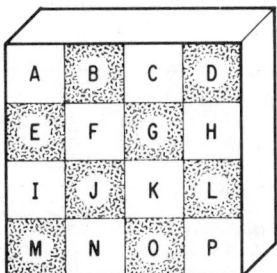

Fig. 6-6 Lettered position of working square

2. Do this for all 16 positions (A through P), and add up the count.
3. If the blank square is one of the shaded squares of Fig. 6–5 (B,D,E,G,J,L,M, or O), add 1 to the sum. Do not change the sum if the blank square was one of the unshaded squares (A,C,F,H,I,K,N, or P).
4. The new array is *possible* if the sum is *even*.
5. The new array is *impossible* if the sum is *odd*.

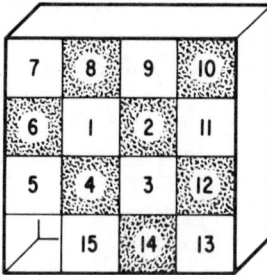

Fig. 6-7 Possible arrangement of the 15 Puzzle

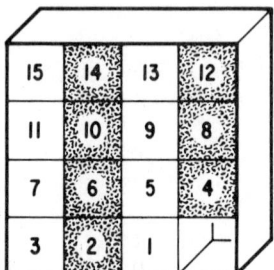

Fig. 6-8 Impossible arrangement of the 15 Puzzle

Proof that the array in Fig. 6–7 can be achieved and that the arrangement in Fig. 6–8 is impossible will be used to illustrate the method just described. Table 6–1 illustrates the sum of the counts for positions A through P. Since the total sum of Fig. 6–7 is even (42), the array is possible to achieve. The array in Figure 6–8 is one of the impossible arrangements since the total sum is odd (105).

The following program determines if a specific arrangement is possible or impossible to achieve.

```
5    REM   15 PUZZLE PROGRAM
10   REM   THIS PROGRAM WILL DETERMINE IF A GIVEN NUMBER
20   REM   ARRANGEMENT IS POSSIBLE OR IMPOSSIBLE
30   REM   PRINT GAME DESCRIPTION
40   PRINT "                    15 PUZZLE"
50   PRINT
60   PRINT " THE 15 PUZZLE WAS INVENTED BY SAM LOYD IN 1878.  IT"
70   PRINT " HAS BEEN AN EXTREMELY POPULAR PUZZLE IN EUROPE AND"
80   PRINT " AMERICA.  THE 15 PUZZLE CONSISTS OF A SQUARE NUMBER"
90   PRINT " ARRANGEMENT WITH THE NUMBERS 1 TO 15 AND A BLANK.  THE"
100  PRINT " BLANK IS REPRESENTED BY THE NUMBER 16.  ANY ONE OF THE"
110  PRINT " NUMBERS TO THE IMMEDIATE RIGHT, LEFT, TOP, OR BOTTOM OF"
120  PRINT " THE BLANK SQUARE CAN BE MOVED INTO THE BLANK POSITION."
130  PRINT " THE OBJECT OF THE PUZZLE IS TO START WITH THE NUMBER"
140  PRINT " CONFIGURATION "
150  PRINT "              1      2      3      4 "
160  PRINT
170  PRINT "              5      6      7      8 "
180  PRINT
190  PRINT "              9     10     11     12 "
```

PUZZLES

Table 6-1 Determining the Sums for the Configurations Shown in Figs. 6-7 and 6-8

Lettered position	Numbers smaller than N	
	Fig. 6-7 arrangement	Fig. 6-8 arrangement
A	6	14
B	6	13
C	6	12
D	6	11
E	5	10
F	0	9
G	0	8
H	3	7
I	2	6
J	1	5
K	0	4
L	0	3
M	3	2
N	2	1
O	1	0
P	0	0
Sum of the above	41	105
Blank position	+1	+0
Total sum	42	105

```
200  PRINT
210  PRINT "                 13   14   15   16"
220  PRINT
230  PRINT " AND FINISH WITH A DIFFERENT NUMBER ARRANGEMENT SAY "
240  PRINT " THE ONE SHOWN BELOW"
250  PRINT
260  PRINT "                  4    8   12   14 "
270  PRINT
280  PRINT "                  3    7   11   16 "
290  PRINT
300  PRINT "                  2    6   10   15 "
310  PRINT
320  PRINT "                  1    5    9   13 "
330  PRINT
340  PRINT " THERE IS ONE SLIGHT CATCH TO THE PUZZLE --- THERE "
350  PRINT " ARE 10,461,394,944,000 NUMBER ARRANGEMENTS THAT "
360  PRINT " ARE IMPOSSIBLE TO OBTAIN.  THERE ARE ALSO THE SAME "
370  PRINT " NUMBER OF POSSIBLE ARRANGEMENTS. "
380  PRINT
390  PRINT " ------------------------------------------------------"
400  PRINT " --- RULES FOR USING THE 15 PUZZLE PROGRAM --- "
410  PRINT
420  PRINT " AFTER THE PROGRAM TYPES A DESCRIPTION AND RULES OF THE "
430  PRINT " 15 PUZZLE THE FOLLOWING MESSAGE WILL BE PRINTED "
440  PRINT
450  PRINT "    TYPE THE NUMBER ARRANGEMENT TO BE "
```

```
460    PRINT "     IN ROW ORDER ( FIRST ROW FIRST, SECOND ROW "
470    PRINT "     NEXT, ETC. ).  SEPERATE EACH NUMBER BY A "
480    PRINT "     COMMA.  THE BLANK SQUARE IS REPRESENTED BY 16."
490    PRINT
500    PRINT " AFTER YOU TYPE THE NUMBER ARRANGEMENT TO BE "
510    PRINT " ACHIEVED AND PRESS RETURN THE PROGRAM WILL "
520    PRINT " DETERMINE IF THE ARRANGEMENT CAN OR CANNOT BE "
530    PRINT " ACHIEVED AND WILL PRINT THE NUMBER ARRANGEMENT "
540    PRINT " AND THE APPROPRIATE OF THE FOLLOWING TWO MESSAGES "
550    PRINT
560    PRINT "     THE FOLLOWING NUMBER ARRANGEMENT "
570    PRINT "     IS IMPOSSIBLE TO ACHIEVE "
580    PRINT
590    PRINT "     THE FOLLOWING NUMBER ARRANGEMENT "
600    PRINT "     IS POSSIBLE TO ACHIEVE "
610    PRINT
620    PRINT " YOU MAY INPUT ANOTHER NUMBER ARRANGEMENT BY "
630    PRINT " TYPING 666 WHEN REQUESTED TO DO SO.  YOU MAY "
640    PRINT " STOP BY TYPING 777 WHEN REQUESTED TO DO SO. "
642    DIM S[4,4]
650    PRINT
660    PRINT
670    PRINT " TYPE THE NUMBER ARRANGEMENT TO BE ACHIEVED"
680    PRINT " IN ROW ORDER ( FIRST ROW FIRST, SECOND ROW"
690    PRINT " NEXT, ECT. ).  SEPERATE EACH NUMBER BY A "
700    PRINT " COMMA.  THE BLANK SQUARE IS REPRESENTED BY 16."
705    PRINT
710    INPUT A,B,C,D,E,F,G,H,I,J,K,L,M,N,O,P
720    LET S[1,1]=A
730    LET S[1,2]=B
740    LET S[1,3]=C
750    LET S[1,4]=D
760    LET S[2,1]=E
770    LET S[2,2]=F
780    LET S[2,3]=G
790    LET S[2,4]=H
800    LET S[3,1]=I
810    LET S[3,2]=J
820    LET S[3,3]=K
830    LET S[3,4]=L
840    LET S[4,1]=M
850    LET S[4,2]=N
860    LET S[4,3]=O
870    LET S[4,4]=P
871    PRINT
872    PRINT A;B;C;D
873    PRINT
874    PRINT E;F;G;H
875    PRINT
876    PRINT I;J;K;L
877    PRINT
878    PRINT M;N;O;P
880    LET T=0
890    IF S[1,2]=16 THEN 980
900    IF S[1,4]=16 THEN 980
910    IF S[2,1]=16 THEN 980
920    IF S[2,3]=16 THEN 980
930    IF S[3,2]=16 THEN 980
940    IF S[3,4]=16 THEN 980
950    IF S[4,1]=16 THEN 980
960    IF S[4,3]=16 THEN 980
970    GOTO 990
980    LET T=T+1
990    FOR I=1 TO 4
1000   FOR J=1 TO 4
1010   FOR K=1 TO 4
1020   FOR L=1 TO 4
```

```
1030    IF S[I,J]>S[K,L] THEN 1070
1040    NEXT L
1050    NEXT K
1060    GOTO 1080
1070    LET T=T+1
1080    LET S[I,J]=16
1082    NEXT J
1084    NEXT I
1090    IF T-2*INT(T/2)=0 THEN 1140
1100    PRINT
1110    PRINT
1120    PRINT " THE ABOVE 15 PUZZLE ARRANGEMENT CANNOT BE ACHIEVED"
1130    GOTO 1170
1140    PRINT
1150    PRINT
1160    PRINT " THE ABOVE 15 PUZZLE ARRANGEMENT CAN BE ACHIEVED"
1170    PRINT
1180    PRINT
1190    PRINT " TYPE 777 IF YOU WANT TO STOP."
1200    PRINT " TYPE 666 IF YOU WANT TO CONTINUE."
1210    INPUT X
1220    IF X=777 THEN 1270
1230    IF X=666 THEN 650
1240    PRINT
1250    PRINT " CAN'T YOU READ ---- TYPE EITHER 777 OR 666."
1260    GOTO 1210
1270    END
```

RUN

15 PUZZLE

THE 15 PUZZLE WAS INVENTED BY SAM LOYD IN 1878. IT
HAS BEEN AN EXTREMELY POPULAR PUZZLE IN EUROPE AND
AMERICA. THE 15 PUZZLE CONSISTS OF A SQUARE NUMBER
ARRANGEMENT WITH THE NUMBERS 1 TO 15 AND A BLANK. THE
BLANK IS REPRESENTED BY THE NUMBER 16. ANY ONE OF THE
NUMBERS TO THE IMMEDIATE RIGHT, LEFT, TOP, OR BOTTOM OF
THE BLANK SQUARE CAN BE MOVED INTO THE BLANK POSITION.
THE OBJECT OF THE PUZZLE IS TO START WITH THE NUMBER
CONFIGURATION

1	2	3	4
5	6	7	8
9	10	11	12
13	14	15	16

AND FINISH WITH A DIFFERENT NUMBER ARRANGEMENT SAY
THE ONE SHOWN BELOW

4	8	12	14
3	7	11	16
2	6	10	15
1	5	9	13

THERE IS ONE SLIGHT CATCH TO THE PUZZLE --- THERE
ARE 10,461,394,944,000 NUMBER ARRANGEMENTS THAT
ARE IMPOSSIBLE TO OBTAIN. THERE ARE ALSO THE SAME
NUMBER OF POSSIBLE ARRANGEMENTS.

```
--------------------------------------------------------
--- RULES FOR USING THE 15 PUZZLE PROGRAM ---

AFTER THE PROGRAM TYPES A DESCRIPTION AND RULES OF THE
15 PUZZLE THE FOLLOWING MESSAGE WILL BE PRINTED

    TYPE THE NUMBER ARRANGEMENT TO BE
    IN ROW ORDER ( FIRST ROW FIRST, SECOND ROW
    NEXT, ETC. ).  SEPERATE EACH NUMBER BY A
    COMMA.  THE BLANK SQUARE IS REPRESENTED BY 16.

AFTER YOU TYPE THE NUMBER ARRANGEMENT TO BE
ACHIEVED AND PRESS RETURN THE PROGRAM WILL
DETERMINE IF THE ARRANGEMENT CAN OR CANNOT BE
ACHIEVED AND WILL PRINT THE NUMBER ARRANGEMENT
AND THE APPROPRIATE OF THE FOLLOWING TWO MESSAGES

    THE FOLLOWING NUMBER ARRANGEMENT
    IS IMPOSSIBLE TO ACHIEVE

    THE FOLLOWING NUMBER ARRANGEMENT
    IS POSSIBLE TO ACHIEVE

YOU MAY INPUT ANOTHER NUMBER ARRANGEMENT BY
TYPING 666 WHEN REQUESTED TO DO SO.  YOU MAY
STOP BY TYPING 777 WHEN REQUESTED TO DO SO.

TYPE THE NUMBER ARRANGEMENT TO BE ACHIEVED
IN ROW ORDER ( FIRST ROW FIRST, SECOND ROW
NEXT, ECT. ).  SEPERATE EACH NUMBER BY A
COMMA.  THE BLANK SQUARE IS REPRESENTED BY 16.

?1,2,3,4,5,6,7,8,9,10,11,12,13,14,16,15

    1     2     3     4

    5     6     7     8

    9    10    11    12

   13    14    16    15


THE ABOVE 15 PUZZLE ARRANGEMENT CAN BE ACHIEVED

TYPE 777 IF YOU WANT TO STOP.
TYPE 666 IF YOU WANT TO CONTINUE.
?555

CAN'T YOU READ ---- TYPE EITHER 777 OR 666.
?666

TYPE THE NUMBER ARRANGEMENT TO BE ACHIEVED
IN ROW ORDER ( FIRST ROW FIRST, SECOND ROW
NEXT, ECT. ).  SEPERATE EACH NUMBER BY A
COMMA.  THE BLANK SQUARE IS REPRESENTED BY 16.

?16,15,14,13,12,11,10,9,8,7,6,5,4,3,2,1

   16    15    14    13

   12    11    10     9

    8     7     6     5

    4     3     2     1
```

PUZZLES

```
THE ABOVE 15 PUZZLE ARRANGEMENT CANNOT BE ACHIEVED

TYPE 777 IF YOU WANT TO STOP.
TYPE 666 IF YOU WANT TO CONTINUE.
?777
```

This program causes the teletype unit to type a short description of the 15 Puzzle and rules for using the program. After the playing rules are typed, the program causes a message to be typed that directs the operator to type the number arrangement that the program will work with. After the operator types the 16 required entries, the program prints the array of numbers and a statement indicating that the chosen number arrangement can or cannot be achieved. The operator can continue playing this program by typing 666 when requested to do so or can stop playing by typing 777. Any other number will cause the message "CANT YOU READ—TYPE EITHER 777 OR 666" to be typed. A flowchart of the 15 Puzzle program is shown in Fig. 6–9.

6.4 Pentominoes

If five squares are arranged edge to edge, twelve different arrangements are possible. These shapes are known as pentominoes, and the twelve arrangements are shown in Fig. 6–10. In a game of pentominoes, a player (or computer) arranges the twelve shapes in a 6 by 10 rectangular box (as also shown in Fig. 6–10).

There are over 2,000 different ways of arranging the 12 pentominoes in a 6 by 10 rectangle. The reader may wish to make a set of pentominoes from cardboard and attempt to find an arrangement different from the one given. The ambitious reader may even wish to write a program to produce several solutions to this problem.

6.5 Buried Treasure

This game is played on a 10 by 10 grid like the one shown in Fig. 6–11. The following program will randomly select a rectangular block of 4 adjacent squares to represent a "buried chest of gold." You are to try to locate the buried treasure by "digging holes." You can dig 10 test holes in an afternoon. You represent the location of each hole by typing x and y coordinates whenever the program requests that you do so.

```
10    REM BURIED TREASURE
20    PRINT "USE A 10 BY 10 GRID WHEN PLAYING"
30    PRINT "THIS GAME. THE COMPUTER HAS BURIED"
40    PRINT "A CHEST OF GOLD IN A FOUR-SQUARE"
50    PRINT "RECTANGULAR AREA WITHIN THE GRID."
60    PRINT "YOU ARE TO TRY TO LOCATE THE GOLD"
70    PRINT "CHEST BY 'DIGGING HOLES'."
80    PRINT
90    LET X=RND(1)
100   LET Z=INT(2*RND(1)+1)
110   IF Z=2 THEN 190
120   LET X[1]=INT(7*RND(1)+1)
130   LET Y[1]=INT(10*RND(1)+1)
140   FOR I=2 TO 4
150   LET X[I]=X[I-1]+1
160   LET Y[I]=Y[I-1]
170   NEXT I
180   GOTO 240
190   LET X[1]=INT(10*RND(1)+1)
200   LET Y[1]=INT(7*RND(1)+1)
210   FOR I=2 TO 4
220   LET X[I]=X[I-1]
```

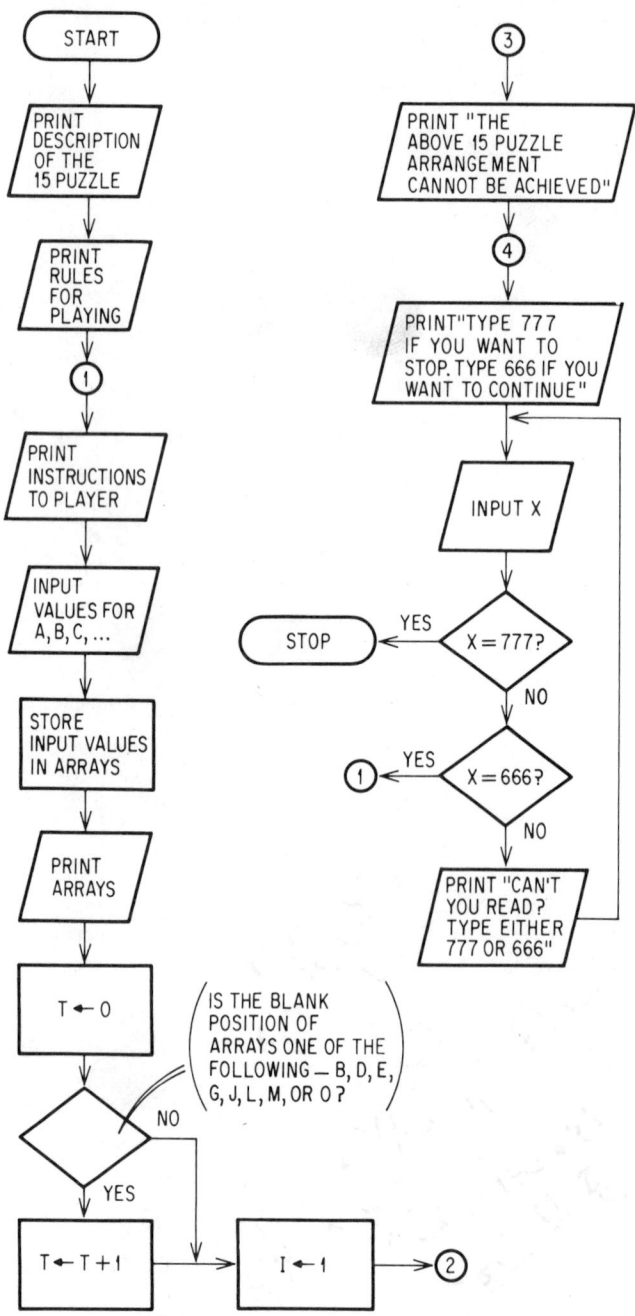

Fig. 6-9 Flowchart of the 15 Puzzle

```
230    LET Y[I]=Y[I-1]+1
240    NEXT I
250    LET S=10
260    PRINT
270    PRINT "WHAT IS THE LØCATIØN ØF THE"
271    PRINT "FIRST HØLE";
```

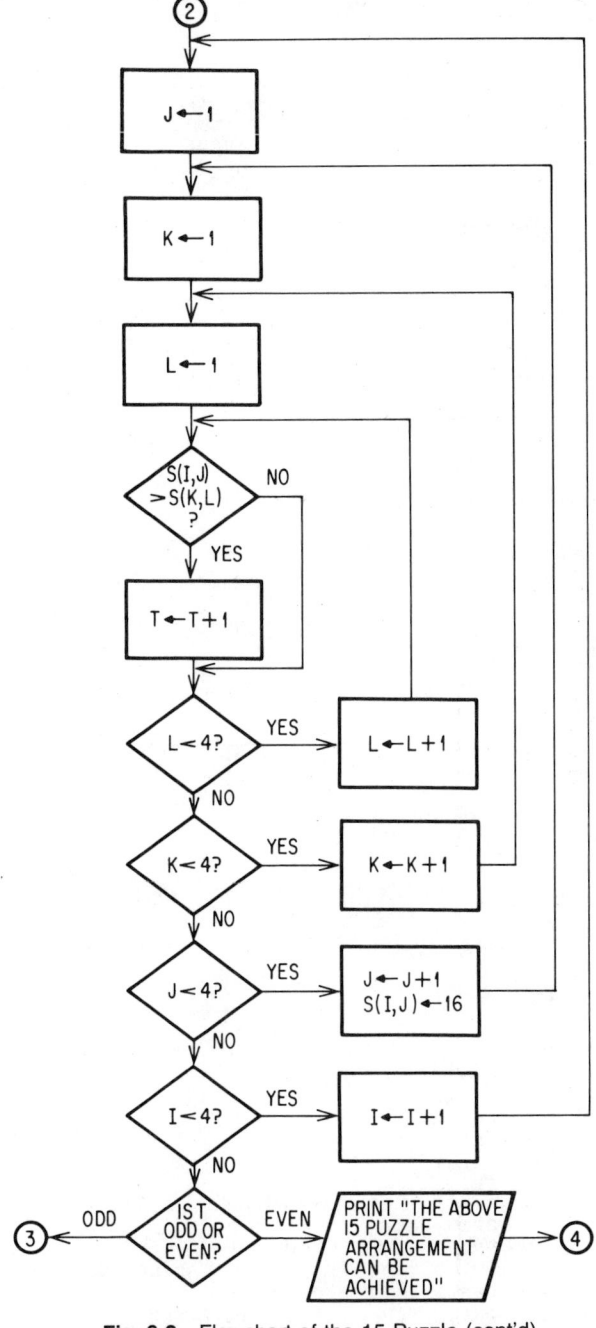

Fig. 6-9 Flowchart of the 15 Puzzle (cont'd)

```
280    INPUT X,Y
290    FOR I=1 TO 4
300    IF X <> X[I] THEN 320
310    IF Y=Y[I] THEN 470
320    NEXT I
330    PRINT "TREASURE NOT THERE"
```

Fig. 6-10 The twelve pentominoes with one possible arrangement

```
340    LET S=S-1
350    IF S=0 THEN 400
360    PRINT "YØU HAVE";S;"TRIES LEFT"
370    PRINT
380    PRINT "LØCATIØN ØF NEXT HØLE";
390    GØTØ 280
400    PRINT "GAME IS ØVER"
410    PRINT "THE GØLD CHEST WAS LØCATED AT "
420    FØR I=1 TØ 3
430    PRINT "(";X[I];",";Y[I];")"
440    NEXT I
450    PRINT "AND (";X[4];",";Y[4];")."
460    GØTØ 480
470    PRINT "HURRAY -- YØU FØUND THE TREASURE"
480    END

RUN
```

PUZZLES

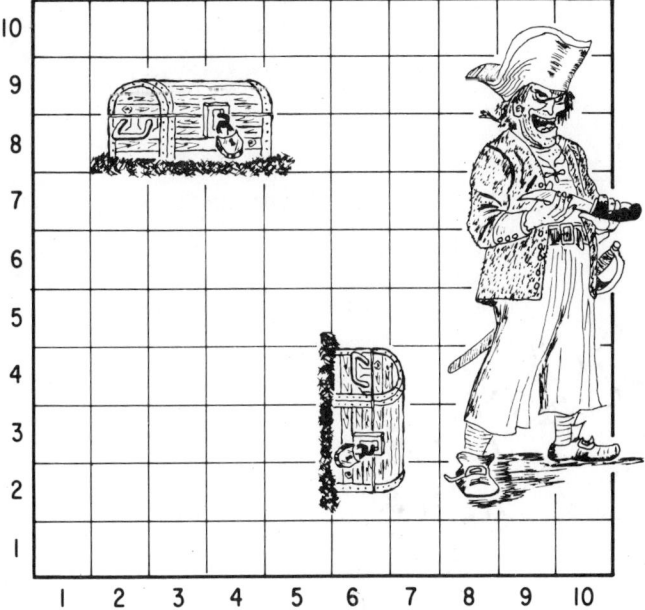

Fig. 6-11 Board for Buried Treasure

```
USE A 10 BY 10 GRID WHEN PLAYING
THIS GAME. THE COMPUTER HAS BURIED
A CHEST OF GOLD IN A FOUR-SQUARE
RECTANGULAR AREA WITHIN THE GRID.
YOU ARE TO TRY TO LOCATE THE GOLD
CHEST BY 'DIGGING HOLES'.


WHAT IS THE LOCATION OF THE
FIRST HOLE?2,3
TREASURE NOT THERE
YOU HAVE 9     TRIES LEFT

LOCATION OF NEXT HOLE?4,7
TREASURE NOT THERE
YOU HAVE 8     TRIES LEFT

LOCATION OF NEXT HOLE?3,9
TREASURE NOT THERE
YOU HAVE 7     TRIES LEFT

LOCATION OF NEXT HOLE?5,1
TREASURE NOT THERE
YOU HAVE 6     TRIES LEFT

LOCATION OF NEXT HOLE?5,10
TREASURE NOT THERE
YOU HAVE 5     TRIES LEFT

LOCATION OF NEXT HOLE?6,8
TREASURE NOT THERE
YOU HAVE 4     TRIES LEFT

LOCATION OF NEXT HOLE?7,3
```

```
TREASURE NOT THERE
YOU HAVE 3    TRIES LEFT

LOCATION OF NEXT HOLE?10,7
TREASURE NOT THERE
YOU HAVE 2    TRIES LEFT

LOCATION OF NEXT HOLE?9,5
TREASURE NOT THERE
YOU HAVE 1    TRIES LEFT

LOCATION OF NEXT HOLE?8,8
TREASURE NOT THERE
GAME IS OVER
THE GOLD CHEST WAS LOCATED AT
( 1   , 5
( 2   , 5
( 3   , 5
AND ( 4    , 5
```

chapter 7

MAGIC SQUARES

Introduction

Magic Squares, an ancient and fascinating amusement, are arrays of numbers such that the sum of the numbers in each row, column, or long diagonal is the same. The simplest magic square is one containing only nine boxes, with numbers from 1 to 9 inclusive, as shown in Fig. 7–1. You will see that each row and each column adds up to 15. Also, the two diagonals add up to 15.

A magic square of order n is defined as n × n array of integers from 1 to n^2 such that the sum of each row, column, and main diagonal is a constant; that is, all the sums are the same. Figure 7–2 shows a magic square of order 4.

So much has been written about the subject that it would appear that stagnation is about to set in. Still, this entertainment exerts a virtually unbreakable hold on the average game enthusiast or recreational mathematician. Generating magic squares by computer is relatively new and interesting. Not only are magic squares fun to construct, they also

8	1	6
3	5	7
4	9	2

Fig. 7-1 The simplest Magic Square containing the numbers from 1 to 9

1	12	7	14
8	13	2	11
10	3	16	5
15	6	9	4

MAGIC NUMBER $= \frac{4(4^2+1)}{2} = 34$
SUM OF ROW $= 34$
SUM OF COLUMN $= 34$
SUM OF MAIN DIAGONAL $= 34$

Fig. 7-2 A Magic Square of order 4

provide excellent programming exercises for the game player. Once you have an understanding of the methods of constructing various magic squares, you will find them quite simple to produce, with or without a computer.

There are endless methods and variations in constructing magic squares. Rather than get involved with all varieties, I will discuss a few of the more direct methods. In my book, *Game Playing with Computers* (Hayden Book Company, 1975), I covered many of the more complex and technically fascinating squares, should you be a more interested student of the subject.

7.1 How to Make Magic Squares

There are two basic methods of making magic squares. One applies to odd-cell (uneven-cell) squares—3, 5, 7, 9, etc.—and the other to even-cell squares—4, 8, 12, 16, etc. To make an odd-cell magic square, we use the *diagonal-arrow method;* to make an even-cell square, we use the *cross-diagonal method*. These methods are described in Sections 7.2 and 7.3.

7.2 Odd-Cell Magic Squares

The *De la Loubere procedure* is used to generate any magic square of odd order. For the sake of simplicity, a 5 by 5 magic square is generated in the following illustrations. The reader should keep in mind that this method of construction may be used equally well for generating 3 by 3, 7 by 7, 9 by 9, 11 by 11, etc., magic squares.

    1. Place the number 1 in the center box of the first row, as shown at the left of Fig. 7–3.

    2. Move in an oblique direction, one square to the right and one square above. This movement results in leaving the top of the box. It is necessary to go to the bottom of the column in which you wanted to place the number. Place the number 2 in this location, as shown at the right of Fig. 7–3.

    3. Now move diagonally to the right again and put the number 3 in the next box you enter, as shown at the left of Fig. 7–4.

    4. If you continue diagonally to the right, you leave the box on the right side. When this occurs you must go to the extreme left of the row in which you wanted to place the number. After crossing over to the left side of the square, put the number 4 into the appropriate box, as shown at the right of Fig. 7–4.

    5. Now, again, go up diagonally to the right and place the number 5. This completes the first group of five numbers, as shown at the left of Fig. 7–5.

MAGIC SQUARES

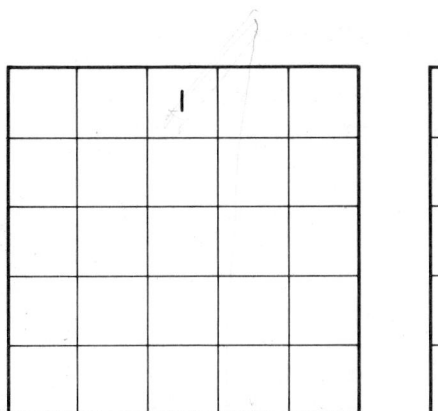
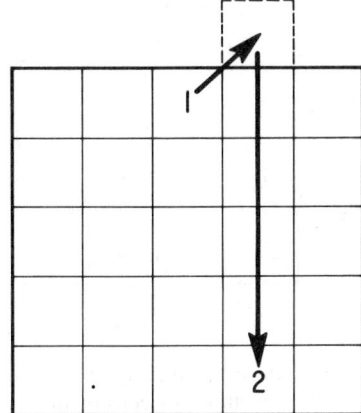

Figure 7-3

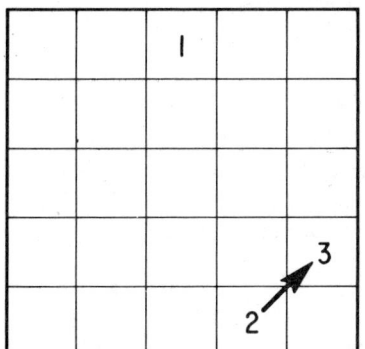
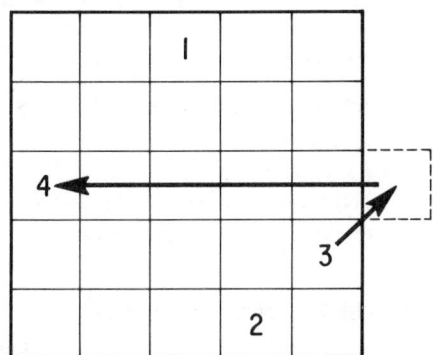

Figure 7-4

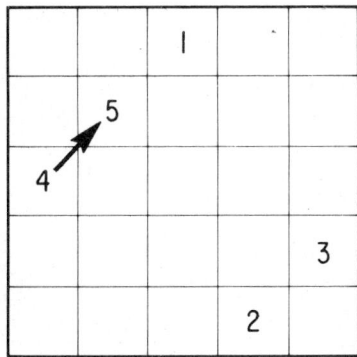
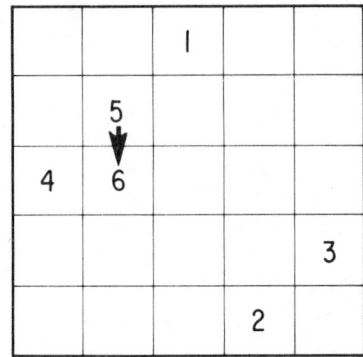

Figure 7-5

6. Since this is a 5 by 5 magic square you must move down one box to generate the next group of five numbers, as shown at the right of Fig. 7–5. If this had been a 3 by 3 square or 7 by 7 square, then you would drop down when you reached a group of three or seven numbers, respectively.

7. Move up diagonally to the right, and place a number into each box you enter. If you leave the box at the top, move to the bottom of the column where you wanted to place the number. If you land outside the box on the right side, move across to the opposite side. After each group of five numbers, go down one box to start the next group of five. When you finish the fifth group of five numbers, the number 25 will occupy the center box of the bottom row, as shown in Fig. 7–6.

17	24	1	8	15
23	5	7	14	16
4	6	13	20	22
10	12	19	21	3
11	18	25	2	9

Figure 7-6

The sum of each of the five rows, five columns and two main diagonals is 65, and the sum of any two numbers which are diametrically equidistant from the center number is 26, or twice the center number.

The following program will generate odd-order Magic Squares using the De la Loubere technique.

```
140  REM MAGIC SQUARE GENERATING PROGRAM
150  REM ORDER OF SQUARE IS N
160  LET N=5
170  LET K=1
180  LET N1=1
190  LET I=1
200  LET J=(N+1)/2
210  REM PLACE ONE IN THE CENTER CELL OF TOP ROW
220  LET M[I,J]=N1
230  LET N1=N1+1
240  REM IS MAGIC SQUARE GENERATION COMPLETE
250  REM TRANSFER CONTROL TO 490 IF LAST
260  REM NUMBER HAS BEEN STORED IN TABLE M
270  IF N1>N*N THEN 490
280  REM IS K AN EVEN MULTIPLE OF N?
290  IF K<N THEN 350
300  REM RESET K TO 1
301  REM SET ROW INDEX TO NEXT ROW
310  LET K=1
```

MAGIC SQUARES

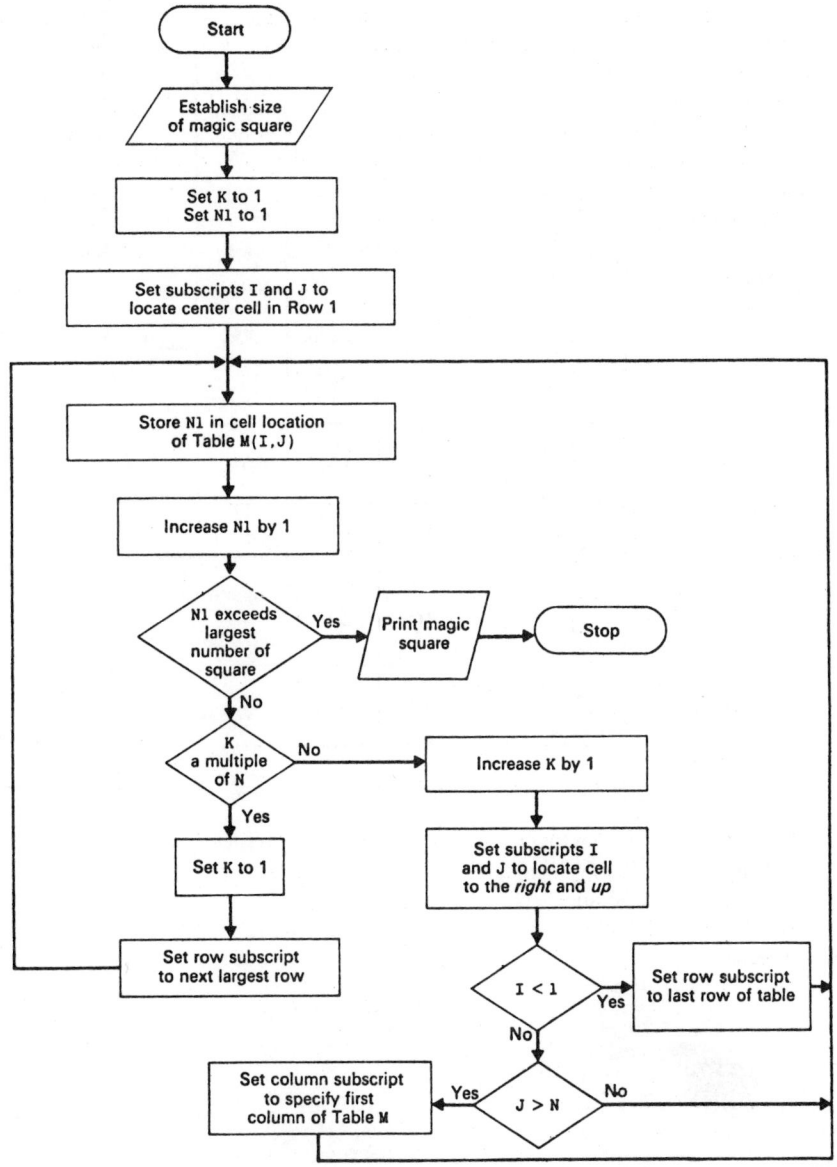

Fig. 7-7 Flowchart to generate an odd-order Magic Square

```
320    LET I=I+1
330    GOTO 220
340    REM INCREASE K BY 1 AND MOVE RIGHT AND UP
350    LET K=K+1
360    LET I=I-1
370    LET J=J+1
380    REM DO NEW SUBSCRIPTS SPECIFY A
```

30	39	48	1	10	19	28
38	47	7	9	18	27	29
46	6	8	17	26	35	37
5	14	16	25	34	36	45
13	15	24	33	42	44	4
21	23	32	41	43	3	12
22	31	40	49	2	11	20

Fig. 7-8 A 7 by 7 Magic Square produced by the De la Loubere technique

```
390   REM LOCATION OUTSIDE OF TABLE M
400   IF I <> 0 THEN 440
410   REM OUTSIDE OF SQUARE - RESET ROW IND TO N
420   LET I=N
430   GOTO 220
440   IF J <= N THEN 220
450   REM OUTSIDE OF SQUARE - RESET COL IND TO 1
460   LET J=1
470   GOTO 220
480   REM PRINT MAGIC SQUARE
490   FOR I=1 TO N
500   FOR J=1 TO N
510   PRINT M[I,J];
520   NEXT J
530   PRINT
540   PRINT
550   PRINT
560   NEXT I
570   END

RUN

      17    24    1     8     15
      23    5     7     14    16
      4     6     13    20    22
      10    12    19    21    3
      11    18    25    2     9
```

The statement at line number 160 establishes the order of the square as 5; that is, the program will generate a 5 by 5 magic square. Starting values for K and N1 are both 1. K is a program counter that is used to determine multiples of N. N1 will vary from 1 to N↑2 and each value of N1 is stored in Table M.

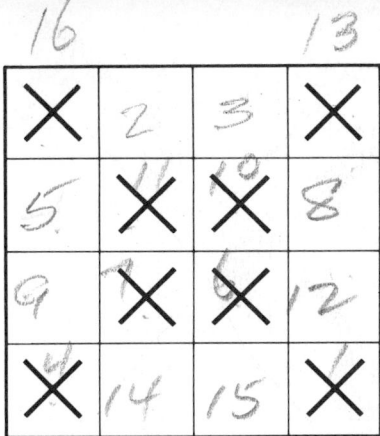

Figure 7-9

The subscripts I and J are first set to 1 and (N+1)/2, which specify the first row and the center cell of the first row, respectively, when appended as subscripts to Table M. After N1 is stored in cell M(I,J), it is incremented by 1 and compared with the largest number to be entered, the square of N. If the value of N1 exceeds the square of N, the program causes an order N magic square to be printed on the teletypewriter. If the value of N1 does not exceed that highest value, the program continues and a check is made to determine whether K is a multiple of N. If so, then K is reset to 1, and the row subscript is set to specify the next row. If K is not a multiple of N, then K is increased by 1, and the subscripts I and J are updated to specify the next cell to the right and up. If the new value of I is less than 1, which indicates that a location outside the top of the square is specified, the row subscript is set to address the last row of Table M. If the new value of J is greater than N, which indicates that a location outside the right side of the square is specified, the column subscript is set to address the first column of Table M. The new value of N1 is then stored in the new cell of M(I,J), and this process continues until N1 exceeds the square of N, when the magic square is complete.

This program generated a 5 by 5 magic square, but the procedure will apply to any square having an odd number of cells in each row and column and requires only a change in the statement at line number 160, where the size of the square is specified. For example, if that statement is revised to read LET N = 7, the program will compute a 7 by 7 magic square. For a square of 81 cells that statement would become LET N = 9.

A flowchart of this procedure is shown in Fig. 7–7. The reader is advised to test this procedure by creating a magic square of 49 cells and comparing his results with Fig. 7–8.

7.3 Even-Cell Magic Squares

The following steps show the generation of an even-cell magic square of four cells:

1. In a blank 4 by 4 square, fill the main diagonal squares with X's, as in Fig. 7–9.

2. Start with the upper left square and move toward the right, obeying the following rules: (a) If the cell is occupied by an X, skip the cell; and (b) if the cell is not occupied by an X, insert a number. Start with the number 1 and increment your count by 1 each time a move is made. On reaching the end of a row, repeat the process in the next row.

3. The first eight numbers would be placed in the square as shown in Fig. 7–10.

4. Now fill in the cells containing an X. Start in the same cell as in step 2 (upper left square) and obey the following rules: (a) If the cell is occupied by an X, insert a number; and (b) if the cell is occupied by a number, skip the cell. Start with the number 16 and decrease the count by 1 each time a move is made. When the end of a row is reached, repeat the same process in the next row.

	2	3	
5			8
9			12
	14	15	

CELL	X's	CONTENTS OF SQUARE
1	X	NOT CHANGED
2		2 → CELL 2
3		3 → CELL 3
4	X	NOT CHANGED
5		5 → CELL 5
6	X	NOT CHANGED
7	X	NOT CHANGED
8		8 → CELL 8
9		9 → CELL 9
10	X	NOT CHANGED
11	X	NOT CHANGED
12		12 → CELL 12
13	X	NOT CHANGED
14		14 → CELL 14
15		15 → CELL 15
16	X	NOT CHANGED

Figure 7-10

16			13
	11	10	
	7	6	
4			1

CELL	X's	CONTENTS OF SQUARE
1	X	16 → CELL 1
2		NOT CHANGED
3		NOT CHANGED
4	X	13 → CELL 4
5		NOT CHANGED
6	X	11 → CELL 6
7	X	10 → CELL 7
8		NOT CHANGED
9		NOT CHANGED
10	X	7 → CELL 10
11	X	6 → CELL 11
12		NOT CHANGED
13	X	4 → CELL 13
14		NOT CHANGED
15		NOT CHANGED
16	X	1 → CELL 16

Figure 7-11

5. The last eight numbers would be placed in the square as shown in Fig. 7-11.
6. The completed magic square would appear as shown in Fig. 7-12.

The following program uses this procedure to generate a 4 by 4 magic square. A flow chart is shown in Fig. 7-13.

```
100   REM 4 BY 4 MAGIC SQUARE
110   LET N=4
120   REM STØRE ZERØS IN ARRAY M
```

MAGIC SQUARES

16	2	3	13
5	11	10	8
9	7	6	12
4	14	15	1

Figure 7-12

```
130  FOR I=1 TO N
140  FOR J=1 TO N
150  LET M[I,J]=0
160  NEXT J
170  NEXT I
180  REM STORE 999 IN EACH CELL OF DIAGONAL 1
190  FOR I=1 TO N
200  LET J=I
210  LET M[I,J]=999
220  NEXT I
230  REM STORE 999 IN EACH CELL OF DIAGONAL 2
240  FOR I=1 TO N
250  LET J=N-I+1
260  LET M[I,J]=999
270  NEXT I
280  REM FIRST PASS THROUGH ARRAY
290  LET K=1
300  FOR I=1 TO N
310  FOR J=1 TO N
320  IF M[I,J] <> 0 THEN 340
330  LET M[I,J]=K
340  LET K=K+1
350  NEXT J
360  NEXT I
370  REM SECOND PASS THROUGH ARRAY
380  LET K=N*N
390  FOR I=1 TO N
400  FOR J=1 TO N
410  IF M[I,J] <> 999 THEN 430
420  LET M[I,J]=K
430  LET K=K-1
440  NEXT J
450  NEXT I
460  REM PRINT MAGIC SQUARE
470  PRINT "4 BY 4 MAGIC SQUARE"
480  PRINT
490  FOR I=1 TO N
500  FOR J=1 TO N
510  PRINT M[I,J];
520  NEXT J
530  PRINT
540  PRINT
550  PRINT
560  NEXT I
570  END
```

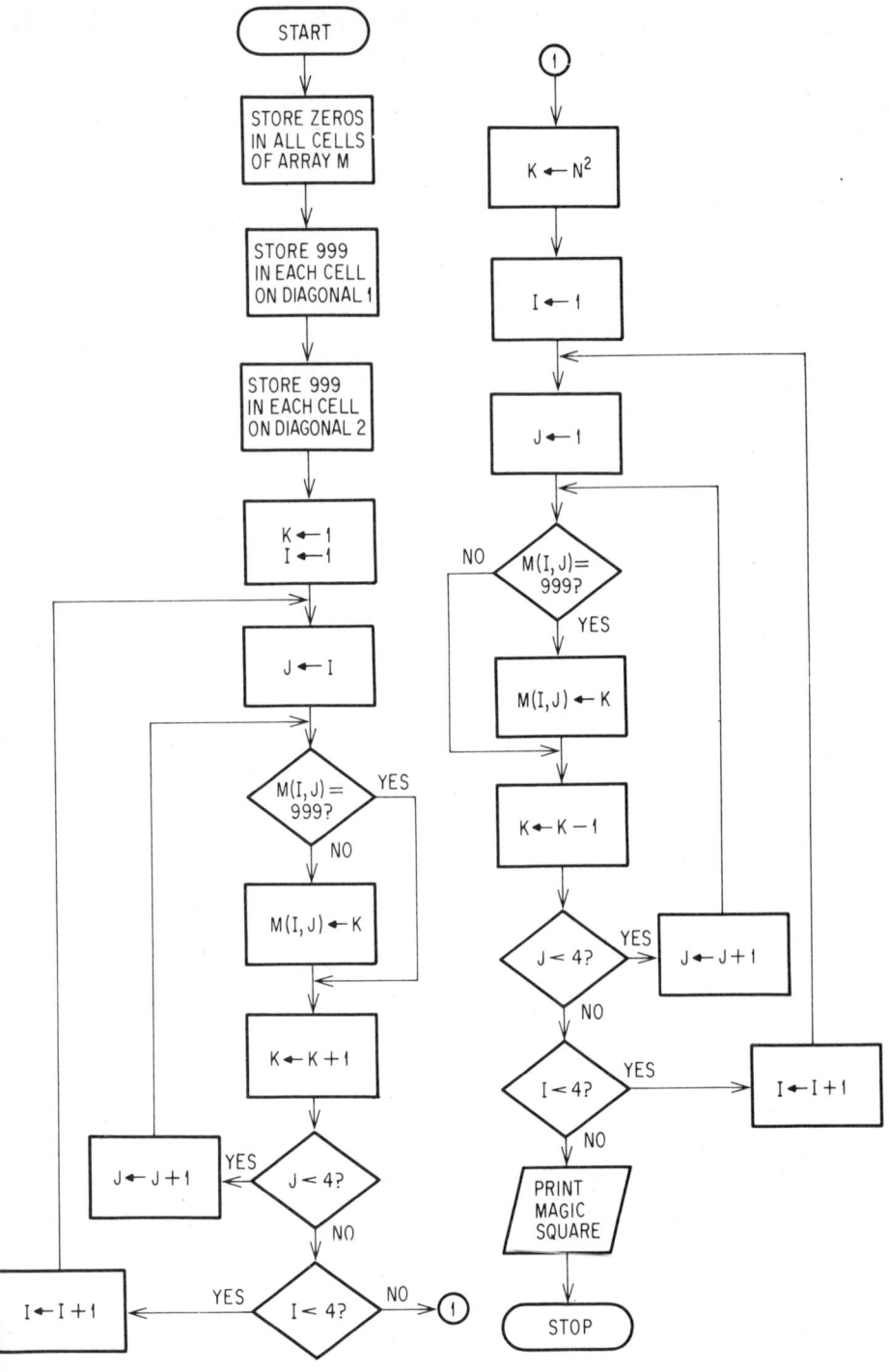

Fig. 7-13 Flowchart to generate a 4 by 4 Magic Square

MAGIC SQUARES

```
RUN

4 BY 4 MAGIC SQUARE
  16    2    3   13

   5   11   10    8

   9    7    6   12

   4   14   15    1
```

7.4 What Numbers Will Magic Squares Add Up To?

We have seen that a magic square of order 3 (3 by 3 cells) has all rows and columns adding up to 15 when numbers from 1 to 9 are used. We have seen that a magic square of order 4 (4 by 4 cells) has rows and columns adding up to 34 when all numbers from 1 to 16 are used. What about squares of order 5, 6, 7, or larger? What will the rows and columns of these add up to? The sum of the rows, columns, and main diagonals, called the *magic constant*, is determined by the formula,

$$\text{Magic constant} = n(n^2 + 1)/2$$

where n is the order of the square. For example, in the magic square of order 3 (9 cells), the magic constant is determined as follows:

$$\text{Magic constant} = 3(3^2 + 1)/2 = 3(9 + 1)/2 = 30/2 = 15$$

In an order 5 square, n = 5:

$$5(5^2 + 1)/2 = 5(25 + 1)/2 = 5(26)/2 = 130/2 = 65$$

That is, all rows, columns and main diagonals add up to 65.
In a square with 25 rows and 25 columns, n = 25:

$$25(25^2 + 1)/2 = 25(625 + 1)/2 = 25(626)/2 = 15650/2 = 7825$$

7.5 Magic Squares Starting with Numbers Other Than One

The magic squares previously discussed all started with the number 1. However, magic squares may be started with any number. The 3 by 3 square in Fig. 7–14 starts with 4.

11	4	9
6	8	10
7	12	5

Figure 7-14

The magic constant of this square is 24 and is computed by the formula,

$$\text{Magic constant} = \frac{n^3 + n}{2} + n(p - 1) = \frac{3^3 + 3}{2} + 3(4 - 1) = 24$$

where n is the order of the square and p is the starting number.

Figure 7–15 shows an order 4 square that starts with 4. The magic constant of this square is 46. A 15 by 15 magic square starting with 7 is shown in Fig. 7–16. The magic constant of this square is 1785.

The following program will generate an odd order magic square starting with any number.

```
100   REM MAGIC SQUARE - STARTING WITH ANY NUMBER
110   DIM M[25,25]
120   PRINT "TYPE SIZE OF SQUARE";
130   INPUT N
140   PRINT "TYPE STARTING NUMBER";
150   INPUT Y
155   LET S=Y
160   PRINT N;"BY";N;"MAGIC SQUARE STARTING"
161   PRINT "WITH THE NUMBER"; S
170   PRINT
180   LET K=1
190   LET I=1
200   LET J=(N+1)/2
210   REM PLACE THE FIRST NUMBER IN CENTER
211   REM CELL OF THE TOP ROW
220   LET M[I,J]=S
230   LET S=S+1
240   REM IS MAGIC SQUARE COMPLETE?
250   REM HAS LAST NUMBER BEEN STORED IN ARRAY M?
260   REM IF YES - PRINT MAGIC SQUARE
270   IF S>N*N+Y-1 THEN 490
280   REM IS K AN EVEN MULTIPLE OF N
290   IF K<N THEN 350
300   REM RESET K TO 1 AND SET ROW INDEX
301   REM TO INDICATE NEXT ROW
310   LET K=1
320   LET I=I+1
330   GOTO 220
340   REM MOVE POSTION TO THE RIGHT AND UP, AND
341   REM INCREASE K BY 1
350   LET K=K+1
360   LET I=I-1
370   LET J=J+1
380   REM DO SUBSCRIPTS NOW SPECIFY A
390   REM LOCATION OUTSIDE OF ARRAY M
400   IF I <> 0 THEN 440
410   REM OUT OF SQUARE - RESET ROW INDEX TO 1
420   LET I=N
430   GOTO 220
440   IF J <= N THEN 220
450   REM OUT OF SQUARE - RESET COL INDEX TO 1
460   LET J=1
470   GOTO 220
480   REM PRINT MAGIC SQUARE
490   FOR I=1 TO N
500   FOR J=1 TO N
510   PRINT M[I,J];
520   NEXT J
530   PRINT
540   PRINT
550   PRINT
560   NEXT I
570   END
```

MAGIC SQUARES

4	15	10	17
11	16	5	14
13	6	19	8
18	9	12	7

Figure 7-15

128	145	162	179	196	213	230	7	24	41	58	75	92	109	126
144	161	178	195	212	229	21	23	40	57	74	91	108	125	127
160	177	194	211	228	20	22	39	56	73	90	107	124	141	143
176	193	210	227	19	36	38	55	72	89	106	123	140	142	159
192	209	226	18	35	37	54	71	88	105	122	139	156	158	175
208	225	17	34	51	53	70	87	104	121	138	155	157	174	191
224	16	33	50	52	69	86	103	120	137	154	171	173	190	207
15	32	49	66	68	85	102	119	136	153	170	172	189	206	223
31	48	65	67	84	101	118	135	152	169	186	188	205	222	14
47	64	81	83	100	117	134	151	168	185	187	204	221	13	30
63	80	82	99	116	133	150	167	184	201	203	220	12	29	46
79	96	98	115	132	149	166	183	200	202	219	11	28	45	62
95	97	114	131	148	165	182	199	216	218	10	27	44	61	78
111	113	130	147	164	181	198	215	217	9	26	43	60	77	94
112	129	146	163	180	197	214	231	8	25	42	59	76	93	110

Fig. 7-16 A 15 by 15 Magic Square starting with 7

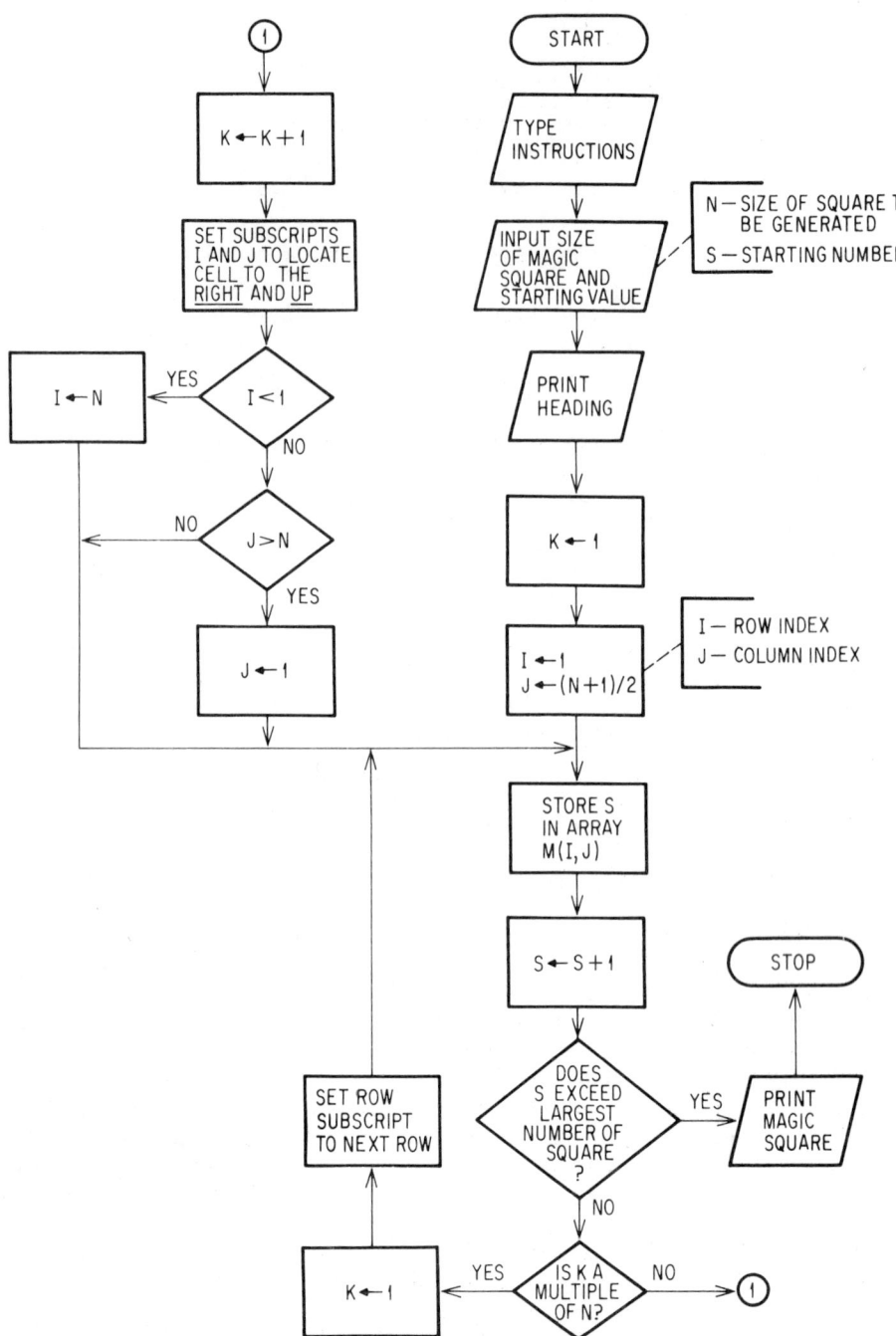

Fig. 7-17 Flowchart to generate an odd-order Magic Square starting with any number

MAGIC SQUARES

```
RUN

TYPE SIZE OF SQUARE??
TYPE STARTING NUMBER?428
 7   BY 7    MAGIC SQUARE STARTING
WITH THE NUMBER 428

    457    466    475    428    437    446    455

    465    474    434    436    445    454    456

    473    433    435    444    453    462    464

    432    441    443    452    461    463    472

    440    442    451    460    469    471    431

    448    450    459    468    470    430    439

    449    458    467    476    429    438    447
```

Input to this program is the order of the square and the starting number. In the example shown, 7 is the order and 428 is the starting number.

After receiving the input information, the program causes the following heading to be typed:

> 7 BY 7 MAGIC SQUARE STARTING
> WITH THE NUMBER 428

The program sets the subscripts I and J to locate the middle cell in the first row of Array M. The starting value is stored in this location. The starting value is increased by 1 and a check is made to see if the program has stored N^2 values in Array M. If all values have been stored, the program will output the magic square. If the program is not through calculating, then another check is made to determine if K is an even multiple of N, and if so, K is reset to 1 and the row indicator I is advanced to the next row. If K is not a multiple of N, the K is advanced by 1, and the subscripts I and J are set to address the next cell of Array M which is to the *right* and *up*. If the new value of J indicates a cell location outside the right side of Array M, then the column indicator J is reset to the first column of the array. If the new value of I is less than 1 then I is reset to N. The program then stores the correct number in the Array M and the program continues until K exceeds the maximum value to be stored in the array. A flowchart is shown in Fig. 7-17.

7.6 Multiplication Magic Square

A 3 by 3 multiplication magic square is shown in Fig. 7-18. The magic constant, obtained by multiplying together the three numbers in any column, row, or diagonal, is 216.

A method based on the De la Loubere odd order constructing method may be used to generate multiplication magic squares of odd order. The construction of a 5 by 5 multiplication square will be used to illustrate the method.

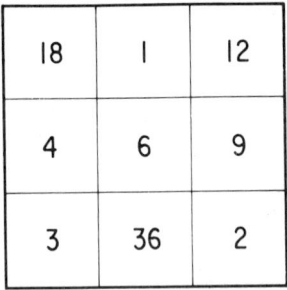

Fig. 7-18 Multiplication Magic Square

    1. Place the number 1 in the center cell of the first row in a blank 5 by 5 square, as shown at the left of Fig. 7–19.

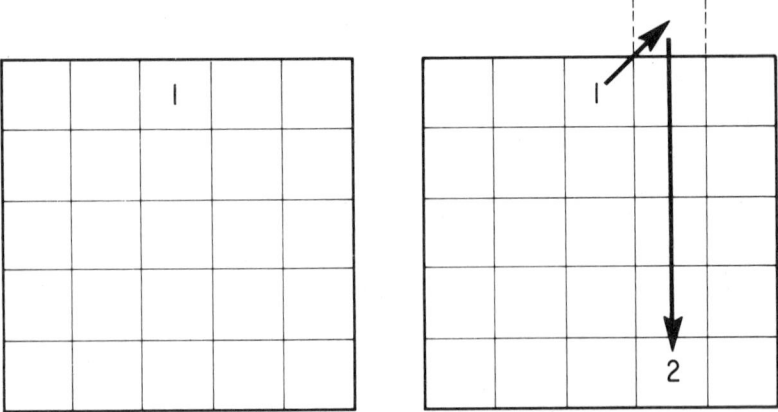

Figure 7-19

    2. Move in an oblique direction, one square above and to the right. This movement results in leaving the top of the box. It is necessary to place the next number in a cell at the bottom of the column in which you attempted to place the number. The number to place at this location is twice the last number, or 2, as shown at the right of Fig. 7–19.
    3. Now move diagonally to the right again, and put a number twice as large as the last, or 4, in the next cell location, as shown at the left of Fig. 7–20.
    4. If you continue diagonally to the right, you will leave the cell on the right side. When this occurs, you must go to the extreme left of the row in which you attempted to place the next number. After crossing over to the left side of the square, place a number twice that of the last, or 8, into the appropriate cell, as shown at the right of Fig. 7–20.
    5. Now, again, go up diagonally to the right and place the next number. This number, determined by doubling the previous number, is 16, as shown at the left of Fig. 7–21.
    This completes the first group of five numbers of a 5 by 5 square. The next group of

MAGIC SQUARES

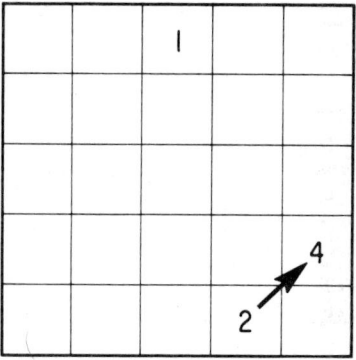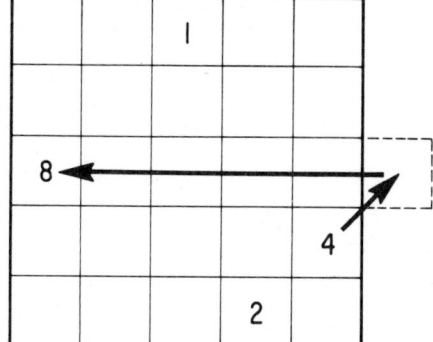

Figure 7-20

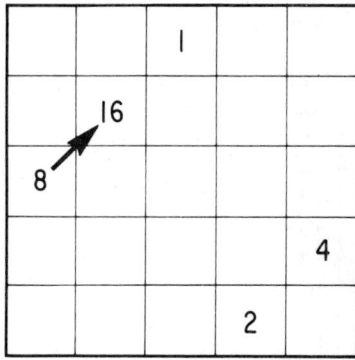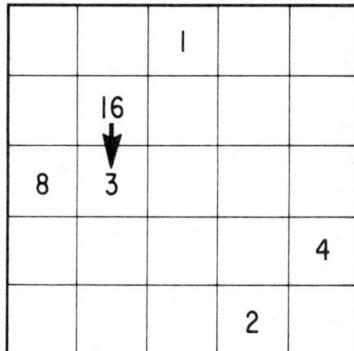

Figure 7-21

five numbers starts with 3, the next group 9, the next group 27, and the last group 81. The reader should note that the starting numbers are all powers of 3:

$$3^0 = 1$$
$$3^1 = 3$$
$$3^2 = 9$$
$$3^3 = 27$$
$$3^4 = 81$$

    6. Since this is a 5 by 5 square, you must move down one cell to place the next group of five numbers. In the case of a 3 by 3 square, you would move down when you reached a group of 3. The number to be placed in this cell is the starting number of the second group of 5 numbers, or 3, as shown at the right of Fig. 7–21.

    7. Move up diagonally to the right and place a number into each cell you enter, always doubling the previous number. When you leave the top of the box, move to the bottom of the column where you attempted to place the number. When you move outside the box on the right side, move across to the opposite side. When you finish the second group of five numbers, the square should appear as shown at the left of Fig. 7–22.

136 GAME PLAYING WITH BASIC

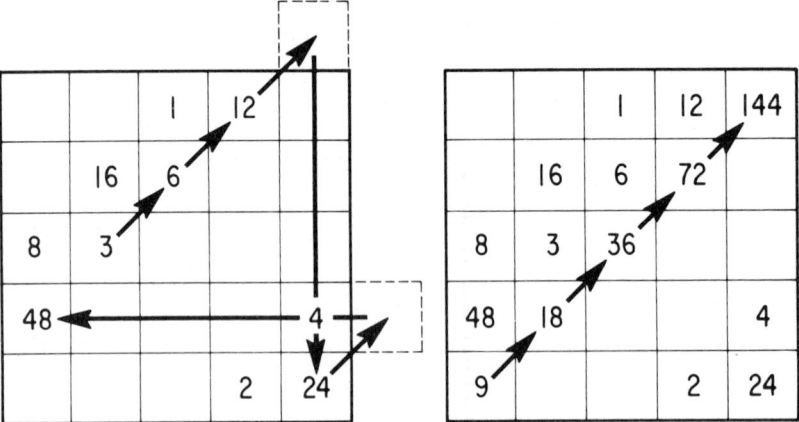

Figure 7-22

8. The square at the right of Fig. 7–22 would result after the third group of five numbers have been placed. The starting number is 9.

9. The fourth group of five numbers would be placed in the manner shown at the left of Fig. 7–23. The starting number is 27.

10. When the twenty-fifth number is placed in the cell opposite the starting cell, the final square will appear as shown at the right of Fig. 7–23.

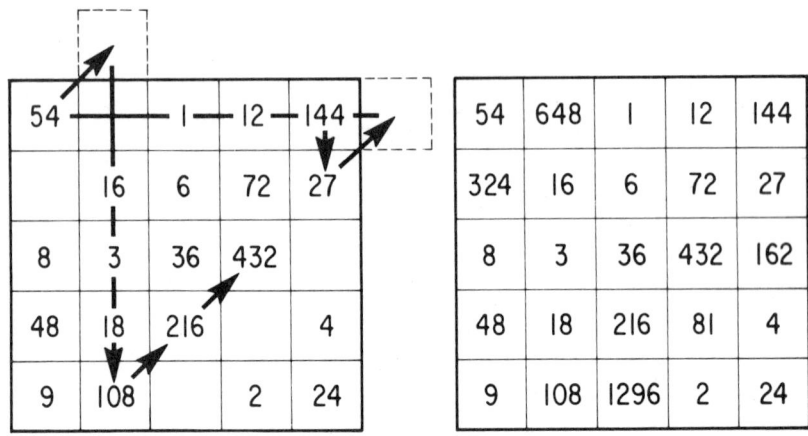

Figure 7-23

Perhaps the reader would like to write a program to generate a multiplication magic square himself.

7.7 Geometric Magic Square

A geometric magic square is an array of numbers where the product of the numbers in every column, row, and main diagonal is the same and where each number of the square is

MAGIC SQUARES

represented by a base value and an exponent. The base value remains the same in all the positions of the square, and the exponent values are the numbers in an ordinary odd order magic square. For example, an order 3 geometric magic square with a base of 2 would appear as shown in Fig. 7-24.

2^8	2^1	2^6
2^3	2^5	2^7
2^4	2^9	2^2

GEOMETRIC MAGIC SQUARE
USING BASE AND EXPONENT
VALUES.

256	2	64
8	32	128
16	512	4

GEOMETRIC MAGIC SQUARE
USING INTEGER VALUES.

Fig. 7-24 Order 3 geometric Magic Square

A flowchart of a geometric square generator is shown in Figure 7-25. A program for a geometric magic square is shown below.

```
10    REM GEOMETRIC MAGIC SQUARE
20    REM PROGRAM GENERATES AN ODD ORDER
21    REM GEOMETRIC MAGIC SQUARE OF SIZE N BY N
30    REM GEOMETRIC MAGIC SQUARE OF SIZE N BY N
40    PRINT "SIZE OF SQUARE TO BE GENERATED IS";
50    INPUT N
60    PRINT "BASE OF SQUARE IS";
70    INPUT B
80    LET K=1
90    LET A=B
100   LET L=1
110   LET I=1
120   LET J=(N+1)/2
130   LET G[I,J]=A
140   LET L=L+1
150   LET A=B↑L
160   IF A>(B↑(N↑2)) THEN 295
170   IF K<N THEN 210
180   LET K=1
190   LET I=I+1
200   GOTO 130
210   LET K=K+1
220   LET I=I-1
230   LET J=J+1
240   IF I <> 0 THEN 270
250   LET I=N
260   GOTO 130
270   IF J <= N THEN 130
280   LET J=1
```

GAME PLAYING WITH BASIC

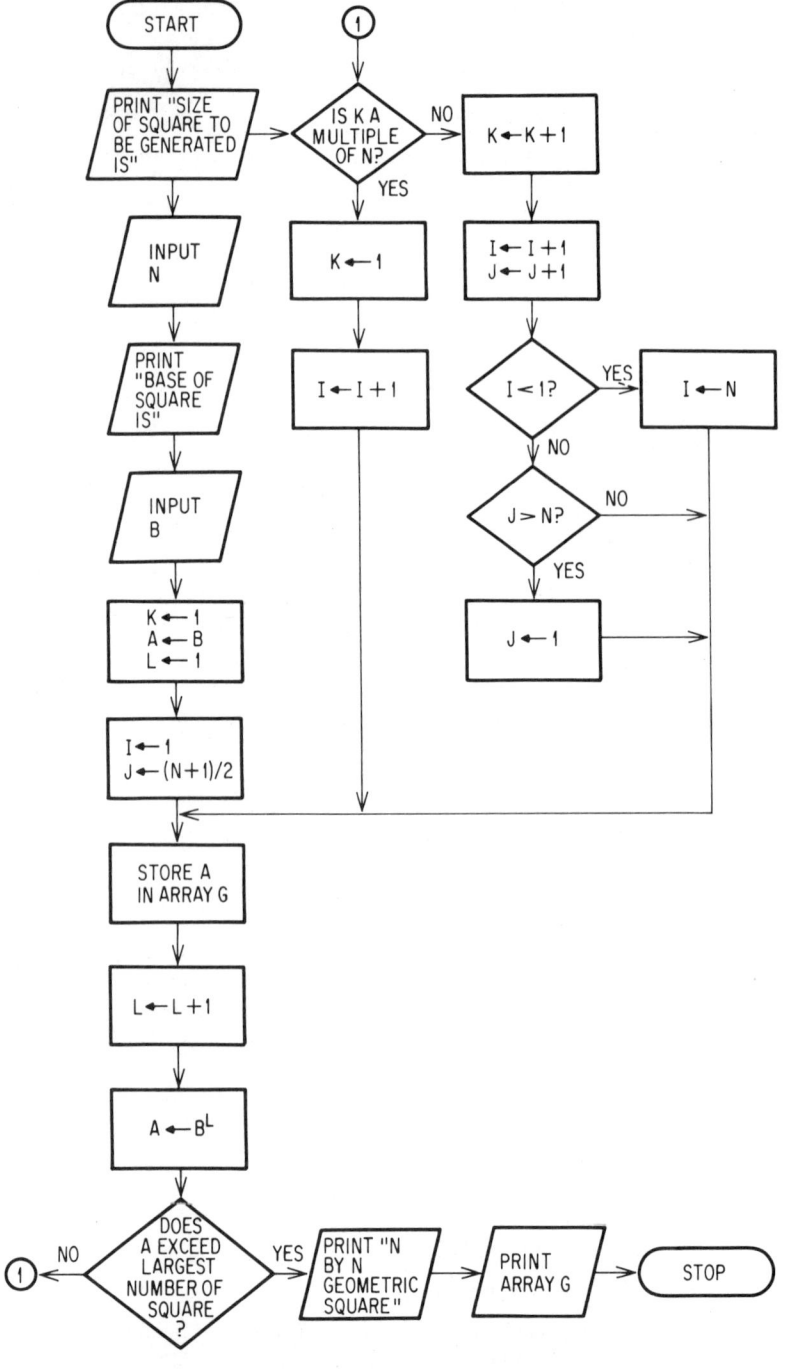

Fig. 7-25 Flowchart of the geometric Magic Square

MAGIC SQUARES

```
290  GOTO 130
295  PRINT
296  PRINT
300  PRINT N;"BY";N;"GEOMETRIC MAGIC SQUARE"
310  PRINT
320  FOR I=1 TO N
330  FOR J=1 TO N
340  PRINT G[I,J];
350  NEXT J
360  PRINT
370  PRINT
380  PRINT
390  NEXT I
400  END

RUN


SIZE OF SQUARE TO BE GENERATED IS?3
BASE OF SQUARE IS?2


 3    BY  3     GEOMETRIC MAGIC SQUARE

256    2      64


 8    32     128


 16   512     4
```

This program causes the following two messages to be printed.

SIZE OF SQUARE TO BE GENERATED IS?

and

BASE OF SQUARE IS?

When the user answers these two questions, the program will generate the requested magic square. For example, assume that you wanted the program to generate an order 3 square using a base of 3. You would answer the first question by typing 3 and the second question by typing another 3. The computer would cause the following magic square to be printed.

256	2	64
8	32	128
16	512	4

Figure 7–26 illustrates two other order 3 geometric magic squares. One of the squares uses a base of 4 and the other a base of 5.

7.8 Other Interesting Magic Squares

A square that is completely magic for both addition and multiplication is shown in Fig. 7–27. The magic constant for addition is 1,200, whereas the multiplication constant is 1,619,541,385,529,760,000.

65536	4	4096
64	1024	16384
256	262144	16

390625	5	15625
125	3125	78125
625	1953125	25

Fig. 7-26 Geometric Magic Squares

17	171	126	54	230	100	93	264	145
124	66	290	85	57	168	162	23	225
216	115	75	279	198	29	170	76	42
261	186	33	210	68	38	200	135	69
50	270	92	87	248	165	21	153	114
105	51	152	150	27	207	116	62	330
138	25	243	132	58	310	95	63	136
190	84	34	184	125	81	297	174	31
99	232	155	19	189	102	46	250	108

Fig. 7-27 A square that is completely magic for both addition and multiplication

Another interesting square, whose magic constant is 2056, is shown in Fig. 7-28. The unusual nature of this square lies in its method of construction. If the numbers are followed consecutively, it is found that the "moves" from one to the next are the moves of a Knight's Tour. The tour in this magic square is closed, since the first and last moves are also connected by a knight's move; an open-tour magic square is one in which the first and last moves are not so related.

The magic square of Fig. 7-29 is made up entirely of prime numbers.

MAGIC SQUARES

184	217	170	75	188	219	172	77	228	37	86	21	230	39	88	25
169	74	185	218	171	76	189	220	85	20	229	38	87	24	231	40
216	183	68	167	222	187	78	173	36	227	22	83	42	237	26	89
73	168	215	186	67	174	221	190	19	84	35	238	23	90	41	232
182	213	166	69	178	223	176	79	226	33	82	31	236	43	92	27
165	72	179	214	175	66	191	224	81	18	239	34	91	30	233	44
212	181	70	163	210	177	80	161	48	225	32	95	46	235	28	93
71	164	211	180	65	162	209	192	17	96	47	240	29	94	45	234
202	13	126	61	208	15	128	49	160	241	130	97	148	243	132	103
125	60	203	14	127	64	193	16	129	112	145	242	131	102	149	244
12	201	62	123	2	207	50	113	256	159	98	143	246	147	104	133
59	124	11	204	63	114	1	194	111	144	255	146	101	134	245	150
200	9	122	55	206	3	116	51	158	253	142	99	154	247	136	105
121	58	205	10	115	54	195	4	141	110	155	254	135	100	151	248
8	199	56	119	6	197	52	117	252	157	108	139	250	153	106	137
57	120	7	198	53	118	5	196	109	140	251	156	107	138	249	152

Fig. 7-28 An order 16 Magic Square constructed with moves of the Knight

83	29	101
89	71	53
41	113	59

Fig. 7-29 Magic Square of Prime Numbers

chapter 8

GAMES FOR READER SOLUTION

The games, puzzles, and mathematical recreations in this chapter, covering a wide range of difficulty, should stimulate creative work and help to demonstrate the reader's understanding of algorithm and program development. Some are little more than elementary exercises, whereas others may require many hours for the development of a suitable solution.

8.1 Magic Square

The following diagram illustrates a form that may be used to generate one of the eight possible number arrangements for a 3 by 3 magic square.

$$
\begin{array}{lll}
a + b & a - (b + c) & a + c \\
a - (b - c) & a & a + (b - c) \\
a - c & a + (b + c) & a - b
\end{array}
$$

Write a program that will accept values for a, b, and c, and generate and print a magic square.

8.2 Buzz

The game of Buzz goes something like this: The players sit in a circle and begin counting, 1, 2, 3, 4, ... Whenever a number either contains a seven (for example, 17 or 72) or is divisible by seven (for example, 14 or 56), the player says *buzz*, rather than the number. If the number meets both conditions (for example, 70 or 77), he says *buzz buzz*. Program the computer to play Buzz while counting to 300.

8.3 Typing Monkey

It has been speculated that if a large group of monkeys were given typewriters and the monkeys hit the keys at random over a long, long, long period of time, they would eventually write every book that has been written, including this one!

Write a program that simulates a monkey typing. Assume that the events consisting of a monkey hitting a key are independent. The procedure should stop when a monkey types the word "game." (Any program that will solve this problem will use a lot of computer time.)

8.4 Prime Number Polynomial

The mathematician Euclid proved that there is an indefinite number of prime numbers. Mathematicians have looked, but in vain, for a formula that would generate all the positive prime numbers. The formula $f(x) = x^2 - x + 41$ will produce all the primes in the range $1 \leq x \leq 40$:

x	$f(x) = x^2 - x + 41$
1	$1^2 - 1 + 41 = 41$
2	$2^2 - 2 + 41 = 43$
3	$3^2 - 3 + 41 = 47$
4	$4^2 - 4 + 41 = 53$
5	$5^2 - 5 + 41 = 61$
⋮	⋮
40	$40^2 - 40 + 41 = 1601$

Write a program that will generate prime numbers using this formula.

8.5 Poker Dice

Five dice are used for playing Poker Dice. These may be either standard dice, marked with numbers, or genuine poker dice, marked with an ace, king, queen, jack, ten, and nine, on their six faces. The rules are the same in either case.

Each player has three rolls. The object is to make the best possible Poker hand. The hands that may be formed on the dice are as follows, from high to low:

1. Five of a kind, as 4-4-4-4-4
2. Four of a kind, as 6-6-6-6-2
3. Full house, as 3-3-3-A-A
4. High straight, as 6-5-4-3-2
5. Low straight, as 5-4-3-2-A
6. Three of a kind, as 5-5-5-6-4
7. Two pairs, as 6-6-2-2-3
8. One pair, as 4-4-A-6-2
9. No pair, as A-6-4-3-2

Aces (1's) rank above sixes, when regular dice are used, and above kings, when poker dice are used.

With his first roll, the player rolls all five dice. He may set aside any of these to be part of his eventual Poker hand and then roll the rest again. From the second roll he again may set aside any and then roll the remaining dice again. He may stand at any time and not take any additional roll due him. When he has made his second roll, he may not pick up dice he set aside from his first roll. The high hand wins. When two players tie, they must play another game.

Write a program that will play poker dice with a human opponent.

8.6 Guessing Game

Write a program for the following game: Enter your guesses for five consecutive throws of a die. Have the program simulate the throwing of a die. If none of your guesses matches the corresponding throw, you pay 5 dollars; with one match, you win one dollar; two matches, 3 dollars; three matches, 10 dollars; four matches, 100 dollars; and five matches, 1,000 dollars. The program should keep track of winnings and losses and print its tosses each time.

8.7 Morra

This finger game is one in which two players simultaneously show one, two, or three fingers at the same time each calls out what he thinks his opponent is showing (see Fig. 8-1). There is no payoff if both guess right or both guess wrong. But if one player guesses right, the other pays him as many chips (dollars, matches, or what have you) as the total number of fingers extended by the two players.

The strategy that John von Neumann worked out mathematically for this ancient game will usually win and should at least break even. You are instructed to keep four as the combined number of fingers and out of each 12 games to show one finger five times, two fingers four times, three fingers three times. Keep the order well-mixed, of course, as

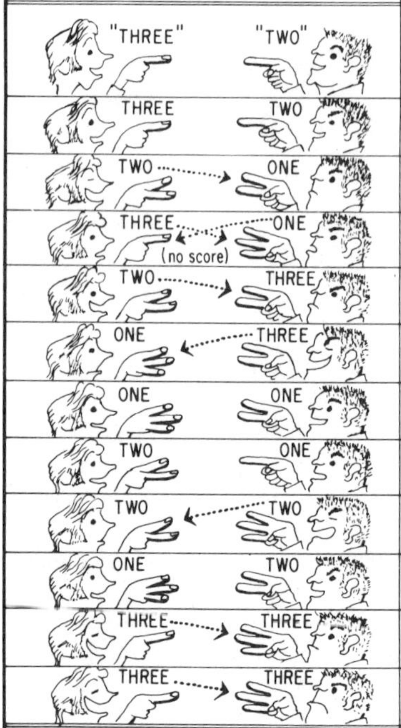

	YOU	OPPONENT
"THREE" "TWO"	0	0
THREE TWO	0	0
TWO → ONE	4	0
THREE ···→ ONE (no score)	0	0
TWO ···→ THREE	4	0
ONE ←··· THREE	0	5
ONE ONE	0	0
TWO ONE	0	0
TWO ←··· TWO	0	5
ONE TWO	0	0
THREE ···→ THREE	4	0
THREE ···→ THREE	4	0
	16	10

Fig. 8-1 A game of Morra

nearly random as you can manage, or your opponent will solve your order of numbers and beat you. In making your calls, of course, you mentally subtract from four the number of fingers you are about to show, and name the difference.

Write a program that will play Morra with a human opponent.

8.8 Twin Primes

Once you know how to generate prime numbers, it is a simple matter to produce *twin primes*. Twin primes are two prime numbers which differ by two. For example, 5 and 7 are twin primes, so are 29 and 31, 149 and 151, and 1,091 and 1,093.

Write a program to produce a list of all twin primes less than 2,000.

8.9 Mersenne Prime Numbers

A number which is prime and of the form $2^p - 1$, where p itself is a prime number, is called a *Mersenne prime:*

$$M_p = 2^p - 1$$

Primes for which M_p is a prime are 2, 3, 5, 7, 13, 17, 19, 31, 61, 89, 107, and 127.

Write a program to find several p's that yield Mersenne primes. The program should produce a printout in the following form:

Prime	Mersenne Prime
2	3
3	7
5	37
7	127
13	8191
•	•
•	•
•	•

8.10 Milkman's Crate

Even at seven o'clock in the morning, the professor was a pretty astute sort of fellow. And when he saw the milkman's crate had just two bottles in it, in the positions shown in Fig. 8–2, it set him thinking.

The professor had ten empty bottles. He promised to pay double for his milk if the milkman could arrange the ten empties in the crate in such a way that no row—across, down, or diagonally—had more than two bottles in it. The milkman wasn't allowed to move the two full bottles.

Write a program that will determine how he did not have to pay double for his milk.

8.11 The 50 Puzzle

Figure 8–3 shows a square containing 36 numbers that have been picked at random. Write a program to connect any three boxes that touch each other at some point—horizontally, vertically, or diagonally—and whose numbers add up to 50.

8.12 Lucky Prisoners

A king once decided to grant amnesty among 1,000 prisoners, each locked in prison cells numbered 1, 2, 3, ..., 1,000. His amnesty included the following provisions: The jailer

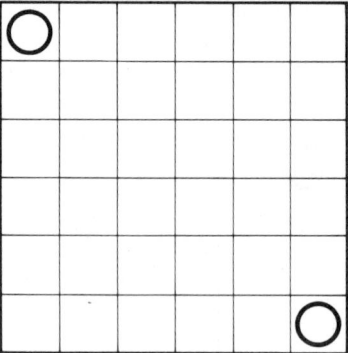

Figure 8-2

12	30	9	17	31	16
7	3	6	21	23	32
2	19	11	8	14	7
13	20	25	28	17	9
26	16	4	18	10	30
1	5	27	9	29	33

Figure 8-3

was first to unlock each of the 1,000 cells. Then starting with the second cell, he was to turn the key in every second cell (2, 4, 6, 8, etc.). Then starting with the third cell he was to turn the key in every third cell; then starting with the fourth, he turned the key in every fourth cell; then starting with the fifth, he turned the key in every fifth cell, and so on. Each turn of the key either locked or unlocked the prison cell door. When the jailor was completely done, those with unlocked doors could leave. Write a program to determine who were the lucky prisoners.

 Hint: Have the program first store a 1 in each of the 1,000 cells. This represents all cells as being unlocked. Now add 1 to every second cell. Then add 1 to every third cell, etc. At the end, those cells containing *odd* numbers are free!

8.13 The Four Checkers

Four checkers are placed on a 36-celled square in such a manner that every one of the checkers is in a separate square and every square on the board is either occupied or in line (horizontally, vertically, or diagonally) with at least one checker (one arrangement is shown in Fig. 8–4). The object of the game is to find the *maximum* number of ways the checkers can be arranged in the squares to produce such an alignment.

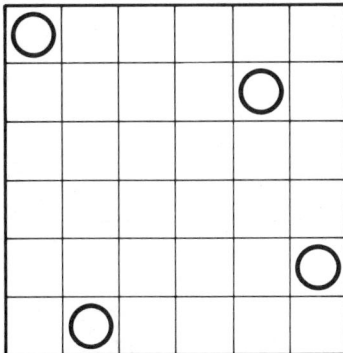

Figure 8-4

Write a program to calculate the maximum arrangements of the checkers. Do not count rotations or mirror reflections of a given arrangement. If your program is written properly, it will determine that seventeen arrangements are possible.

8.14 Poker

It was the study of games of chance that first led Pascal and Fermat to their discovery of probability. So it is not surprising that probability plays a role in a familiar card game, Poker. An interesting problem results from counting the different possible Poker hands and computing various related probabilities, such as the following.

How many different five-card Poker hands can be dealt from a deck of 52 cards? The answer is the combination of 52 things taken five at a time, or 2,598,960 hands. This may not seem like very many. However, if you were able to deal out a different five-card Poker hand every second, working day and night, it would take about one month to deal them all.

Why is a flush better than a straight and a straight better than three of a kind in Poker? The answer is that the ranking of Poker hands is based upon the probabilities of their occurring; the better the hand, the lower the probability of its being dealt.

Write a program to compute and print out the probabilities of the various Poker hands.

8.15 Palindromic Numbers

A palindromic word, sentence, or number is one that is symmetric. It reads the same from either end. For example, *dad, deed,* and *madam* are palindromic words. *Was it a cat I saw?* is a palindromic sentence. And 432696234 and 129637736921 are palindromic numbers.

Numbers that are not palindromic may be made palindromic in the following way. Reverse a number's digits, and add the original number and the reverse number together. Continue this procedure (reverse and add) until the sum is a palindromic number, as follows:

	723 number
	327 reversed
	1050 added
	0501 reversed
Palindromic in two steps	1551 added
	43 number
	34 reversed
Palindromic in one step	77 added
	86 number
	68 reversed
	154 added
	451 reversed
	605 added
	506 reversed
Palindromic in three steps	1111 added

For all two-digit numbers in which the sum of the digits is less than 10, the first reversal and addition gives a two-digit palindrome. If the digits add to 10, 11, 12, 13, 14, 15, 16 or 18 (note that 17 is missing here), a palindrome results after two, one, two, two, three, four, six, and six reversals, respectively. If the two digits add to 17, it takes a long time for that number to become palindromic.

Research has shown that only 249 integers smaller than 10,000 have failed to generate a palindrome after 100 reversals. However, it has not yet been proved whether these integers will or will not become palindromic eventually.

Write a program to produce palindromic numbers. You may want to use Table 8–1 to check your results.

8.16 Magic Square Checker

Write a program to determine if the number arrangement in Fig. 8–5 is a magic square.

15	16	22	3	9
8	14	20	21	2
1	7	13	19	25
24	5	6	12	18
12	23	4	10	11

Figure 8-5

Table 8-1 Palindromic Numbers

Number	Number of steps	Palindrome
43	1	77
723	2	1,551
86	3	1,111
94	2	484
6294	2	13,431
847	4	44,044
87	4	4,884
372	4	5,115
563	11	88,555,588
8707	15	5,233,333,325
4087	6	293,392
9479	7	9,912,199
738	5	99,099
6987	7	12,455,421
79	6	44,044
985	8	1,136,311
837	5	99,099
7084	6	293,392
4078	5	583,385
739	17	5,233,333,325
639	5	99,099
561	3	4,884
4897	6	293,392
4327	6	1,136,311
89427	5	7,296,927
489	3	9,339
95	3	1,111
589	8	1,136,311
223	1	545
89	24	8,813,200,023,188

8.17 Boule

Boule is a game similar to Roulette. It is very popular in casinos in Europe and the Caribbean. Boule is played with a stationary wheel that is divided into 18 compartments numbered from 1 to 9 twice. A croupier spins a small ball around the rim of the bowl. The ball will eventually come to rest in a number compartment which is considered to be the winning number. The number 5 is reserved for the house; therefore, the house expects to win one-ninth, or slightly over 11 percent of all money bet.

Figure 8-6 illustrates the wheel and layout used in this game. The following bets may be placed by the players:

Bet	Payoff odds
Any number (1,2,3,4,5,6,7,8,9)	7 to 1
Odd numbers, *impair* (1,3,7,9)	Pays even

Bet	Payoff odds
Even numbers, *pair* (2,4,6,8)	Pays even
First four numbers, *manque* (1,2,3,4)	Pays even
Last four numbers, *passe* (6,7,8,9)	Pays even
Black numbers (1,3,6,8)	Pays even
Red numbers (2,4,7,9)	Pays even

Write a program to simulate play at Boule.

8.18 Craps

Read the section on Craps in Chapter 5 and then write a program to play this game. Have your program produce a printout similar to the one that follows:

```
YOU ARE GIVEN 70 DOLLARS TO PLAY WITH.

YOU ROLL FIRST....

HOW MUCH DO YOU BET? 20

YOU ROLL    5    AND    3    SO YOUR POINT IS 8
YOU ROLL    2    AND    4    ...ROLL AGAIN.
YOU ROLL    3    AND    2    ...ROLL AGAIN.
YOU ROLL    2    AND    1    ...ROLL AGAIN.
YOU ROLL    3    AND    1    ...ROLL AGAIN.
YOU ROLL    1    AND    3    ...ROLL AGAIN.
YOU ROLL    3    AND    6    ...ROLL AGAIN.
YOU ROLL    2    AND    4    ...ROLL AGAIN.
YOU ROLL    5    AND    3    AND MAKE YOUR POINT

YOU NOW HAVE 90      DOLLARS
HOW MUCH DO YOU BET? 90

YOU ROLL    6    AND    4    SO YOUR POINT IS 10
YOU ROLL    5    AND    4    ...ROLL AGAIN.
YOU ROLL    3    AND    1    ...ROLL AGAIN.
YOU ROLL    6    AND    5    ...ROLL AGAIN.
YOU ROLL    1    AND    4    ...ROLL AGAIN.
YOU ROLL    3    AND    4    AND LOSE...

YOU HAVE RUN OUT OF MONEY....SORRY ABOUT THAT.
```

This printout illustrates two plays of the program. The program assigns the player some money to play with. In the first example, the player bets $20.00 and makes his point of 8. In the second example, the player bets and loses $90.00 as he did not make his point of 10 before he rolled a 7.

8.19 Five Field Kono

This game is played using the layout of Fig. 8–7. One player has seven black stones and the other seven white stones. The player with the black stones always makes the first move. The players move one piece at a time, in alternate plays, either backward or forward or diagonally across the squares. The object of the game is to get the pieces across to the other side in the place of those pieces of the other player. The player who does this first wins the game. Write a program that will play this game.

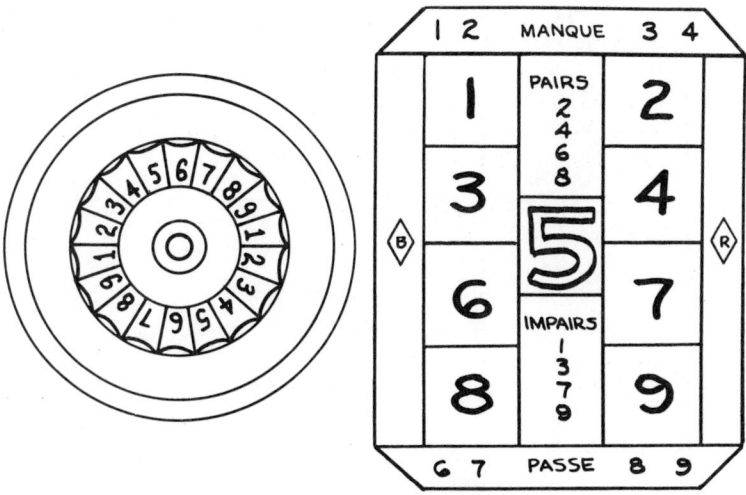

Fig. 8-6 Boule wheel and table layout

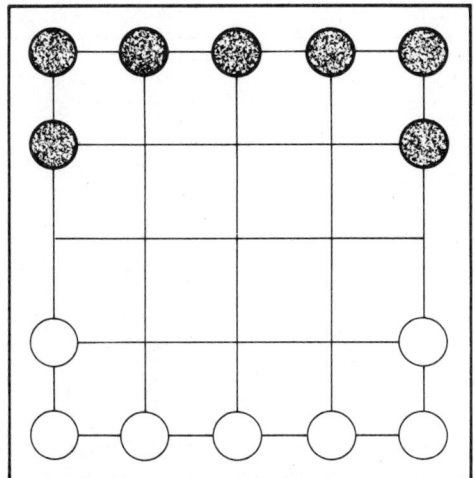

Fig. 8-7 Layout for Five Field Kono

8.20 Knight Interchange

Write a program that will determine the minimum number of moves that are necessary to make the white and black knights change places on the board shown in Fig. 8–8.

A knight's move consists of one square in a vertical or horizontal direction plus one square diagonally. The knight can also jump over any piece on the board. The interchange can be accomplished with 16 individual moves.

8.21 Symmetry Game

Here is a game that has a winning strategy based on symmetry. An object, such as a coin, is placed on each corner of a regular polygon, say a nonagon, for example (see Fig. 8–9).

Fig. 8-8 Layout for Knight Interchange

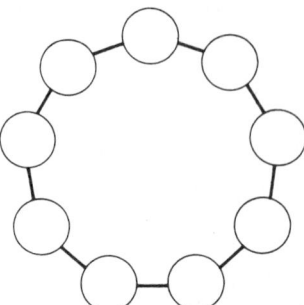

Figure 8-9

The two players take turns removing either one object or two objects that are next to each other. The player who picks up the last object wins.

The game isn't fair because the player who goes second can always win. Suppose the first player picks up two objects, leaving the board as shown at the left in Fig. 8-10. The second player should then take the object exactly opposite so that the board looks like the diagram at the right in Fig. 8-10.

What should the second player do from this point on to be sure of winning the game? If the first player picks up only one object at the start, what should the second player's original move be? After answering the previous questions, write a program to play this game.

GAMES FOR READER SOLUTION

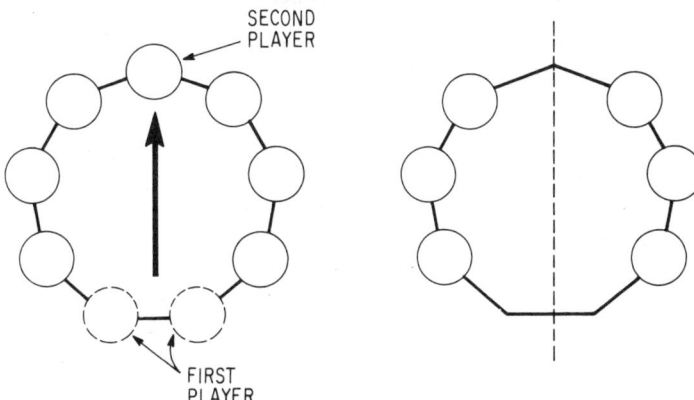

Figure 8-10

8.22 Nine Men's Morris

This is a very ancient game, played in various forms in many parts of the world. It is a game for two players, each starting with nine counters. The players take turns in placing a counter on an empty vertex of the board, trying to form a row of three along one of the lines or to block the movement of the opponent's men. Each time a player forms a row, he may remove one of his opponent's men from the board. When all the men have been entered, play continues, each player taking turns to move one of his men along a line to a neighboring empty vertex, the object still being the same. The game ends when one player has been reduced to too few men to form a line or has been blocked from making any further moves.

Figure 8–11 illustrates the game board. Write a program to play this game.

8.23 King's Tour of the Chessboard

The King's power of movement on the chessboard is very limited. He can move only one square at a time. He can go into any of the squares—front, back, or side—adjacent to the square on which he stands, as shown in Fig. 8–12.

To complete a King's Tour, the King must move successively to every cell on the board. Figure 8–13 illustrates such a tour. An interesting thing about this tour is that the numbers indicating the path form a magic square.

Write a program that will produce the King's Tour of the chessboard.

8.24 Hexapawn

The game of Hexapawn is described by Martin Gardner in the March, 1962 issue of *Scientific American*. It is played on a 3-by-3 board like that used for Tic-Tac-Toe. The play starts with three chess pawns for each player located as shown in Fig. 8–14.

A player moves one of his pawns either straight ahead one place to an empty square or diagonally one place to a square occupied by an opponent's pawn, thereby capturing that pawn (which is removed from the board). These moves are basic moves for the pawn in chess, hence the name Hexapawn. The game is won by (1) capturing all of the opponent's pawns, or (2) moving into the third row, or (3) placing the opponent in a position from which there is no legal move. There can be no draw in the game.

Write a program that plays Hexapawn. Let the human player play first.

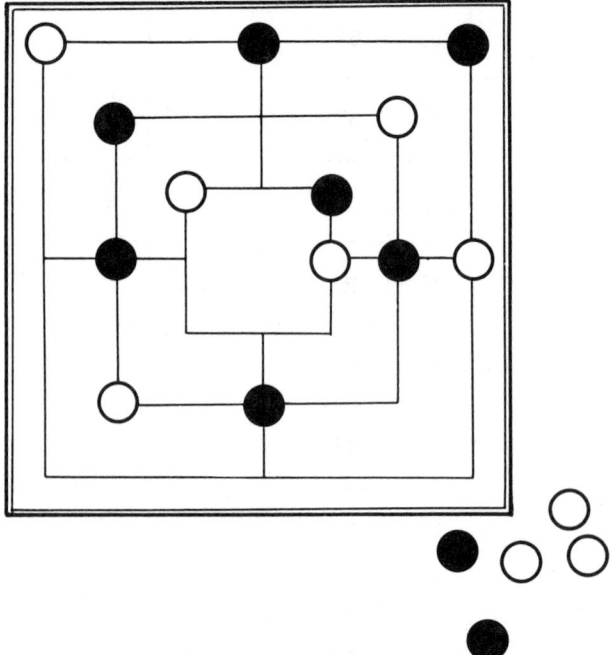

Fig. 8-11 Nine Men's Morris

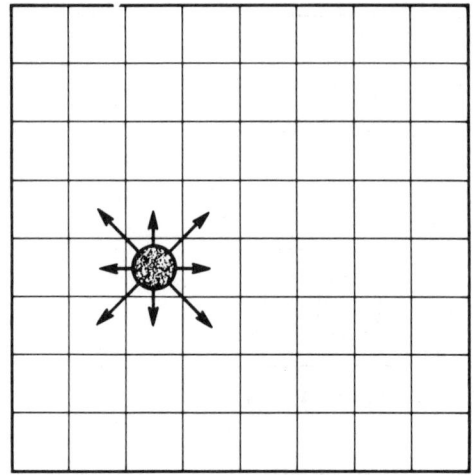

Fig. 8-12 Moves permitted the King

8.25 Nim

The game of Nim is usually played with piles of counters between two players, one of which could be a computer. Each player draws alternately one or more counters, up to the whole of one pile if he chooses. He can take from only one pile at a time but for each turn can choose the pile from which to take. The player to take the last counter is the winner.

GAMES FOR READER SOLUTION

61	62	63	64	1	2	3	4
60	11	58	57	8	7	54	5
12	59	10	9	56	55	6	53
13	14	15	16	49	50	51	52
20	19	18	17	48	47	46	45
21	38	23	24	41	42	27	44
37	22	39	40	25	26	43	28
36	35	34	33	32	31	30	29

Fig. 8-13 King's Tour that forms a Magic Square

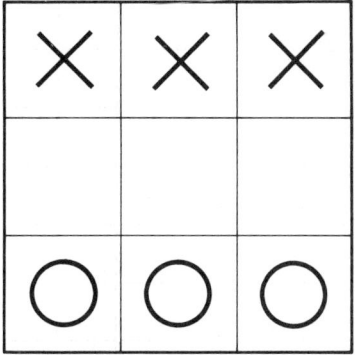

Fig. 8-14 Layout for Hexapawn

Like so many games, the outcome, if there are no mistakes, is predictable. For example, once one pile has been exhausted, the player drawing next can take from the biggest pile enough counters to leave the same number in each of the remaining piles. He must then win if he copies his opponent's moves exactly, always leaving two piles the same.

This is not the only winning position, however. Surprisingly, a winning position can best be expressed in binary terms, in the following way. The numbers contained in each pile are first written in the binary scale and the three numbers set out as an addition

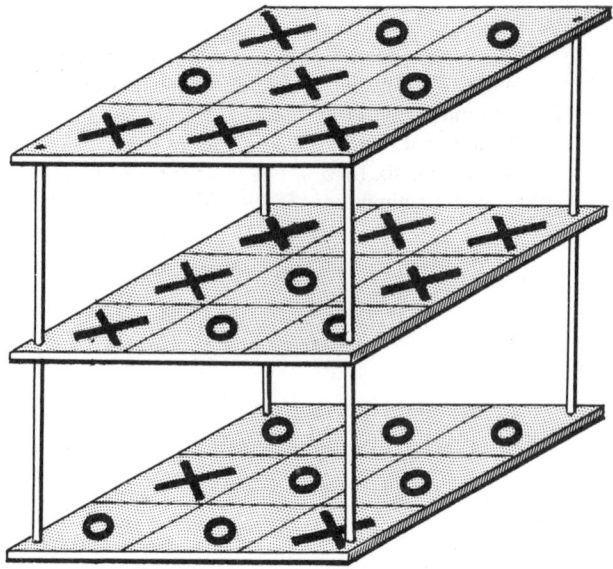

Fig. 8-15 3-D Tic-Tac-Toe

sum. Each column is then added separately, the results being expressed as decimal numbers. The total of each column will be 0, 1, 2, or 3. If at the outset, any of the totals is either 1 or 3, then the player drawing first can put himself in a winning position. He does this by taking sufficient counters from one pile to make the totals for all columns even, that is either 0 or 2. If at the outset, all the totals are even, then the first player is in a losing position. An example will make all this more clear.

If the piles start off as 12, 7, 13, these will be written in the binary notation as:

$$
\begin{array}{rr}
12 & 110 \\
7 & 111 \\
13 & 1101
\end{array}
$$

Column total (in decimal scale)   2312

There are odd totals in two of the columns. This situation can be converted into a winning position by the first player subtracting sufficient counters from one of the piles to make the column totals all even. There are several possibilities; for instance, six counters from the pile of seven would make the column totals 2202; or two counters from the pile of twelve would make the totals 2222. An example of a losing position is a game in which the piles start off as 6, 9, 15. The column total of the binary equivalents is 2222, and there is nothing that the first player can do that will keep all four columns even. Any number of counters removed will leave a 1 or 3 in the totals, enabling the second player to convert it to a winning position. The only possibility of gaining the initiative is by subtracting such a number that will make as difficult as possible the task of deciding what can be taken to leave the column totals all even, then relying on the inferior skill of the opponent.

Write a program to play Nim.

8.26 3-D Tic-Tac-Toe

Tic-Tac-Toe played on a nine-square board is familiar to all. Adding a third dimension to the game makes it considerably more interesting (and difficult from a programming standpoint). The possibilities of forming rows of three are greatly increased, as they will occur not just in three horizontal planes but in the vertical planes as well. In the game shown in Fig. 8–15, the zeros have won with six lines against four for the crosses.

Write a program to play three-dimensional Tic-Tac-Toe.

BIBLIOGRAPHY

Many books contain excellent chapters or sections that deal with the field of computerized game playing. Some books cover the subject thoroughly, and I have listed a few of these basic volumes. I have also listed a few good general computer books as well as books that discuss the BASIC language.

Ahl, D. H., *BASIC Computer Games,* Digital Equipment Corp., 1973.
Coan, J. S., *Basic BASIC: An Introduction to Computer Programming in BASIC Language,* 2nd ed., Hayden, 1970, 1978.
Coan, J. S., *Advanced BASIC: Applications and Problems,* Hayden, 1976.
Dwyer, T. A. and M. S. Kaufman, *A Guided Tour of Computer Programming in BASIC,* Houghton Mifflin, 1973.
Epstein, R. A., *The Theory of Gambling and Statistical Logic,* Academic Press, 1967.
Fults, J. L., *Magic Squares,* Open Court, 1974.
Gross, J. L. and W. S. Brainerd, *Fundamental Programming Concepts,* Harper & Row, 1972.
Kemeny, J. G. and T. E. Kurtz, *BASIC Programming,* John Wiley, 1973.
Noir, Jacques, *Casino Holiday,* Oxford Street Press, 1970.
Revere, L., *Playing Blackjack as a Business,* Lyle Stuart, 1973.
Sage, E. R., *Fun and Games with the Computer,* Entelek Inc., 1975.
Smith, R. E., *Discovering BASIC: A Problem Solving Approach,* Hayden, 1969, 1970.
Spencer, D. D., *A Guide to BASIC Programming,* 2nd ed., Addison-Wesley, 1975.
———, *Computers in Action,* Hayden, 1974.
———, *Computers in Society,* Hayden, 1974.
———, *Game Playing with Computers,* 2nd ed., Hayden, 1975.
Thorp, E. O., *Beat the Dealer,* Alfred A. Knopf, 1966.
What to Do After You Hit Return, People's Computer Company, 1975.
Wilson, A. N., *The Casino Gambler's Guide,* Harper & Row, 1975.

INDEX

INDEX

ABS function, 24
Absolute value, 24
Algorithms, 5
Amicable Numbers, 72–74
   program for, 74
Argument of a function, 22
Armstrong Numbers, 77
   program for, 77
Arrays, 24–26
   one-dimensional (lists), 25
   two-dimensional (tables), 25–26
Artificial intelligence, 2

Babbage, Charles, 6
Baccarat, 99–101
BASIC:
   arrays, 24–26
   functions, 22–24
   language, 1, 12–30
   line number, 13–14
   statements, 14–30
   subroutines, 29–30
   variables, 14, 24
BASIC commands:
   DATA, 18–20
   DIM, 26
   END, 15
   FOR, 14
   GO TO, 15–18
   GOSUB, 30
   IF-THEN, 17–18
   INPUT, 20–21
   LET, 14
   NEXT, 14
   PRINT, 14–15
   READ, 18–20
   REM, 14, 18

RESTORE, 26–29
RETURN, 30
BASIC statements, 14–30
BASIC programs:
   Armstrong Numbers, 77
   Battle of Numbers, 42–45
   Blackjack, 86–89
   Buried Treasure, 113–118
   Chinese Remainder Theorem, 68–69
   Coin Tossing, 31–32
   Fibonacci Numbers, 71–72
   Fifteen Puzzle, 108–113
   Guess the Number, 62–64
   Knight's Tour, 57–60
   Magic Square (even-cell), 126–127, 129
   Magic Square (geometric), 137, 139
   Magic Square (odd-cell), 122, 124, 130–133
   Mountain of Paper, 12–13
   Mouse in a Maze, 36, 38
   Number Guessing, 24
   Perfect Numbers, 70
   Poker, 47–48
   Prime Numbers, 66, 68
   Rolling a Die, 33
   Rolling Two Dice, 33–34
   Roulette, 91–92
   Sam the Drunk, 39–40
   Seven or Eleven, 34
   Sharky, the Card Player, 60
   Sieve of Eratosthenes, 66
   Slot Machine, 81–82
   Square Numbers, 76–77
   Tic-Tac-Toe, 53–54
   Tossing a Coin, 31–32
   Tower of Hanoi, 103

BASIC system commands, 13–14
  LIST, 10
  RUN, 10, 14
Battle of Numbers, 40–46
  program for, 42–45
Blackjack, 3, 9, 82–89
  program for, 86–89
Boule, 149–150
Buried Treasure, 113–118
  program for, 113–118
Business games, 6
Buzz, 142

Casino gambling games; see Gambling games
Checkers, 2, 6, 8–9
Chess, 2–3, 6, 8
Chinese Remainder Theorem, 68–69
  program for, 68–69
Coding, 5
Coin tossing simulation, 31–33
Colored Cubes puzzle, 105–106
Column, array, 25
Comments; see REM statement
Computer, 1, 3–6
Craps, 3, 92–97, 150
  program for, 93, 96–97

DATA statement, 18–20
Dealing a Poker hand, 46–49
  program for, 47–48
Debugging, 6
Dice problems, 33–34
DIM statement, 26

END statement, 15

Fibonacci Numbers, 70–72
  program for, 71–72
Fifteen (15) Puzzle, 3, 7, 106–113
  program for, 108–113
Fifty (50) Puzzle, 145
Five Field Kono, 150–151
Flowcharts, 5
FOR statement, 14
Four Checkers game, 146–147
Fox and Geese, 49–50
Functions, library, 22–24

Gambling games, 78–101
  Baccarat, 99–101
  Blackjack, 3, 9, 82–89
  Craps, 3, 92–97
  Keno, 98–99
  Roulette, 89–92
  slot machines, 78–82
  Wheel of Fortune, 101
Games for reader solution, 142–157
Games, puzzles, and recreations:
  Amicable Numbers, 72–74
  Armstrong Numbers, 77
  Baccarat, 99–101
  Battle of Numbers, 40–46
  Blackjack, 3, 9, 82–89
  Boule, 149–150
  Buried Treasure, 113–118
  business, 6
  Buzz, 142
  casino, 78–101
  Checkers, 2, 6, 8–9
  Chess, 2–3, 6, 8
  Chinese Remainder Theorem, 68–69
  Coin Flipping, 31–33
  Colored Cubes, 105–106
  Craps, 3, 92–97, 150
  dealing a Poker hand, 46–49
  dice, 33–34
  Fibonacci Numbers, 70–72
  Fifteen Puzzle, 3, 7, 106–113
  Fifty Puzzle, 145
  Five-Field Kono, 150–151
  Four Checkers, 146–147
  Fox and Geese, 49–50
  gambling games, 78–101
  games for reader solution, 142–157
  Go, 2, 6–7
  Go-Moko, 2–3, 7–8, 56
  Guess the Number, 62–64
  guessing, 144
  Hexapawn, 153
  Keno, 98–99
  King's Tour of the chessboard, 153
  Knight Interchange, 151
  Knight's Tour, 7, 24–27, 56–60, 140–141
  Lucky Prisoners, 145–146
  Magic Square (even-cell), 125–129
  Magic Square (geometric), 136–139

INDEX

Magic Square (multiplication), 133–136
Magic Square (odd-cell), 120–125, 129–133, 142
Magic Square checker, 148–149
Mersenne Primes, 145
Milkman's Crate, 145
mind-reading tricks, 74–76
Morra, 144
Mountain of Paper, 12–14
Mouse in a Maze, 35–39
Nim, 6, 8, 154–156
Nine Men's Morris, 153
Number Guessing, 24
Palindromic Numbers, 147–148
Pentominoes, 6–7, 113, 116
Perfect Numbers, 3, 69–70
Poker, 46–49, 147
Poker Dice, 143
Prime Numbers, 3, 7, 64–68, 140–141, 143, 145
prime number polynomial, 143
Rolling a Die, 33
Rolling Two Dice, 33–34
Roulette, 6, 89–92
Russian Roulette, 9–10
Sam the Drunk, 39–40
Seven or Eleven, 34–35
Sharky, the Card Player, 60
Sieve of Eratosthenes, 64–66
Slot Machine, 6, 78–82
Square Numbers, 76–77
Symmetry, 151–152
Thinking of a Number, 61
Three-D Tic-Tac-Toe, 157
Tic-Tac-Toe, 3, 6, 52–56, 157
Tossing a Coin, 31–33
Tower of Hanoi, 3, 102–105
Typing Monkey, 142
war, 6, 8
Wheel of Fortune, 101
Game classifications, 2–3
Game playing with computers, 1–11
Go, 2, 6, 7
Go-Moko, 2, 3, 7–8, 56
GOSUB statement, 30
GO TO statement, 15–18
Guess the Number, 62–64
Guessing game, 144

Hexapawn, 153

IF–THEN statement, 17–18
INPUT statement, 20–21
INT function, 22–24

Keno, 98–99
King's Tour of the chessboard, 153
Knight Interchange, 151
Knight's tour, 7, 24–27, 56–60, 140–141
  program for, 57–60

LET statement, 14
Library functions, 22–24
  ABS, 24
  INT, 22–24
  RND, 22–24
Line numbers, 13–14
LIST command, 10
Lists, 25
Looping, 14
Lucky Prisoners, 145–146

Magic Square, even-cell, 125–129
  program for, 126–127, 129
Magic Square, geometric, 136–139
  program for, 137, 139
Magic Square, multiplication, 133–136
Magic Square, odd-cell, 120–125, 129–133, 142
  program for, 122–124, 130–133
Magic Square checker, 148–149
Magic Squares, 3, 6, 9, 119–141, 142, 148–149
  how to make, 120
  magic constant, 129
Mathematical recreation, 3
Mersenne Primes, 145
Milkman's Crate, 145
Mind-reading tricks, 74–76
Minicomputers, 3
Morra, 144–145
Mountain of Paper program, 12–14
Mouse in a Maze, 35–39
  program for, 36, 38

NEXT statement, 14
Nim, 6, 8, 154–156
Nine Men's Morris, 153

Number Guessing program, 24
Number recreations, 61-77

Palindromic Numbers, 147-148
Pentominoes, 6-7, 113, 116
Perfect Numbers, 3, 69-70
   program for, 70
Poker, 46-49, 147
Poker Dice, 143
Prime number polynomial, 143
Prime Numbers, 3, 7, 64-68, 140-141, 143, 145
   program for, 66-68
PRINT statement, 14-15
Programs; see BASIC programs
Program debugging, 6
Programming language, 5
Puzzles, 3, 102-118

Random numbers, 22-24
READ statement, 18-20
Relational operators, 17
REM statement, 14, 18
RESTORE statement, 26-29
RETURN key, 10
RETURN statement, 30
RND function, 22-24
Rolling a Die, 33
   program for, 33
Rolling Two Dice, 33-34
   program for, 33-34
Roulette, 89-92
   program for, 91-92
Row, array, 25
RUN command, 10, 14
Russian Roulette, 9-10

Sam the Drunk, 39-40
   program for, 39-40

Seven or Eleven, 34-35
   program for, 34
Sharky, the Card Player, 60
   program for, 60
Sieve of Eratosthenes, 64-66
   program for, 66
Simulation, 3
Slot machine, 78-82
   program for, 81-82
Solitaire, 3
Square Numbers, 76-77
   program for, 76-77
Subroutines, 29-30
Subscripted variable, 24-25
Symmetry game, 151-152
System commands, 13-14
   LIST, 10
   RUN, 10, 14

Tables, 25-26
Tac Tix, 50-51
Terminals, 3
Thinking of a Number game, 61-62
Three-D Tic-Tac-Toe, 157
Tic-Tac-Toe, 3, 6, 52-56, 157
   program for, 53-54
Time-sharing system, 4
Tossing a Coin, 31-33
   program for, 31-32
Tower of Hanoi, 3, 102-105
   program for, 103
Twin primes, 145
Typing Monkey, 142-143

Variable, 14
   subscripted, 24

War games, 6, 8
Wheel of Fortune, 101